IMAGES
*of America*

THE SILVER VALLEY

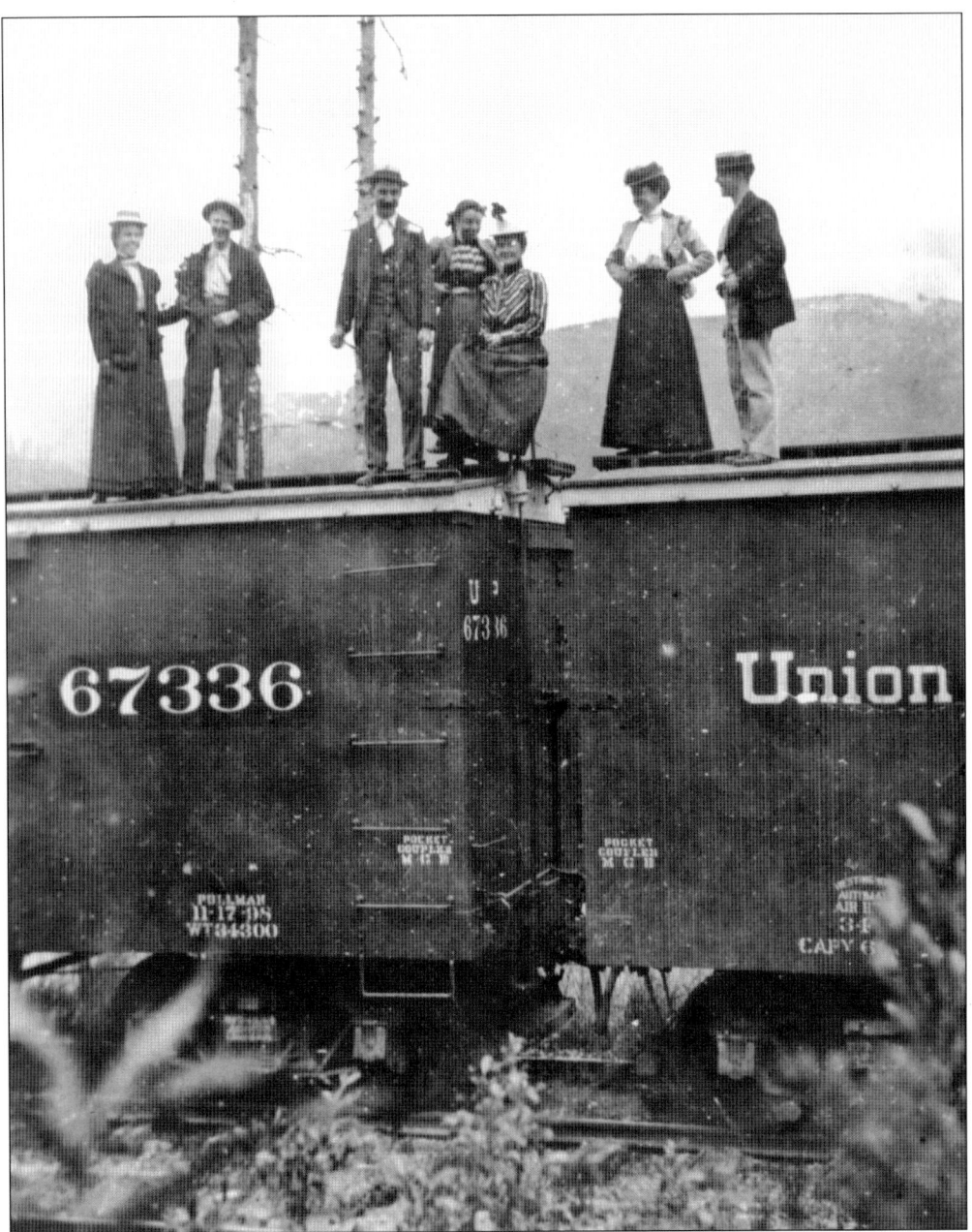

Trains became the center of Silver Valley life. Goods came in, and ore was shipped out. Trains brought families in and made getting out to the big city for a weekend possible. This photograph shows a Union Pacific train at the Gold Hunter Mine.

ON THE COVER: Looking north up Sixth Street from the intersection at Bank Street in 1918, the John Mullan statue is prominent in the center of the street. Transportation still is a mix of horse and wagon and cars. The streets are paved, and the sidewalks are concrete. Electricity on the streets, in homes, and businesses makes Wallace a very progressive community. (Courtesy of the Historic Wallace Preservation Society.)

# IMAGES of America
# THE SILVER VALLEY

Historic Wallace Preservation Society

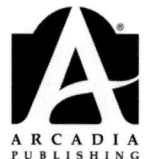

Copyright © 2010 by Historic Wallace Preservation Society
ISBN 978-0-7385-8175-0

Published by Arcadia Publishing
Charleston, South Carolina

Printed in the United States of America

Library of Congress Control Number: 2010932072

For all general information, please contact Arcadia Publishing:
Telephone 843-853-2070
Fax 843-853-0044
E-mail sales@arcadiapublishing.com
For customer service and orders:
Toll-Free 1-888-313-2665

Visit us on the Internet at www.arcadiapublishing.com

*This book is dedicated to the men and women who built this valley, who built lives around hard work and love of family and country.*

# Contents

| | | |
|---|---|---|
| Acknowledgments | | 6 |
| Introduction | | 7 |
| 1. | From Lookout to Fourth of July | 9 |
| 2. | Hospitals | 33 |
| 3. | Schools, Churches, and Courthouses | 39 |
| 4. | Valley Life | 55 |
| 5. | Bars and Furnished Rooms | 71 |
| 6. | Trains | 77 |
| 7. | Mother Nature at Work | 83 |
| 8. | Famous and Infamous | 93 |
| 9. | Silver Valley Mines | 101 |
| 10. | Mining Wars and Disasters | 121 |

# ACKNOWLEDGMENTS

In the late 1960s, the Idaho and United States transportation departments proposed to blast a section of Interstate 90 right through the middle of Wallace, devastating its business district and historic 19th-century aesthetics. Wallace native Nancy Lee Hanson went to work on founding the Historic Wallace Preservation Society, and through this vehicle secured first the Northern Pacific Railway depot, then the entire one-square-mile town, for listing on the U.S. Park Service National Register of Historic Places, saving the town from destruction.

Hanson was joined by Wallace mining magnate Harry F. Magnuson, another native son, in successful litigation to halt the freeway-engineering plan to level Wallace. A compromise was reached in the mid-1980s that moved the freeway bypass north of, and above, the downtown, and at the same time funding the move of the Northern Pacific Railroad Depot across the South Fork of the Coeur d'Alene River to its current location, and a full restoration of this historic landmark.

Its primary mission accomplished, the Historic Wallace Preservation Society's goal is to collect photographs, written information, and oral information about our past, and to make it available for everyone. Without our past we have no future.

Historic Wallace, which is a nonprofit 501(c)3 corporation, also supports local organizations through fundraisers such as the Children's Christmas Fund, volunteer firefighters, chamber of commerce, Wallace Business Community Association, the Art of Fun Series, Sixth Street Theater, Wallace City Swimming Pool, and other community benefits.

The Historic Wallace Preservation Society, Inc., is Nancy Lee Hanson, founder; Rich Asher, president; Shauna Hillman, photographer and archival printer of black-and-white gold; David Bond, codirector and romancer of the written word; Leonarda Sabey, codirector and file-writer; James Taylor, codirector; and Donna Westmorehouse, codirector. The Pinehurst Historical Society was founded by Lawanna Watts.

Thank you to all the people who have over the years brought their family photo archives to us as gifts to the collection. And thank you for all the stories you have shared with us.

All photographs, unless otherwise stated, are the property of the Historic Wallace Preservation Society, Inc.

# Introduction

Welcome to the Silver Valley. Its very name lures you in with its promise of riches, of fortunes won and lost.

A decade after the Civil War, dreams of the mother lode brought men from all over the world to the heart of the Bitterroot Mountains in what would become the continental United States' last gold rush. Tent cities with names like Delta, Eagle, Prichard, and Murray sprang up along the Coeur d'Alene River's headwaters as word of "gold in them there hills" spread around the lower 48. Once the Shoshone County seat, Murray is home of the Bedroom Gold Mine saloon and the Sprag Pole Museum and Saloon, both well-tended points of historic interest.

While the easy findings of gold panning played out within the ensuing decade, gold mining remained a staple of that district's economic diet into the 1930s with a Guggenheim-owned dredge responsible for the boulder piles still visible on Prichard Creek today. However in 1884, silver, lead, and zinc were discovered on the Coeur d'Alene River's South Fork, prompting a "silver rush." Among the discoveries were the famed Sunshine, Hercules, and Bunker Hill mines and the ensuing production of more than 1 billion ounces of silver. Trains operated by the Oregon Navigation Company, Northern Pacific, and Union Pacific ran up and down the rivers, and to and from Wallace and Burke, linking the communities before there was even talk of a road. During the first and second decades of the 1900s, Bunker Hill built lead and zinc smelters to purify ores and get around the high tariffs imposed by the railroad cartels.

Today numerous mines still operate along the Osburn Fault that runs beneath the South Fork, including Hecla's Lucky Friday mine in Mullan, U.S. Silver's Galena mine near Osburn, the New Bunker Hill Mining Company in Kellogg, and the New Jersey Mining Company Mill just east of Kellogg. Geologists say there remain another billion ounces of silver, still in the ground, along the Silver Valley.

The wealth from our ore went to work building the cities of Spokane, Washington, and Coeur d'Alene, Idaho, and endowed chairs at the University of California. To this day many of the streets and prominent buildings in Spokane bare the names of the mine owners from our valley, and their mansions stand as residences, museums, restaurants and even a bishopric. Coeur d'Alene and the South Fork of the Coeur d'Alene River became places for summer homes and vacations. The rail bed is now a paved bike trail, the Trail of the Coeur d'Alenes that takes travelers down 72 miles along the Coeur d'Alene River to the bottom of Lake Coeur d'Alene through the chain lakes, and through the lake city of Harrison and timber town of St. Maries. The old Milwaukee Road bicycle ride takes its riders through tunnels and over trestles that will amaze on the Route of the Hiawatha, the route of the million-dollar silk trains.

Each of the towns in the valley has its own colorful history. They include stories of ghosts like Miss Maggie, who keeps the employees on their toes at The Jameson on Sixth Street in Wallace. In the early days, if two folks wanted to move a road or a line, a handshake at a lodge meeting took care of it. Why spend time and money at the courthouse recording it when a man's word was all you needed? There's the story of how Wallace stole the county seat from Murray. There were the mining wars of early days that pitted workers against the mine owners and the U.S. Army, giving birth to the union movement and incidentally women's suffrage. The valley's St. Valentines Day shoot-out that left two dead and two wounded was over a woman who, by today's standards, would not get a second look. Thankfully, we don't take ourselves too seriously. Kellogg for years had a sign at its western entrance welcoming visitors with the slogan "The town which was discovered by a jackass and which is inhabited by its descendants."

Cataldo offers its Catholic mission, the oldest standing building in Idaho, beckoning visitors to the history of the native people who called it the Dark Valley. When they hunted here, they would not spend the night in the narrow canyons where the sun touches the floor of the valley for only short periods of time.

I have childhood memories of placing my hands in the dried mud handprints that Native American children left behind. They mixed mud with straw and plastered it against the inside walls of the mission. Fitting my fingers into the impressions that their hands left in the wall gave me an overwhelming need to protect our local history. History, its truths and its legends, link everyone together. Hopefully, history teaches us that life and the world around us is forever changing and forever the same. We can stand still and watch it go by, or like the men and women who built our valley, we can move ahead, sometimes with overwhelming speed to new horizons. We hope readers enjoy this walk through time as much as the Historic Wallace Preservation Society enjoys delivering it.

—Leonarda Sabey

# One

# From Lookout to Fourth of July

Lookout Pass is the eastern doorway into the Silver Valley. At a height of 4,725 feet, and right on the state line, Lookout Pass boasts the Lookout Ski Resort. From its heights, you get your first look into the valley below. It is a beautiful sight; in summer it is a green that would make an Irishman think he was coming home. In winter, under a blanket of snow, a peaceful quiet envelops you.

Each town along the way from Lookout Pass and into the Silver Valley offers its own past, present, and future. Many of the places in the area would come to carry names that refer to people or events in their histories. Some of these names carry legends that can no longer be proved but are accepted as local gospel. True or not, they tell in themselves of the dangerous lives the builders of our part of the world lived.

A 1910 atlas lists Wallace, Burke, Page, Kellogg, and Wardner as the principal towns in order of population in Shoshone County. Together, they hosted more people than Ada County and Boise, Idaho. Until the crash of silver prices in the 1980s, the area between Lookout Pass and Fourth of July Pass in Shoshone County paid a third of all the taxes for the state. We will again.

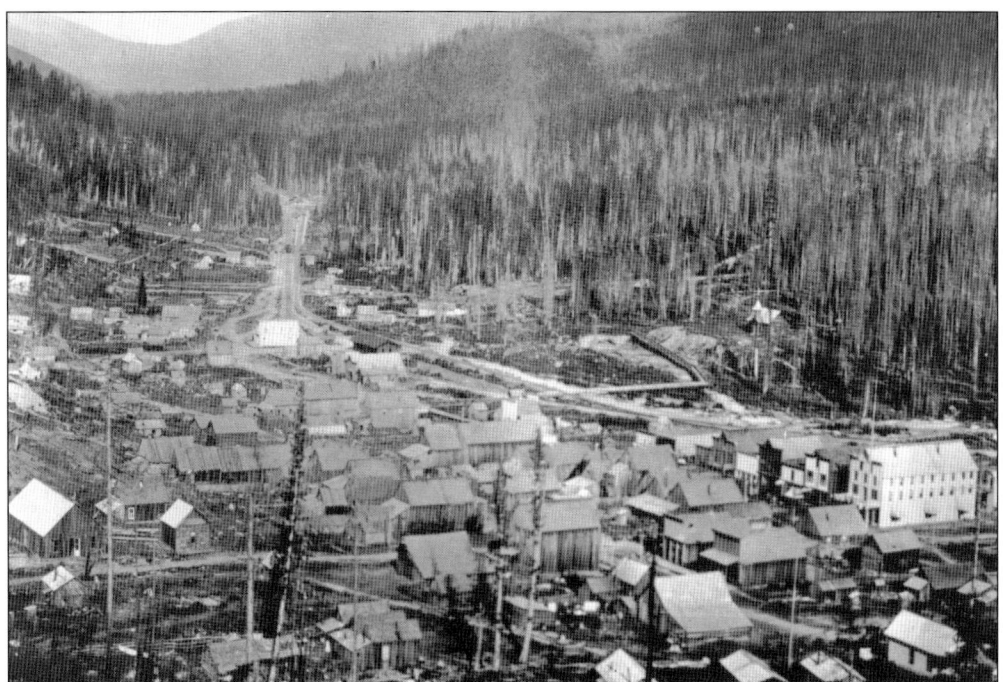

In this c. 1892 photograph, Mullan is already a growing community. To the right in the trees is the school, which was also probably a church. The three-story hotel in this mining camp shows that many people in the town were just passing through.

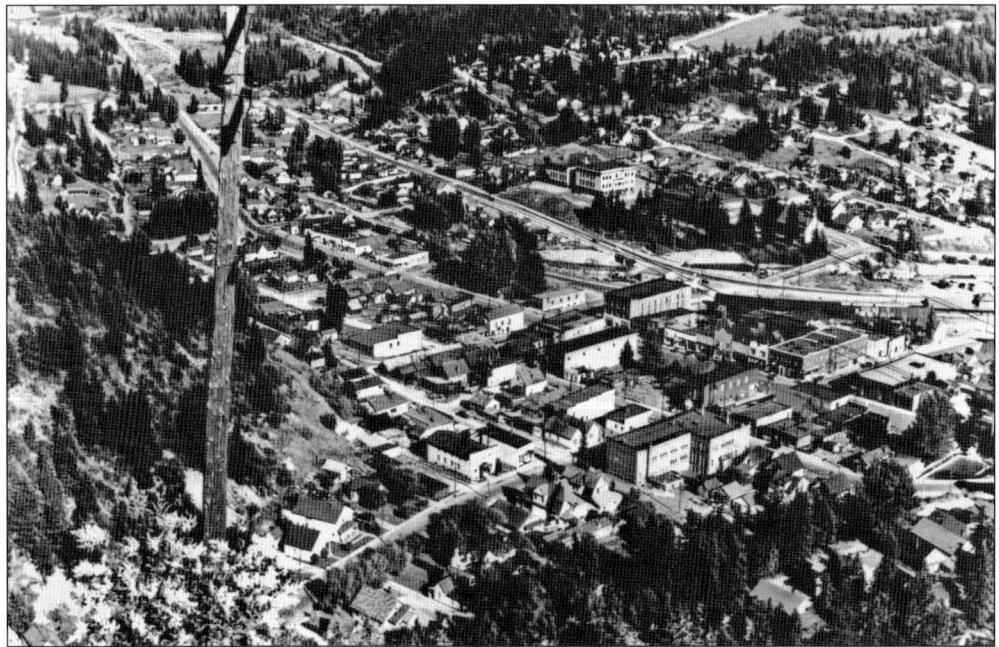

The town has grown a lot in the 50 years between the photograph above and this one taken in 1942. Buildings are now being built using brick. Roads are being laid out in square grids. Business and residential areas are more divided. The school is now a large brick structure. There are now around 2,000 people who live and work here.

Burke Canyon is so narrow in places that the train tracks, road, and creek took up the same space along the canyon floor. The Tiger Hotel in Burke, also called the "Beanery" by locals, made the *Guinness Book of World Records* because it was built so that the train ran "through" it; the Beanery was also noticed by Ripley's Believe It or Not. The canyon was home to a number of little towns that grew up around the mines. Some carried colorful names that make one wonder what was happening at the time. Others were named for the mines they grew up around: Gem, Yellowdog, Frisco, Mace, Burke, Black Bear, and Cornwall. Most of these little towns were made up of a single row of homes clinging to the canyon walls.

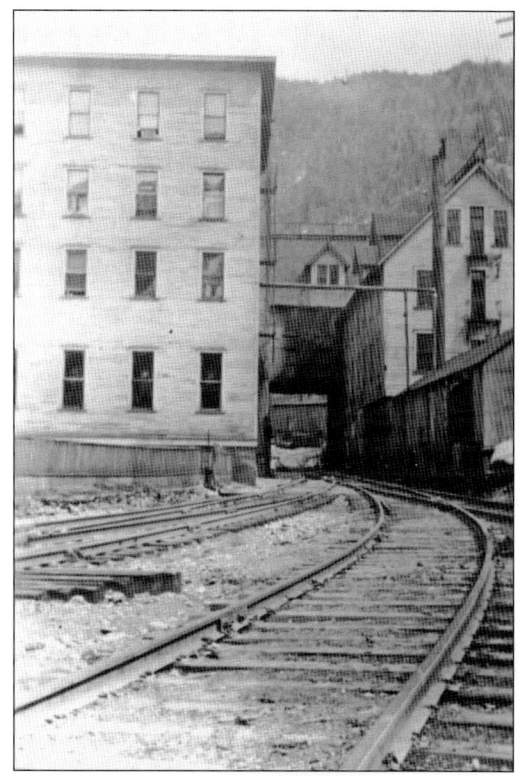

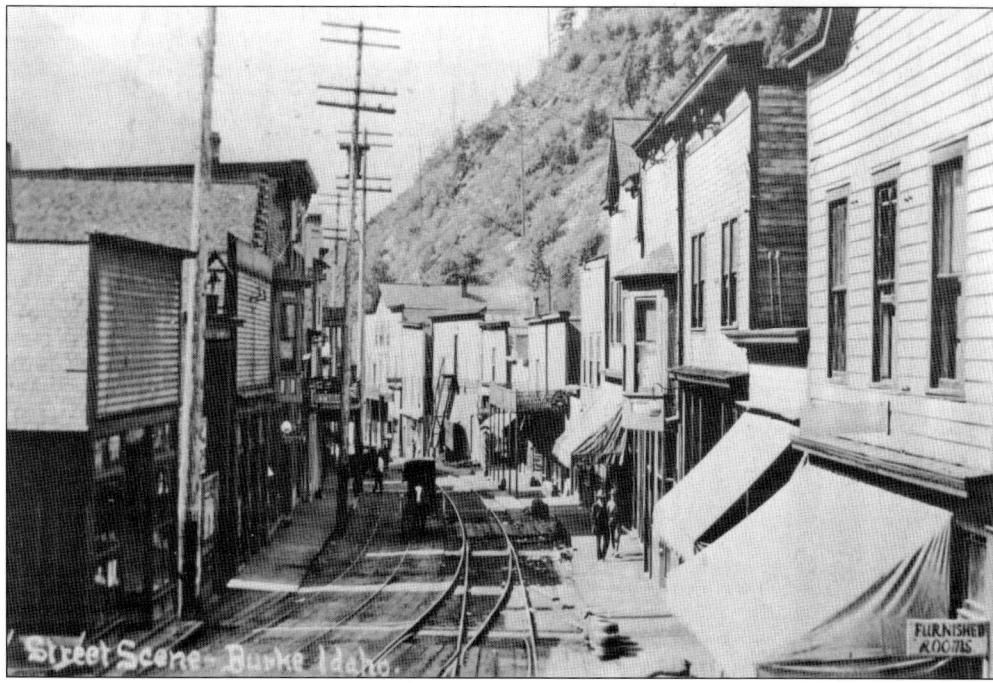

This *c.* 1912 photograph shows the Burke business district. Notice how little room there is between the storefronts and the train tracks. Businesses would have to roll in their awnings when the trains came through to keep them safe from the hot embers of the coal-fired train engines.

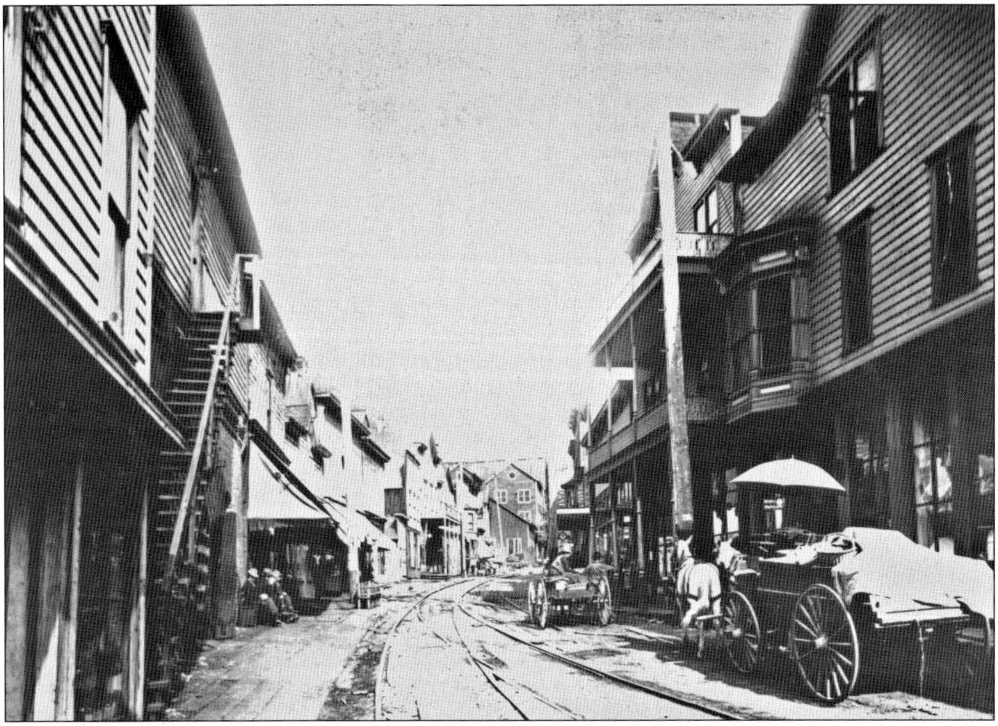

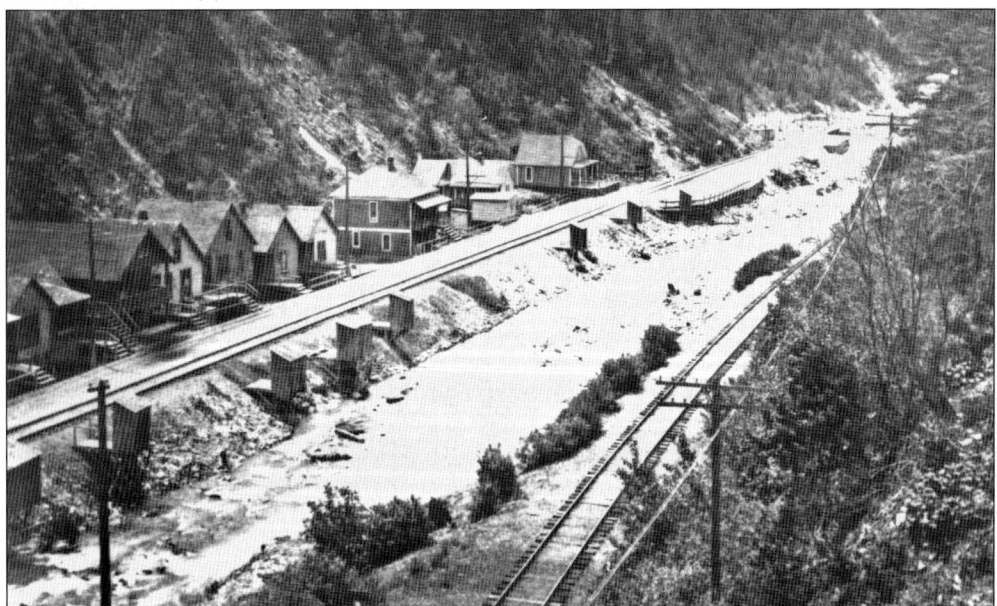

Notice the bay window above the umbrella in this 1913 Burke Street scene. In the distance, the Mammoth Mine is visible. The men sitting in front of one of the businesses are probably talking about the shift they just finished at the mine.

For many years, the homes in Burke Canyon had no indoor plumbing. Outhouses built over the creek were used. These homes are at Cornwall on Canyon Creek in the 1920s, and their toilets were "flushed" every spring during the runoff. Notice the railroad tracks on both side of the creek, serving the Union Pacific and the Northern Pacific Railways.

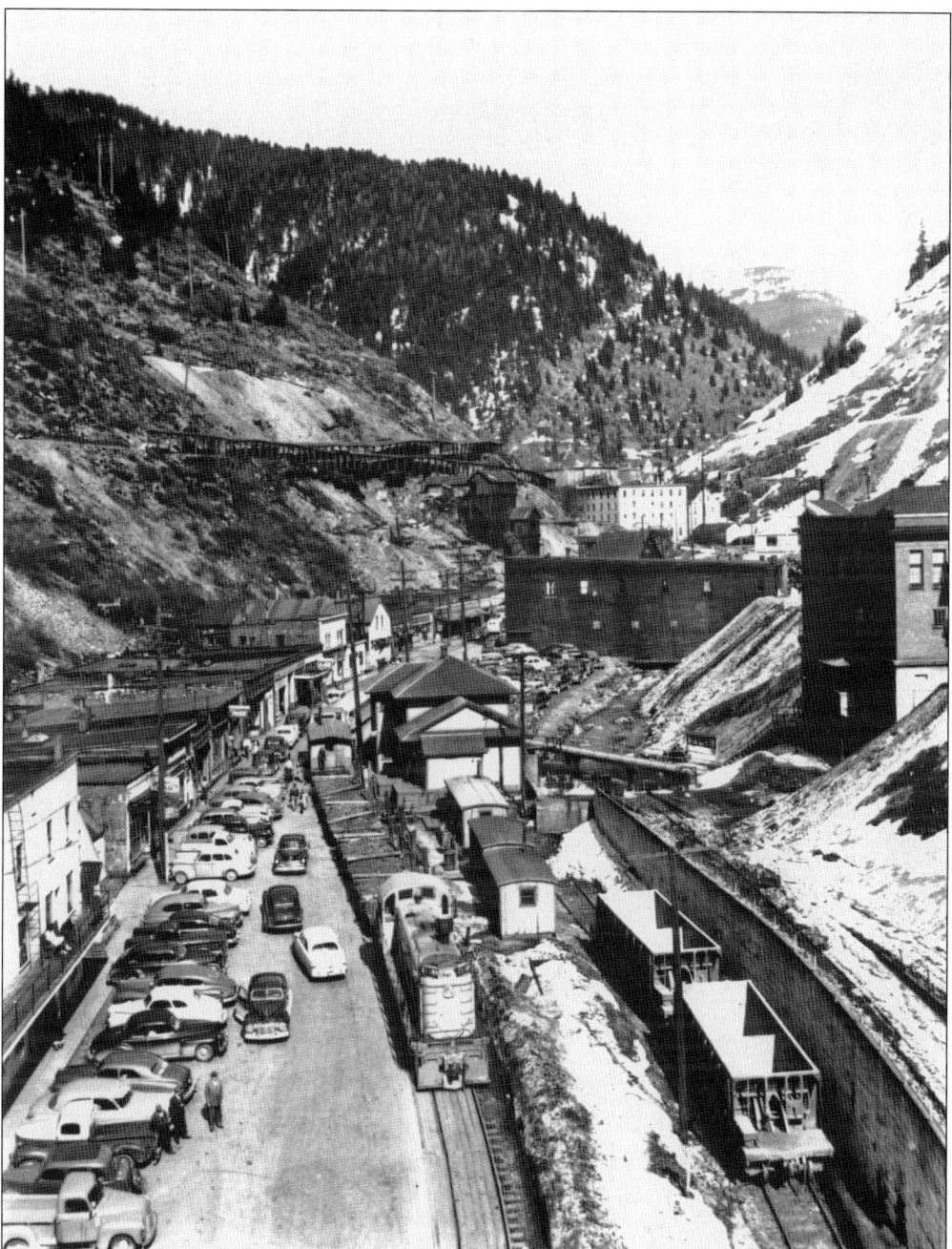

The Burke business district, seen here in 1949, had everything the folks of Burke Canyon needed. In this shot, over 17 businesses are visible. The Burke Hotel and in the distance the Tiger Hotel, may be seen. Eight places served liquor: the Combination Bar, Vic's Bar, Tunnel Bar, the liquor store, Paskevich's, Otto Olson's Bar, Silver Club Bar, and the B&B Bar. There were men's and ladies' clothing stores, barber and beauty shops, a grocery store, theater, churches, and restaurants. On the right, at about the middle of the photograph, is the Union Pacific Depot.

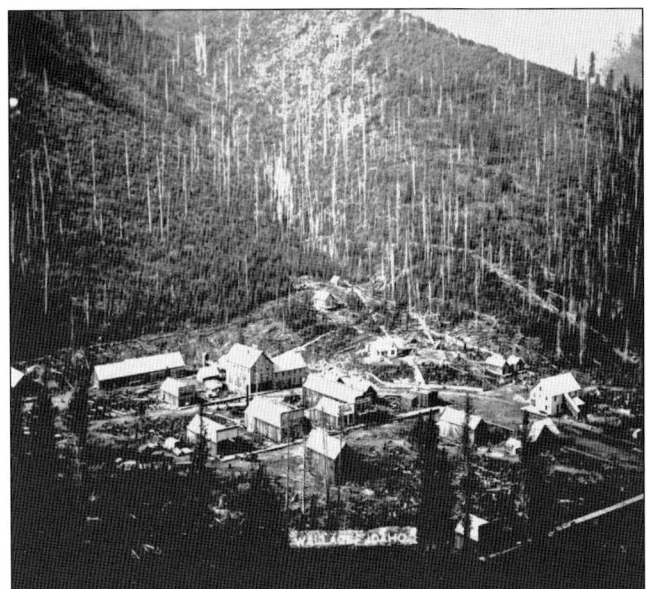

Taken in 1887, this is the earliest photograph featured in this book. It shows Wallace two years before the fire that would level the town. In 1908, the city fathers decided that all structures built in the business district would be of brick. The trees on the hillsides that look dead are Western Larch. Unlike most conifers that stay green year-round, "tamarack" turn gold in the fall and drop their needles. This photograph was taken either early in the spring or very late in the fall. Colonel Wallace's home is the second from the top on the hillside.

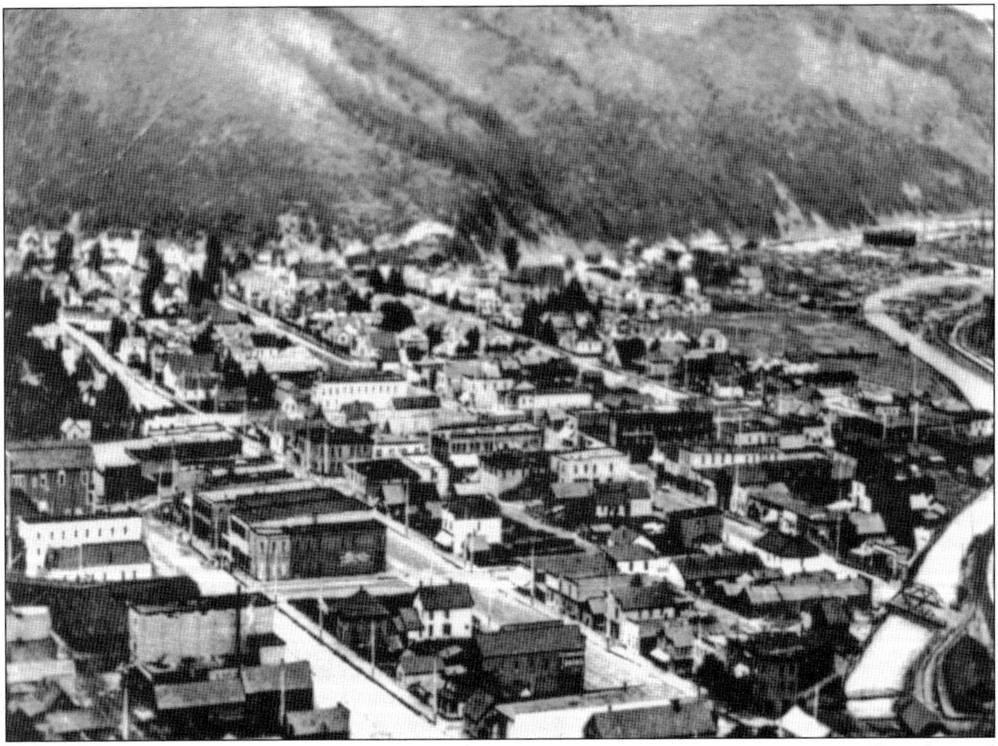

The business district is only few blocks square. To the left is the Opera House. Wallace hosted many theater productions, as it was the halfway stop between Spokane and Missoula. The small bridge is on Cedar Street, the building with the bell tower is the fire department. The right side of Cedar Street is where the businesses of the "ladies of the evening" were located for years. Against the mountain is the hospital, and in the foreground by the river is the Pacific Hotel. Note the footbridge from the Union Pacific Depot to the hotel. The courthouse would later be built where the two-story white house stands at the bottom of this 1904 photograph.

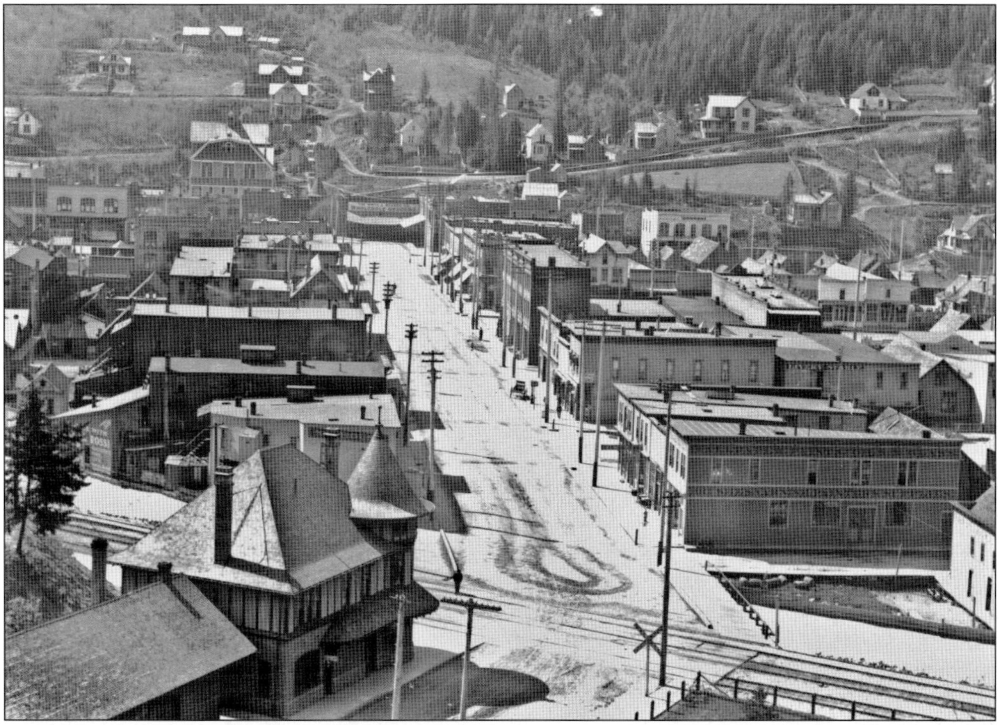

In the foreground of this shot, taken by Arthur Fay in 1905, the Northern Pacific Depot is seen in its original setting. The large building in the background is the Opera House. Looking up Sixth Street, the three stories of the Wallace Corner are visible. A close inspection reveals that its wall is not straight. After the fire of 1889, the town was in a rush to rebuild. The story goes that halfway through its building, they realized its eastern wall was leaning out. Because of the need to finish quickly they just brought the wall in the rest of the way up. This early, sunny Sunday morning shot finds the streets and sidewalks nearly empty.

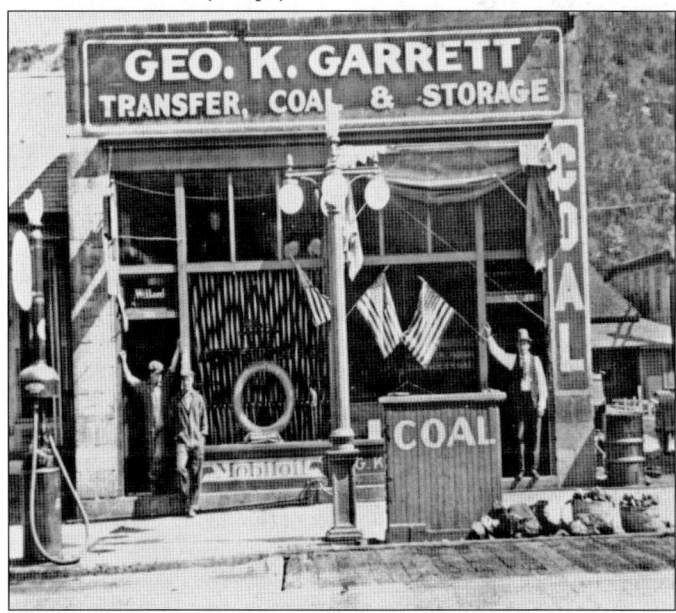

Located at 513 Pine Street in 1916, George K. Garrett would fill your coal order or store your belongings. Here they are preparing to watch the Fourth of July parade.

15

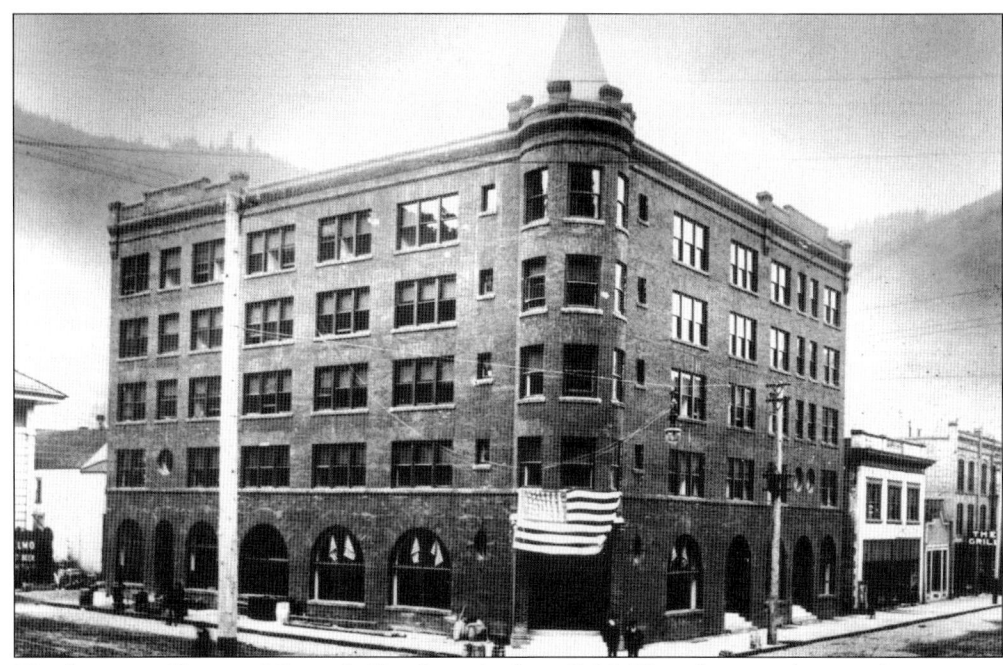

The five-story "five star" Samuels Hotel was built in 1906. This photograph was taken near its completion; nail kegs sit on the sidewalk and street along with other building tools. To the left is a billboard advertising St. Elmo beer from the Sunset Brewery. To the right of the Samuels Hotel is the studio of T. N. Barnard. This hotel was removed when the freeway was planed to go through it. The ground floor boasted stores, a café, and a bar. A birdcage elevator complete with operator took guests to the rooms on the upper stories. The tower was reminiscent of a castle, inviting guests to be treated like royalty from the moment they checked in. On its site is now a community park.

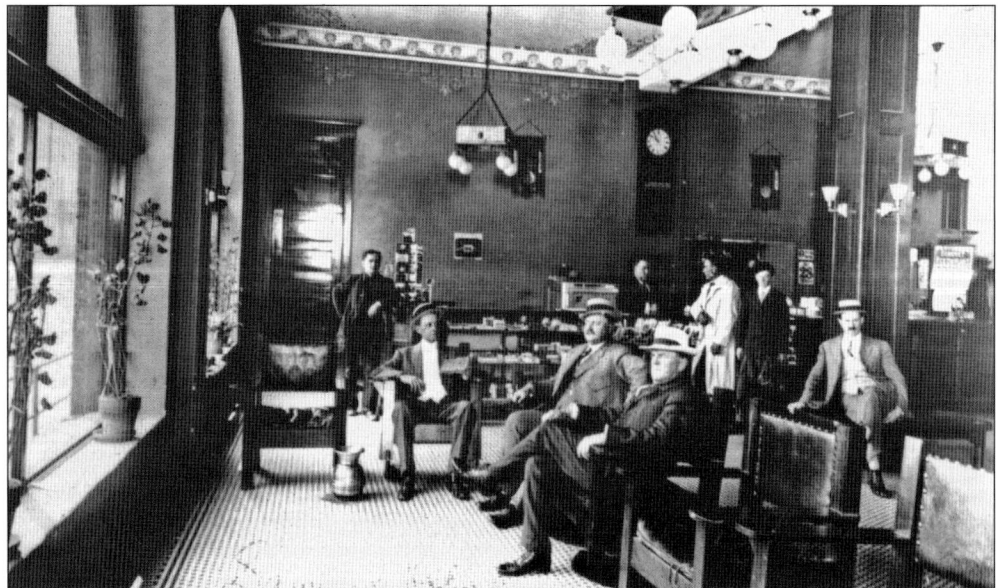

This is the interior of the Samuels Hotel in 1907. Gentlemen could enjoy the comfort of the lobby for a smoke or a chew (notice the spittoon).

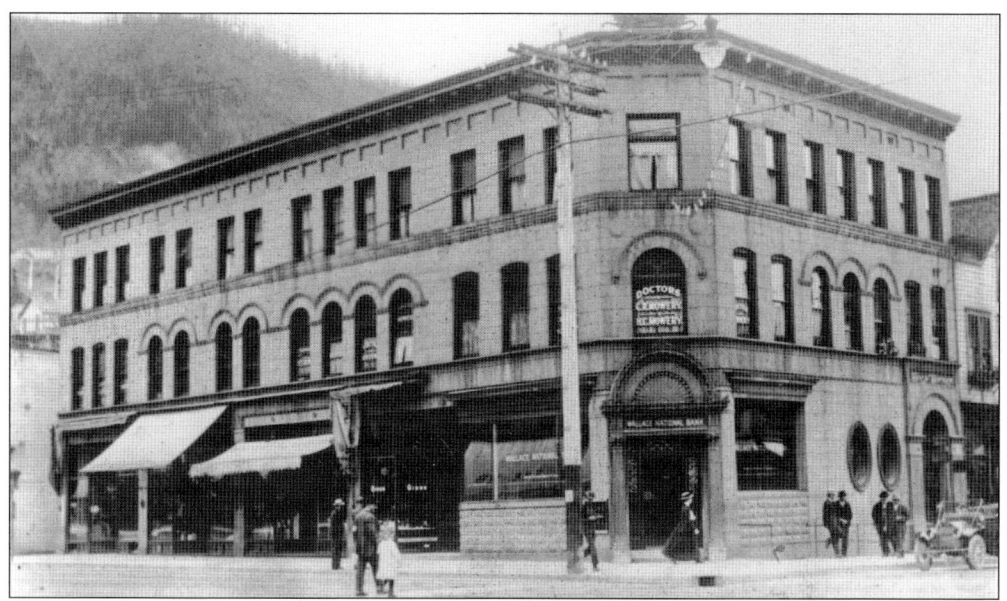

In 1915, around when this photograph was taken, this was known as the O'Neil-Samuels building. At the time, it was the Wallace National Bank—or the "second national bank," as one of Wallace's forefathers called it as a child when his father tried to get a loan to buy a delivery truck at the First National Bank and was turned down because "automobiles were just a fad." The boy suggested that they go to the "second national bank" to get the loan instead. They walked over to the Wallace National Bank and qualified. On the ground floor adjacent to the bank were five separate stores, including a cigar store and a jewelry store. The second floor housed Dr. C. R. Mowery and Dr. R. C. Mowery's offices. On the third floor were the Kozy Korner apartments. Notice the round windows; these were removed in one of the bank remodels. Look at the elaborate detail on top of the building where "O&S" is proudly displayed. The building would later be named the Holohan McKinlay Building and is now a U.S. Bank branch.

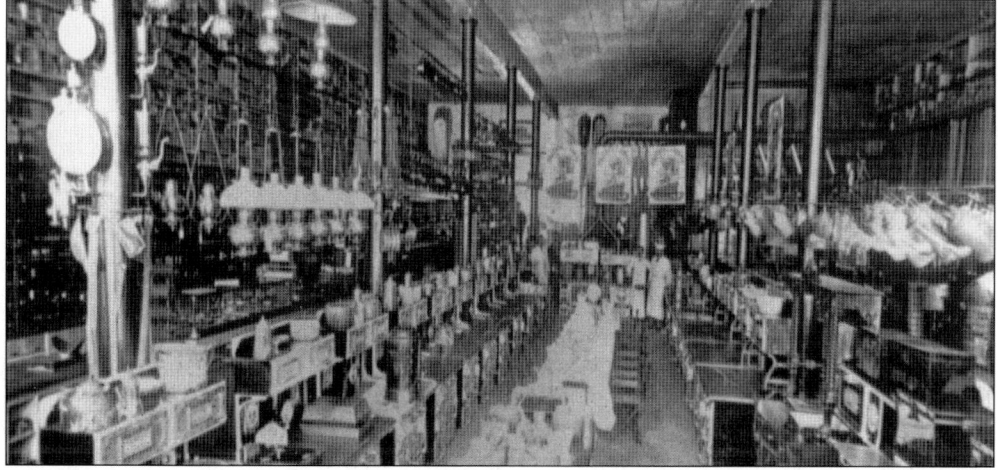

Mason, Marks, and Company, seen in this 1890s photograph, stocked everything to get a new home up and running. These beautiful Queen Anne wood stoves were the top of the line. With the upper warming ovens and some even had tanks behind that heated water so running hot water was possible. Dishes and cookware are lined up on the tables down the center, and oil lamps are hanging from the ceiling.

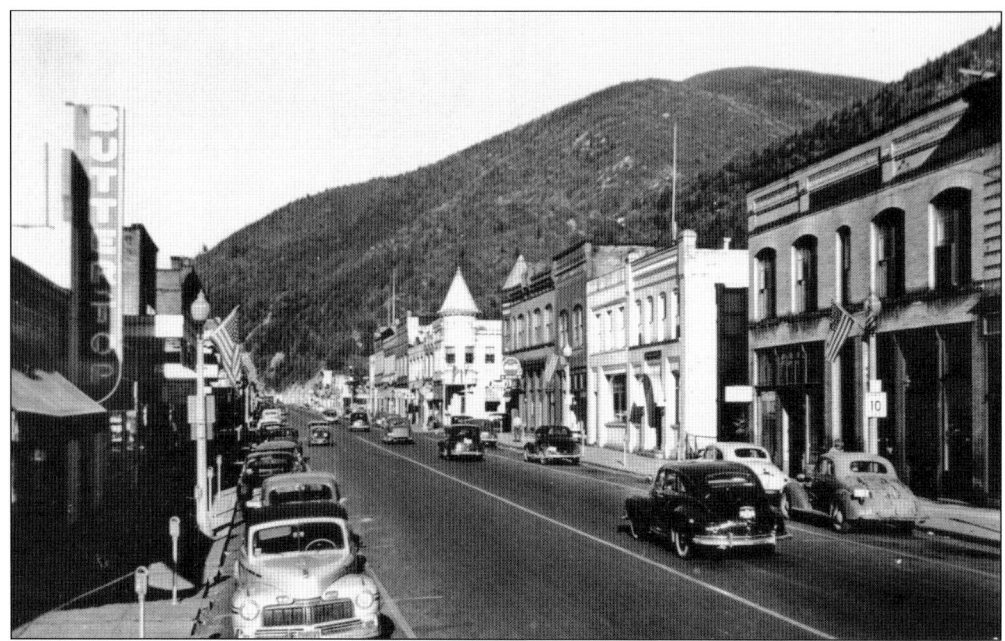

For many years, Bank Street in Wallace was Highway 10. Mrs. Rice's Bakery with the large "BUTTERTOP" sign was the first neon sign created by the Williams Brothers, soon to be called American Sign and Indicator. This was also the first home of the Coeur d'Alene Mines Corporation. The intersection about two blocks up the street is where the last stoplight on Interstate 90 was located for many years.

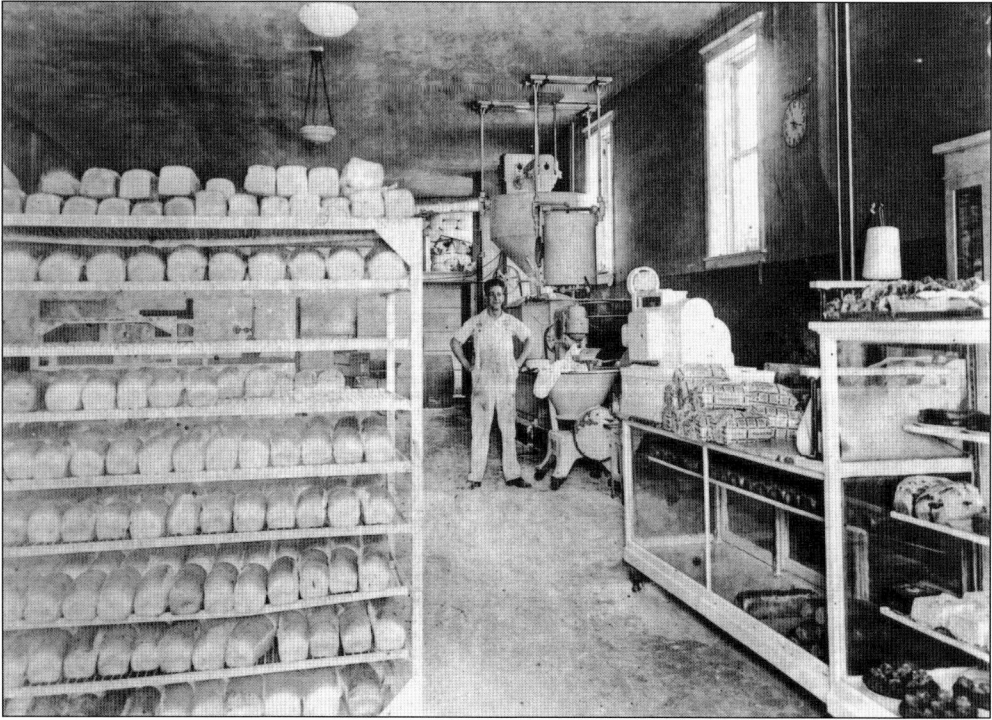

Can't you just smell the fresh bread?

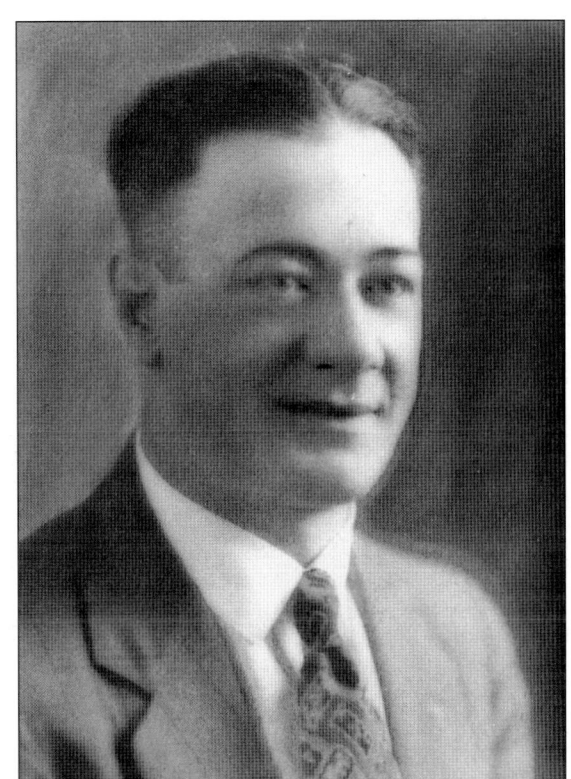

Harlow Rice and Anna Rice were the owners of the Rice Bakery in Wallace. It would be the base for Coeur d'Alene Mines. Their son, Justin L. Rice, would take the company to amazing heights before he retired in the 1980s. Known as the "mine finder," J. L. Rice is still active in the mining industry at the young age of 92.

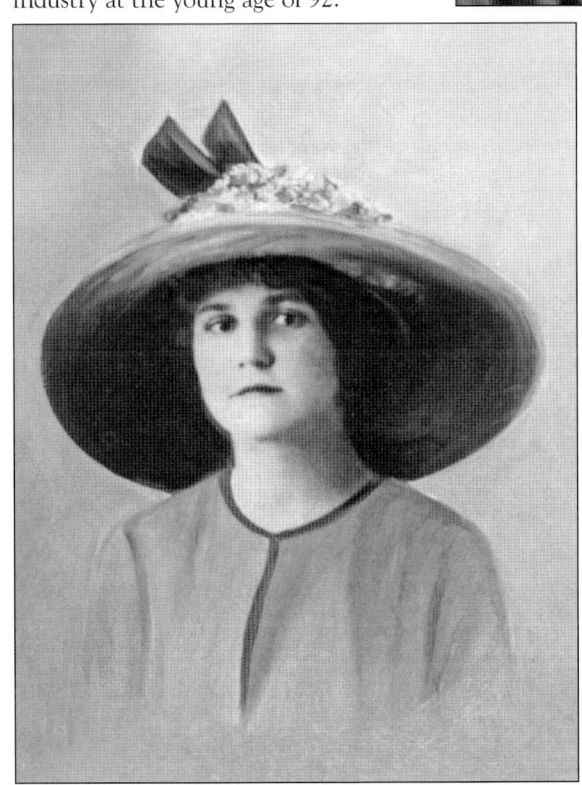

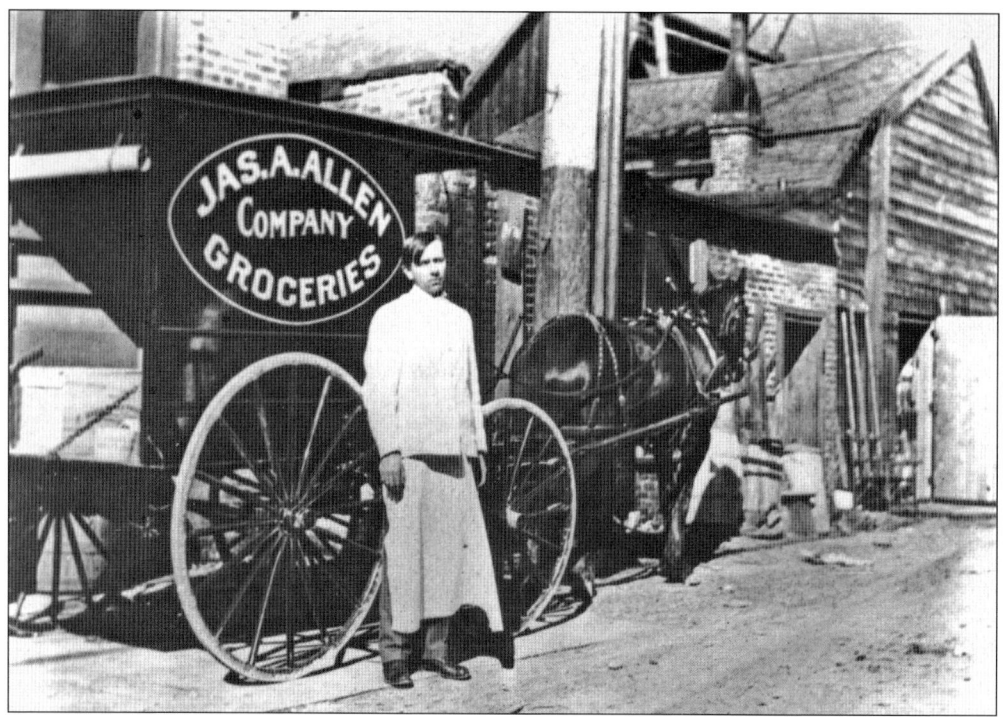

Oh, for the good old days when shops delivered to your door. Here the Jas. A. Allen Groceries Company makes its deliveries by horse and wagon in Mullan.

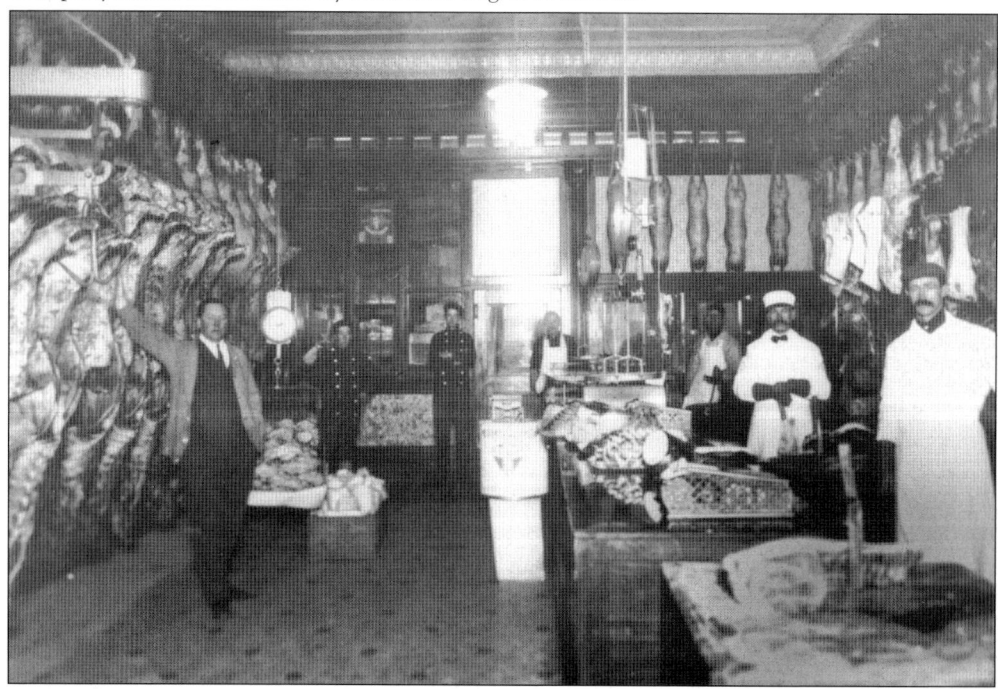

It is hard to believe that meat was sold this way at the Wallace Meat market, featured in this c. 1900 image. Customers could stop by or, after telephones came to town, could call in an order for home delivery. Pick out not just the cut, but which animal you wanted it from.

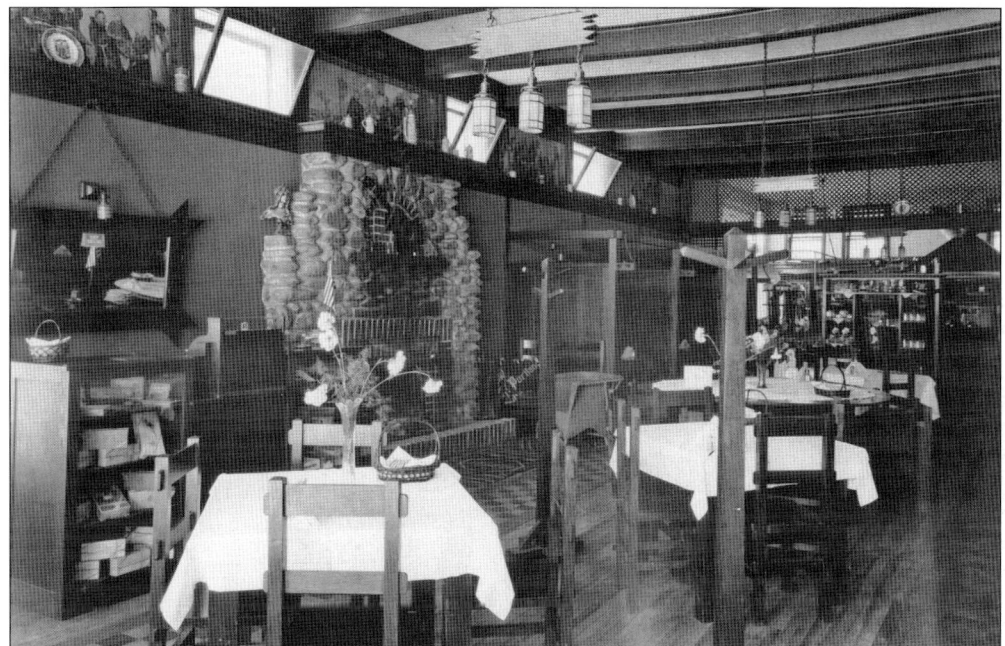

The Grotto was an elegant restaurant in Wallace, located in the Shoshone Building at Bank and Fifth Street. The flowers on the tables are real. Along the top of the walls are murals featuring monks, wine, and feasting. The beams and decor give the Old World feeling that the food was probably French or German.

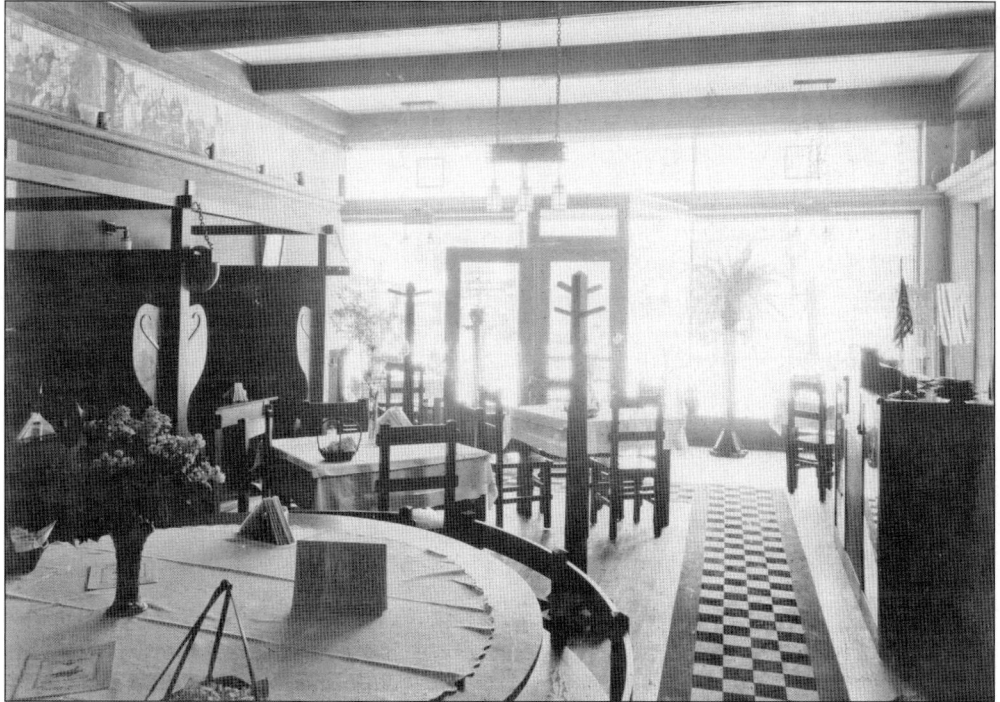

This photograph of The Grotto shows the booths along the wall that gave privacy from the neighboring tables. Brilliant sunshine streams through the front windows.

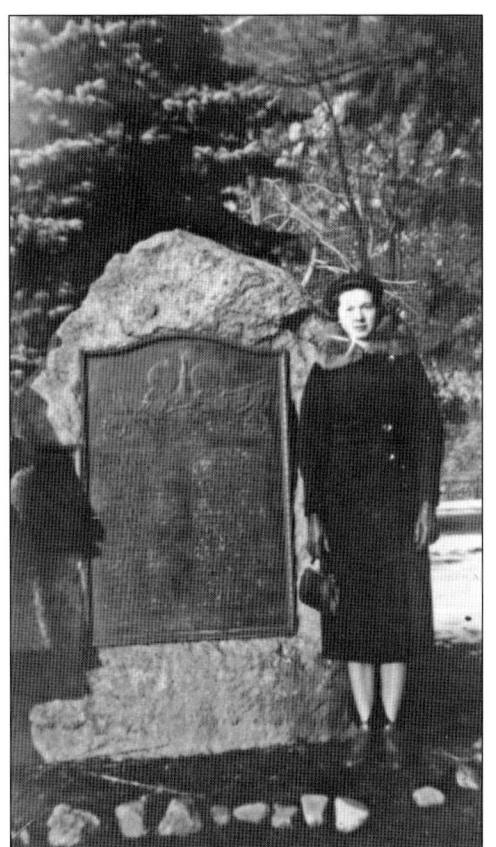

This photograph shows the memorial to the World War II solders from Wallace. Sometime in the last 40 years, it had been removed when the park was taken out and the school gym was built. The plaque was stored away and forgotten. When the local VFW started working on a Veterans' Memorial to be built in Kellogg they started a search for the plaque. When arguments about whether it had ever been in the city park on a rock started, this photograph was used to show where and how it was displayed, proving once again that photographic and written history are important for today. It is back now where it belongs, proudly sitting next to the Carnegie Library in Wallace.

It is believed that the cannon in Wallace City Park was melted down during World War II when the scrap-metal drives were going on all over America. At any rate, it disappeared along with the fountain. No one is sure where it went.

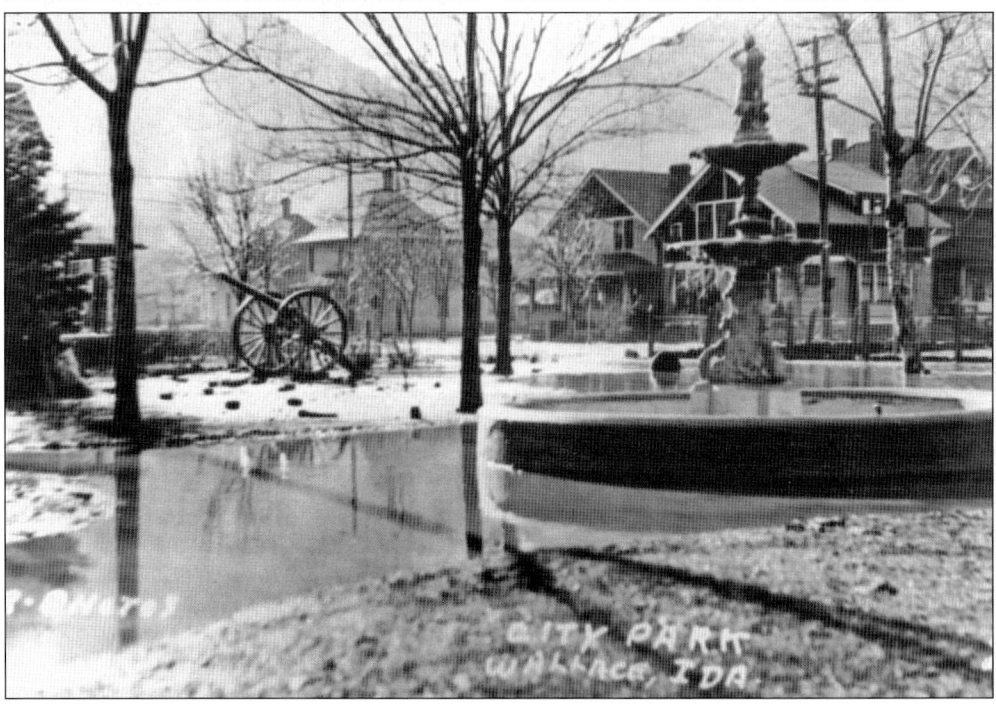

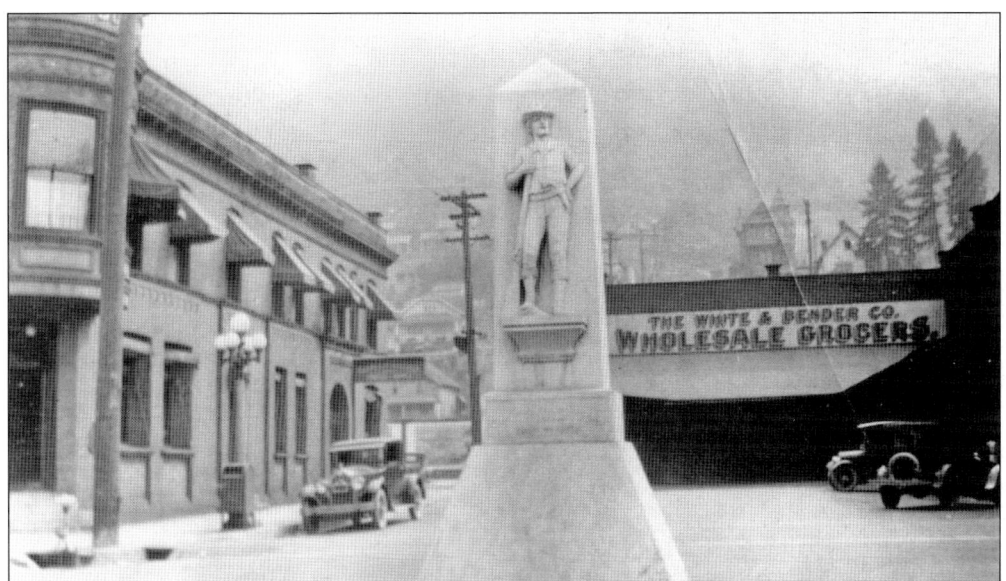

The Capt. John Mullan statue, pictured here in 1918, along with others, marks the trail that the then Lieutenant Mullan blazed through the valley as he cut the wagon road for the military. Being the first road into the valley made it possible to have freight wagons bring in goods and people. This statue stood at the intersection of Bank and Sixth Streets. When Bank Street became part of U.S. Highway 10 it was moved to a small park on Fifth Street, still on the Mullan Trail but no longer in the traffic lane. The Capt. John Mullan statue was a gift from William A. Clark, the Pioneers of Montana, and the Idaho Historical Society.

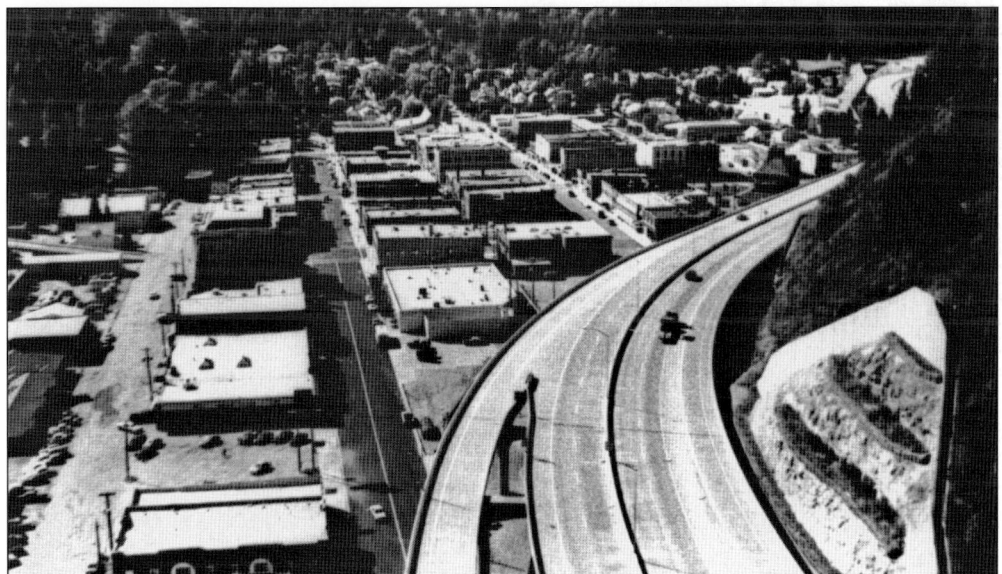

This is the freeway that started the Historic Wallace Preservation Society. The highway hugs the mountain on the north side of town and is raised on supports that have allowed for a paved bike path and walkway underneath. The Trail of the Coeur d'Alenes is an Idaho State Park. It is 72 miles long, following the original railroad line that moved the mined ore out of the Silver Valley to the smelters. On Labor Day weekend every year, the Under the Freeway Flea Market is held. (Courtesy of Shauna Hillman.)

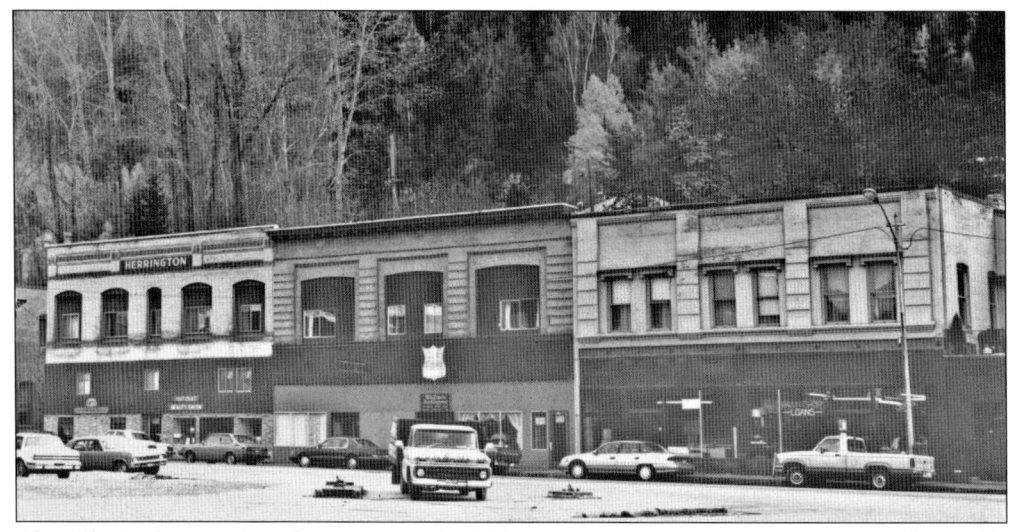

The Elks Lodge, instituted on January 4, 1896, was in the middle building in this block. On the sidewalk in front, elk tracks can be seen in the cement. The first building to the left is the Harrington, built by a dentist in 1898. The Elks Lodge was built in 1905; the down stairs was originally a general mercantile. The building on the far right is the Morbeck Building, built in 1902. This building served as the post office until the new Federal Building was finished in 1935. (Courtesy of Shauna Hillman.)

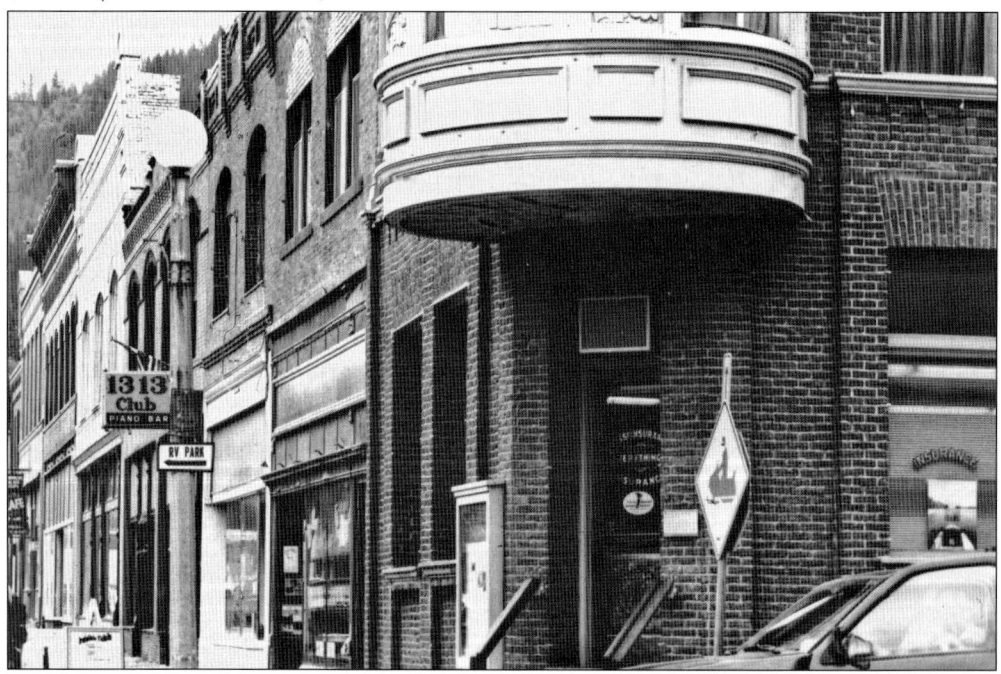

Notice the snowmobile sign. Snowmobiles and All Terrain Vehicles (ATVs) may legally run on the streets of Wallace. These riders enjoy about 600 miles of roads and trails in the mountains of the Silver Valley. The sign above the "RV Park" sign tells drivers to park 2 feet from the curb. For many years, Wallace had the streets swept twice a day. In order to keep the curbs clean, cars had to park far enough out so that the cleaning crew could get between them and the sidewalk. Even the alleys were paved with sidewalks in Wallace. (Courtesy of Shauna Hillman.)

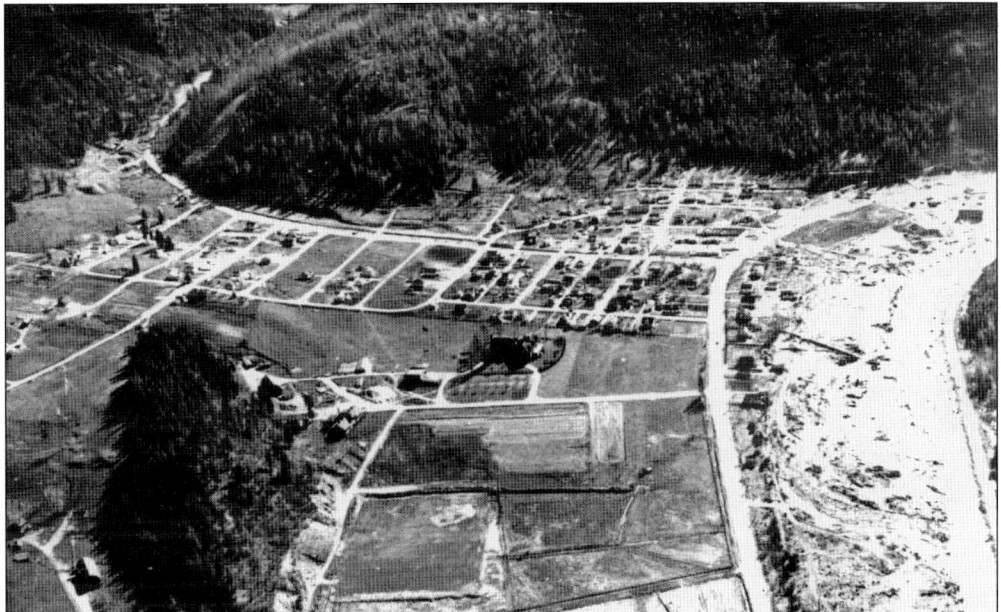

The large building in this 1920s photograph of Silverton is the Poor Farm. In later years, it would be used as the county hospital. The brickyard that supplied the bricks used in building the business districts for the most part came from here. Markwell's Dairy and Orchards provided food for the local stores or delivered to homes in Wallace. The road running along the right side is the Yellowstone Highway.

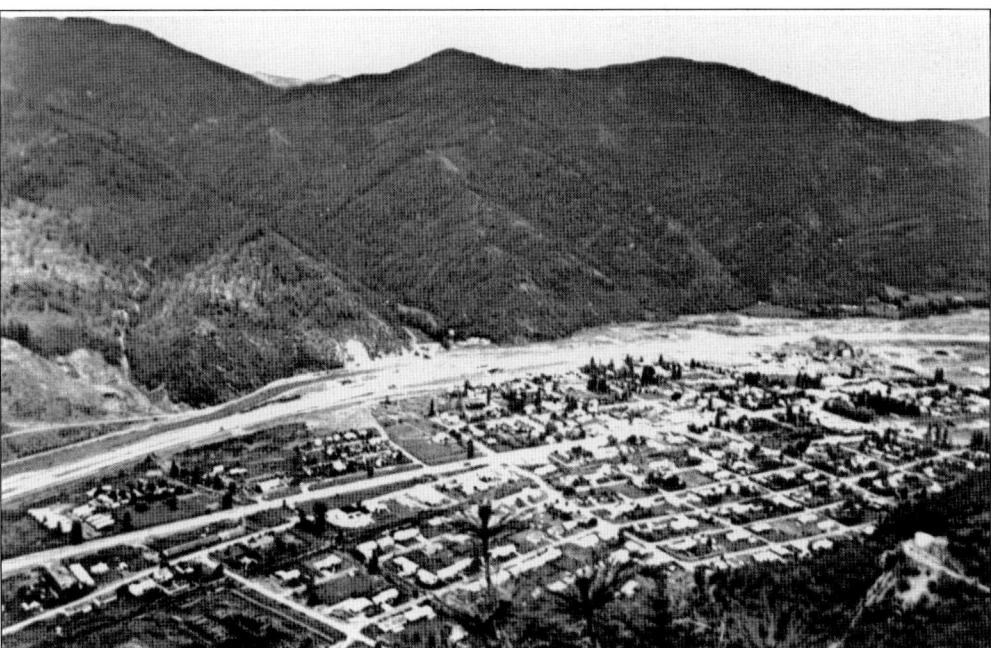

Osburn, in the 1920s, started out with just a trading post. Legend has it that this was the destination for the Shoshone County seat and that the records were "hijacked" at the top of Two Mile Creek during the transfer and moved to Wallace, making it the third county seat for Shoshone County, Idaho.

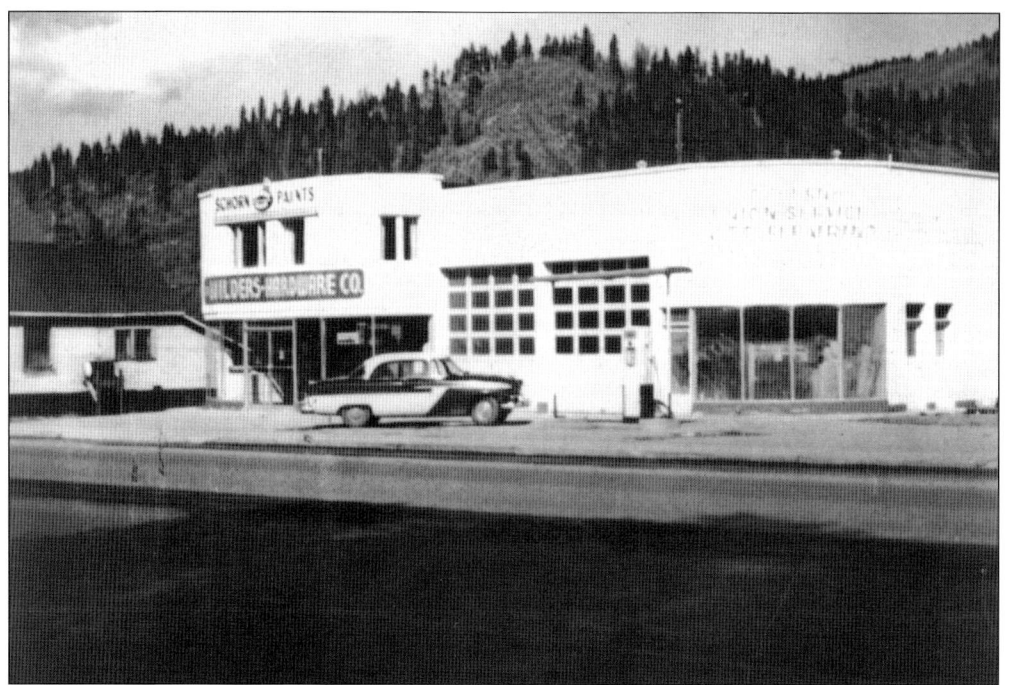

Builders Hardware was located on Mullan Avenue in Osburn and was the base of operations for McKim and Kaiser Construction Company. They built many of the schools and businesses as well as homes in the Silver Valley.

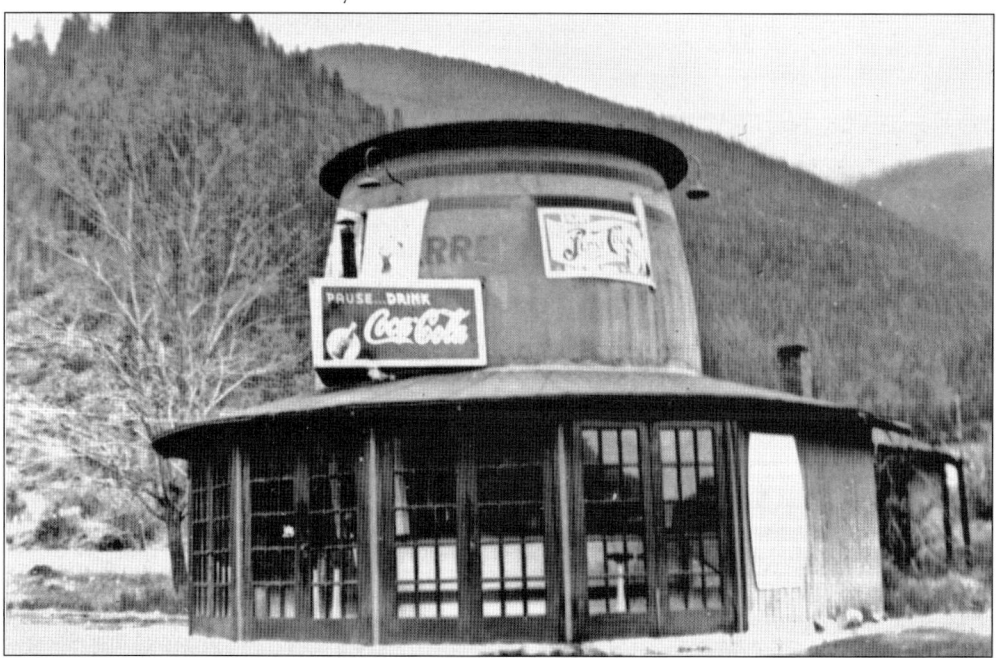

During the 1930s and 1940s, it became popular to build buildings that looked like their businesses name. Restaurants and bars were especially big on this fad. The Barrel was one of these, located on original route of U.S. Highway 10. You could get a great burger and Coke here with carhop service.

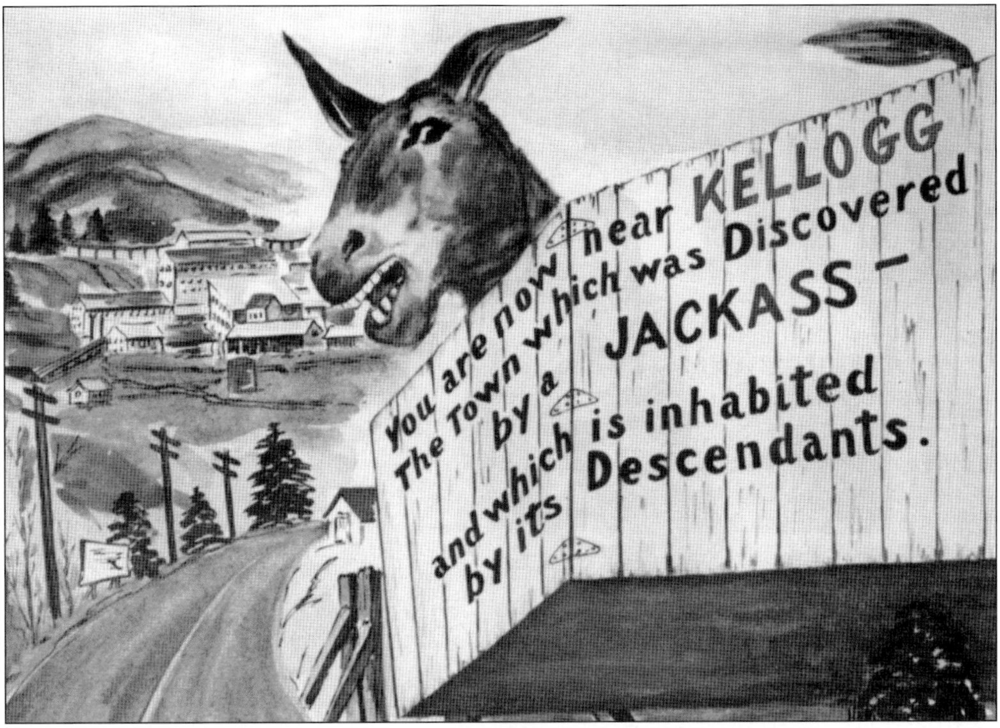

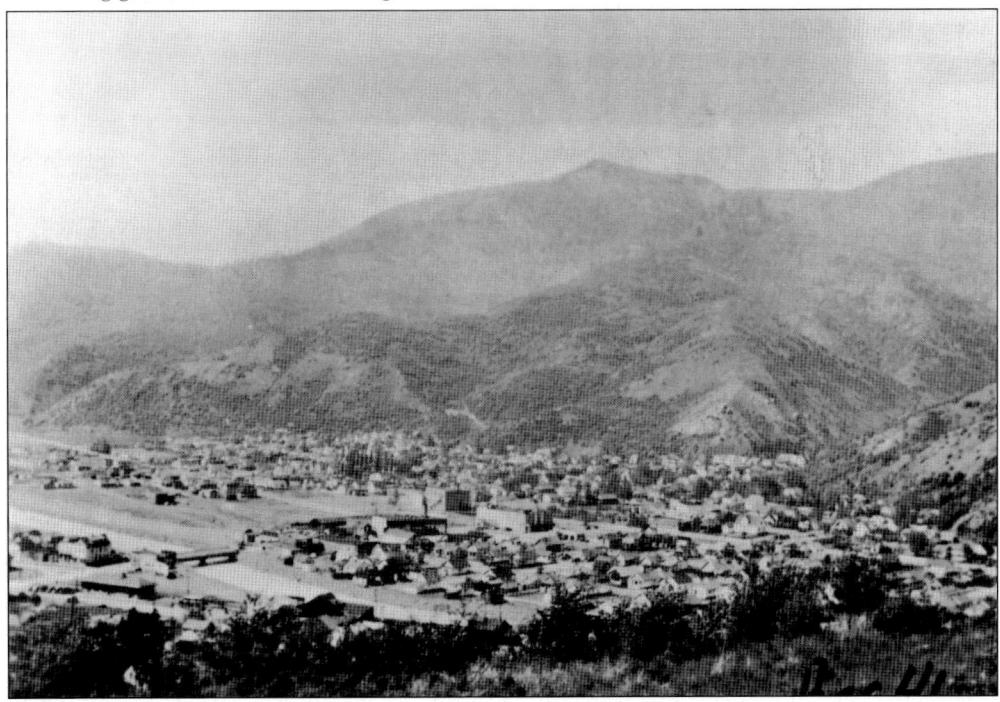

For many years, this billboard greeted travelers as they entered Kellogg from the west. After years of it being gone, it is back welcoming one and all.

This overview of Kellogg in 1941 shows the Sunnyside School and the Rena Theater building. They are the two large buildings in the center of the photograph.

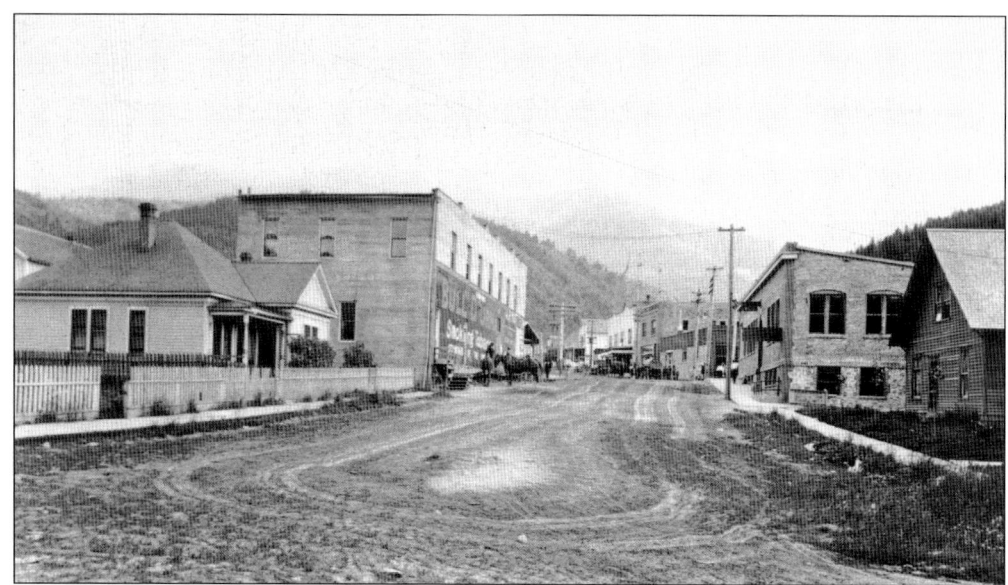

This c. 1900 photograph shows Main Street in Kellogg, looking south. The Bull Durham sign is on the side of the Hutton Department store. This store would continue to operate into the 1970s, when it was lost to a fire. Across the street the brick building was a bank. The dark house to the right will become the funeral home.

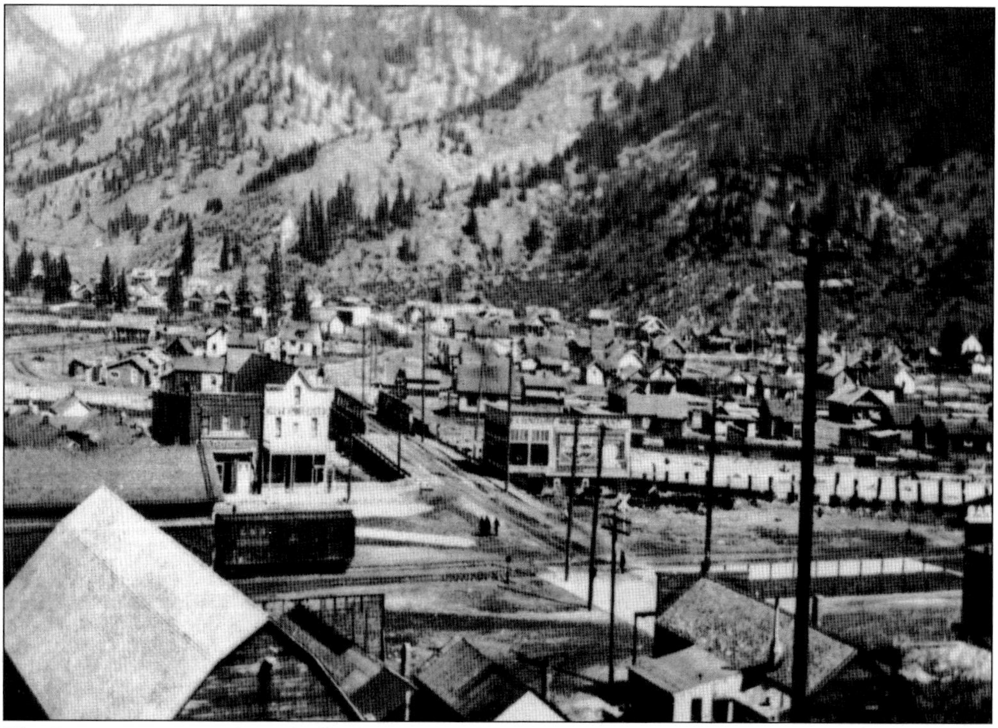

The furniture store to the right by the river in this c. 1890 photograph is now a dry cleaner. Across the street is the Idaho Hotel. The building with the ladder on the roof is the freight depot for the Northern Pacific; today this is Excelsior Bicycle Shop located on the Trail of the Coeur d'Alenes, a beautiful green belt through the community.

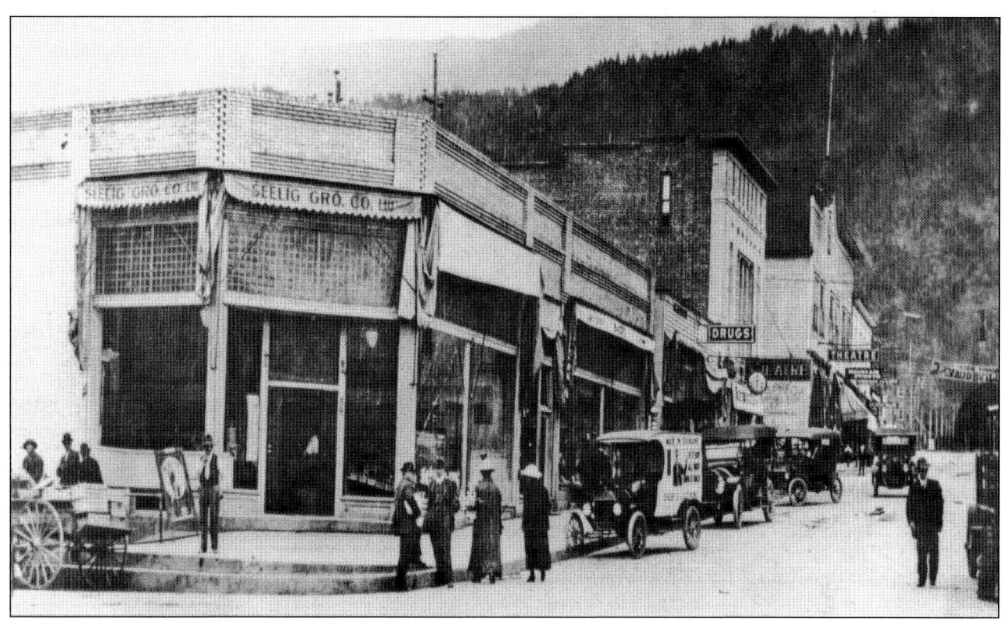

This is the corner of Main Street and McKinley Avenue in Kellogg, pictured in 1914. Seelig Groceries later had a store in Wallace at the south end of Sixth Street. Down the street are two theaters, a billiards hall, and a sign advertising a vaudeville show in the theater on Main Street. Kellogg was known as the "twin city" to Wardner for many years. Several businesses established in Wardner started a second store in the Kellogg business district. Today Twin City Furniture on McKinley Avenue still bears the name.

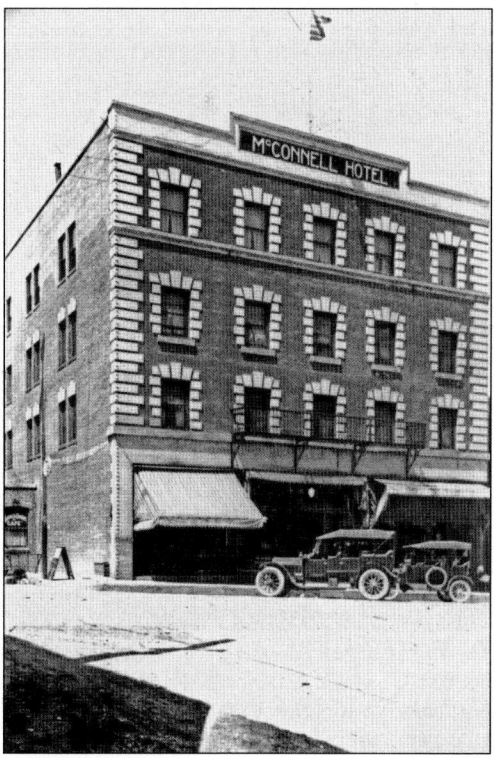

This c. 1917 photograph shows McConnell Hotel, which was the home of KWAL radio station for many years. Being four stories high and on the upper part of Main Street gave the antennas the height needed to broadcast. From the 1920s to the 1950s, part of the romance of radio was when the announcer would say, "KWAL. Brought to you live from the roof top of the McConnell Hotel." On the ground floor was a café, the hotel lobby, and another business.

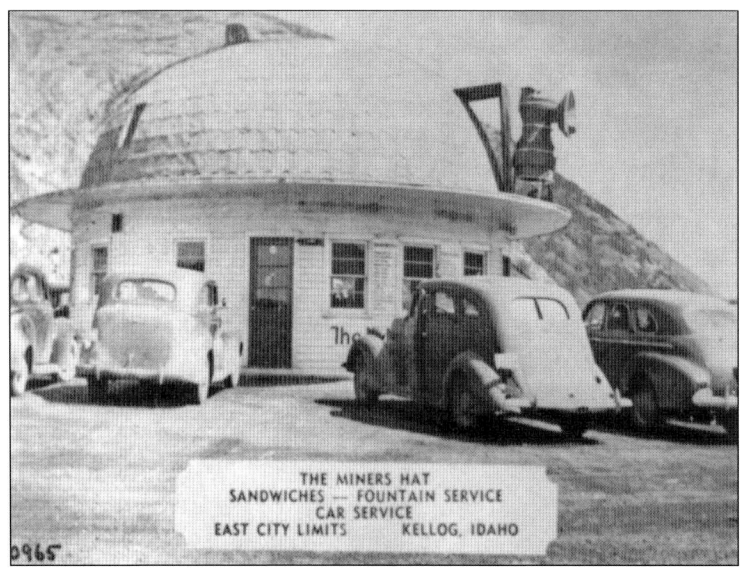

Like Osburn's Barrel, Kellogg had the Miners Hat, featured in this c. 1920 photograph. Carhops on roller skates took orders and brought around burgers, fries, and milkshakes. The building is shaped like the helmets miners wear underground and is complete with a headlamp that lit up the night sky. The lamp still lights the nighttime sky. By day, it is Miners Hat Realty.

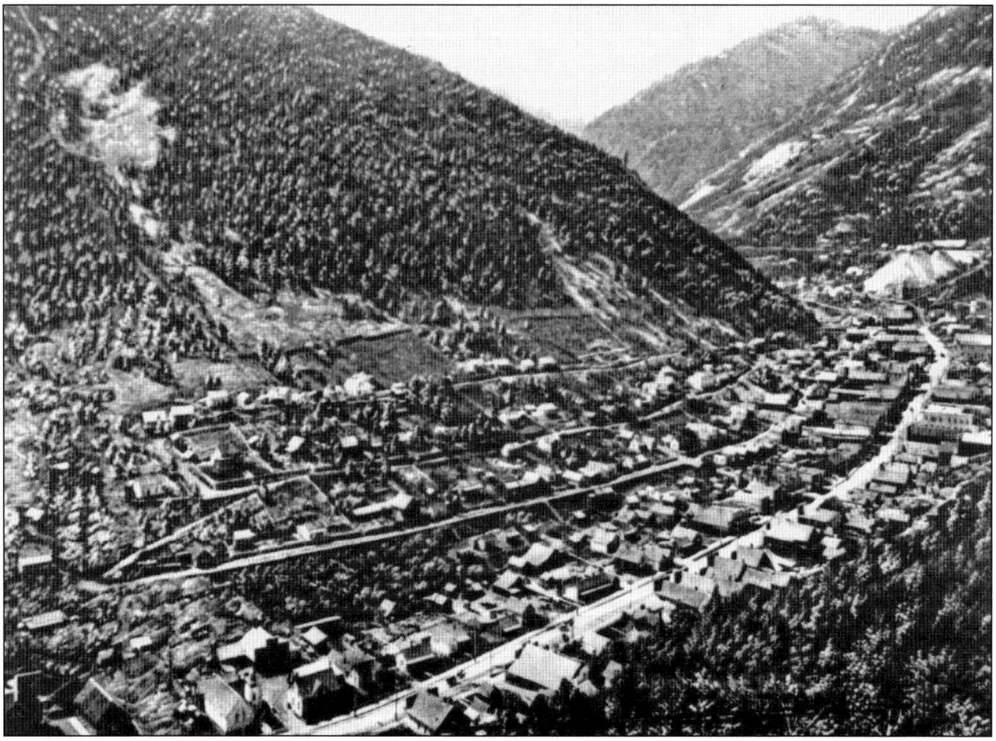

This c. 1900 photograph shows Wardner. South of Kellogg, Wardner grew up around the Bunker Hill and Sullivan Mining Company holdings. Like the towns up Burke Canyon, homes were built up the mountainsides. But after forest fires and the clearing of timber for housing and the mines, there was nothing to hold the snow back and a snow slide would devastate Wardner in the coming years. Wardner's business district ran along the valley floor while homes were built up the mountainside. In the 1940s, a snow slide coming down in the two areas that were clear-cut would wipe out homes and take lives. The Bunker Hill mine workings moved around the ridge, and so did its "twin city," Kellogg.

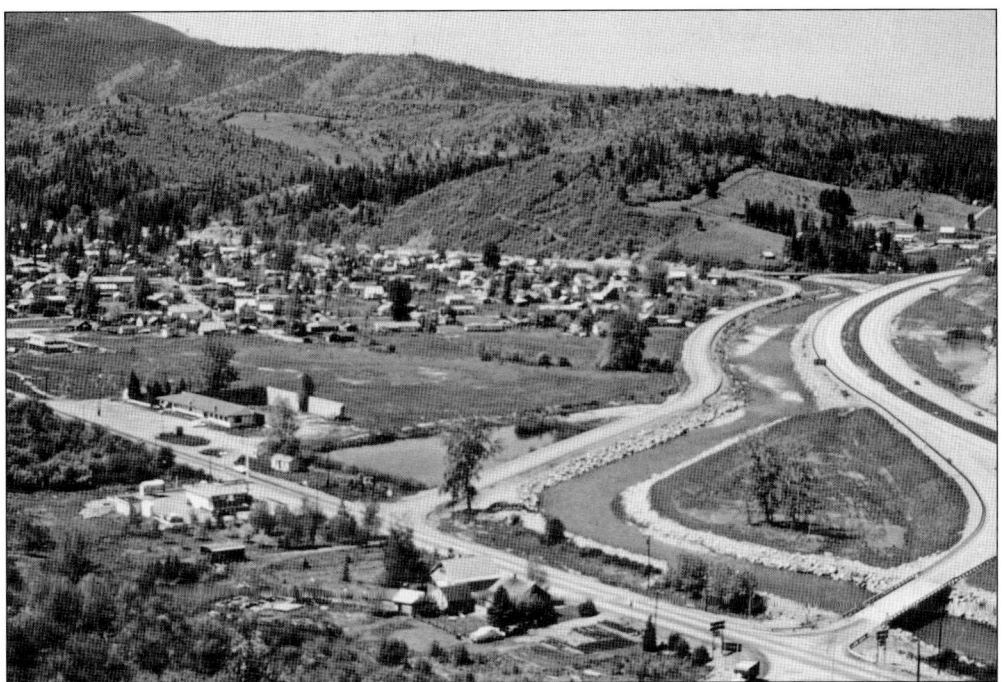

This shows Pinehurst in 1971. The second house on the way into town was where The Dutchman had a flower nursery. It was fun to visit there because you had to take your shoes off and put on wooden shoes before you could come into the home. Just down the road is Shiplett's Chevron service station on the left. This is still a full service gasoline and auto maintenance facility. On the right is the Tee Off Bar. These photographs were taken shortly after the new freeway was built. (Courtesy of Lawanna Watts.)

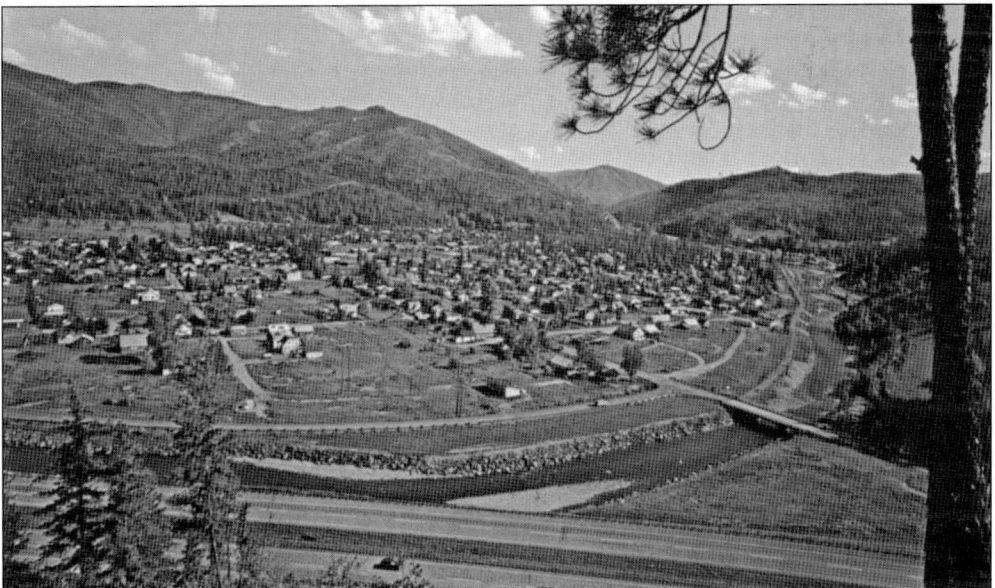

This photograph of Pinehurst shows the bridge on the west side of town. In the 40 years since Dr. Wallace planned out the town and sold the first lots in 1920s, the town has really grown. (Courtesy of Lawanna Watts.)

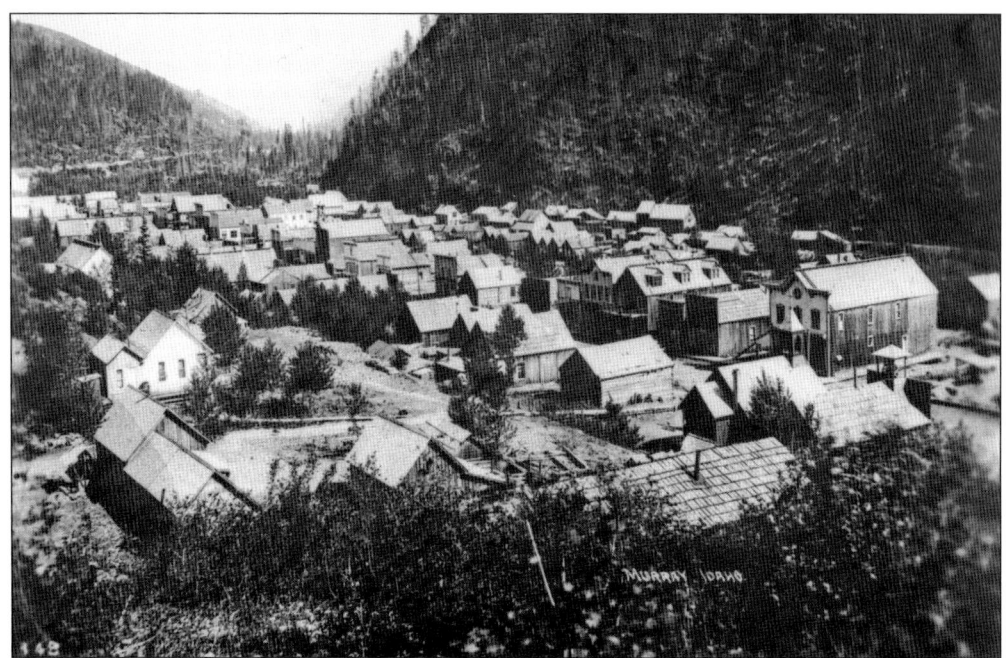

This c. 1887 photograph shows Murray, the heart of the last gold rush of the lower 48. The church and school are in the lower right corner. Gold Street next to the mountain was the location of businesses that were more then happy to take a miner's gold as payment for services.

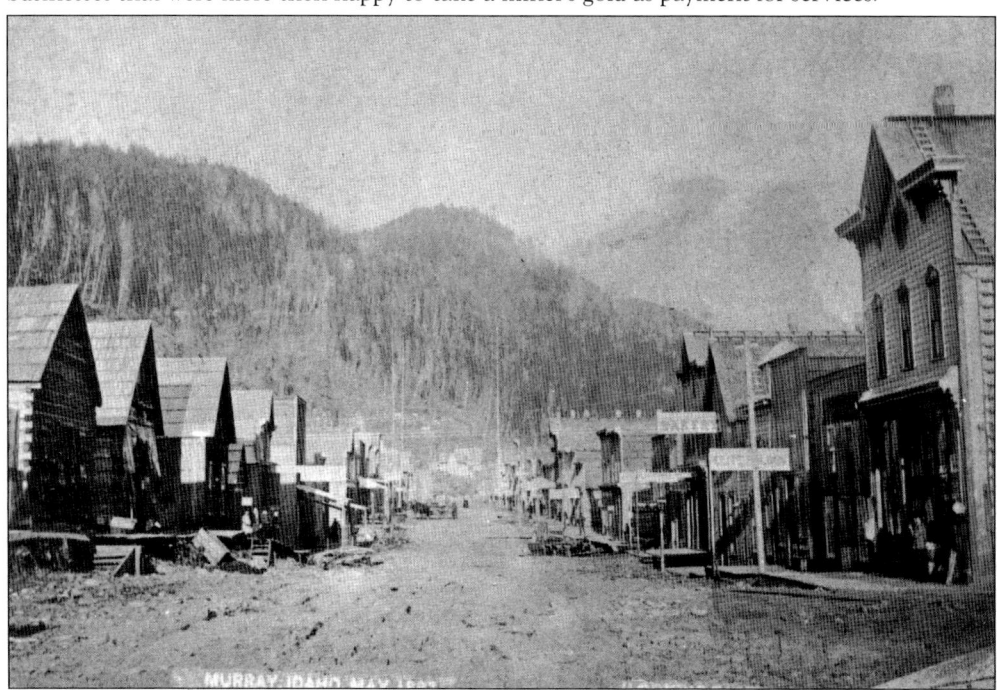

Like most mining towns, Murray, pictured in May 1887, was built by two types of people: those who saw a future here and those who came to get rich and leave. This picture clearly shows on the right those planning to stay: well-built and well-maintained buildings. On the left are log cabins with piles of junk out front.

# Two

# Hospitals

Building a new community is a dangerous business. Men can be injured in mining, construction, logging and hunting accidents—as well as in the occasional fight. There were also, of course epidemics, illnesses, and births. These needs brought doctors to the camps in their early days. With doctors first working out of their homes, offices, and small clinics, the communities' need for hospitals became overwhelming.

Because of the distance between Mullan and Kellogg, the valley boasted multiple hospitals for years, including three in Wallace. Among them was the Hope, on the upper floor of the Morrow Department Store building. This space would later be occupied by mining offices and is currently the Brooks Hotel.

The Frances Holland Memorial Hospital was built at the west end of Cedar Street. This beautiful white building was built with the funds donated by a woman from back east. Mrs. Holland, wished to leave a legacy of her husband where it would be most needed. Over the years this hospital would be rebuilt and renamed until the final building no longer resembled its original design. It ended its service to the community as the Wallace City Hospital in 1964.

Providence Hospital was operated by The Sisters of Providence and built by deductions from the pay of Central Miners Union members, often referred to as the miners' hospital. The Providence, while having been built with miners' money, did not give free services to those same miners who could not pay for care.

Silverton was home to the County Poor Farm where the county hospital was located for many years. This large brick building operated as a nursing home and hospital for those who could not afford the treatment. Later this building would house U.S. Forest Service offices. Today it is awaiting its next adventure in serving the valley. Henry L. Day Hospital, also known as East Shoshone Hospital, was built next-door to the county hospital. It is a flat-roofed building that had a short life span. With the lowering price of silver and rising costs of healthcare, mismanagement of the hospital caused its closing. It is now a publishing company's office space.

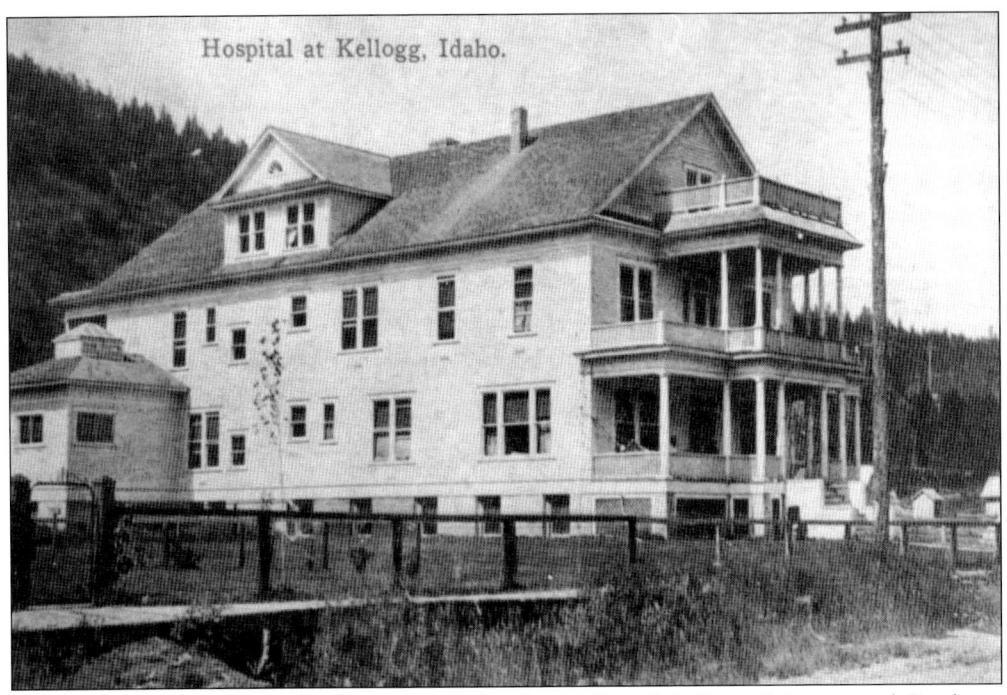

This is Wardner Hospital in Kellogg. The Bunker Hill and Sullivan Mining and Smelting Company garnished a fee from the miner's union to pay for the construction during the same time as Providence Hospital was constructed in Wallace.

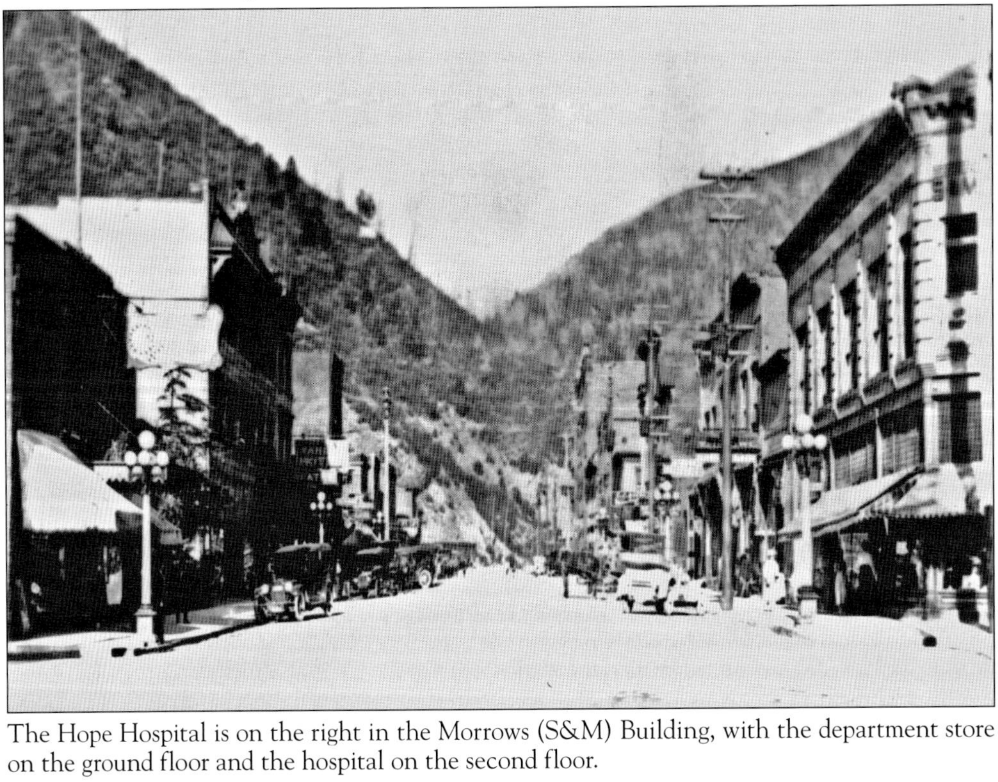

The Hope Hospital is on the right in the Morrows (S&M) Building, with the department store on the ground floor and the hospital on the second floor.

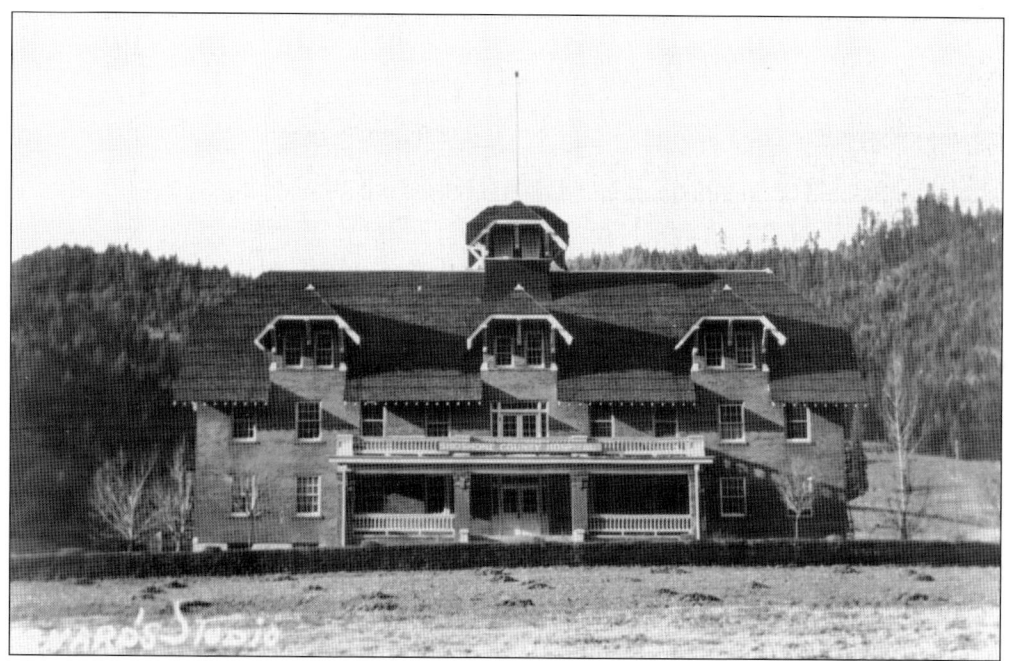

The County Poor Farm located in Silverton would later be called the County Hospital. The smaller building to the left was the Veteran's Home; later it would become one of the best schools for children with challenges. The woman who ran the school said, "No child was unteachable; there were simply teachers that did not know how to reach them."

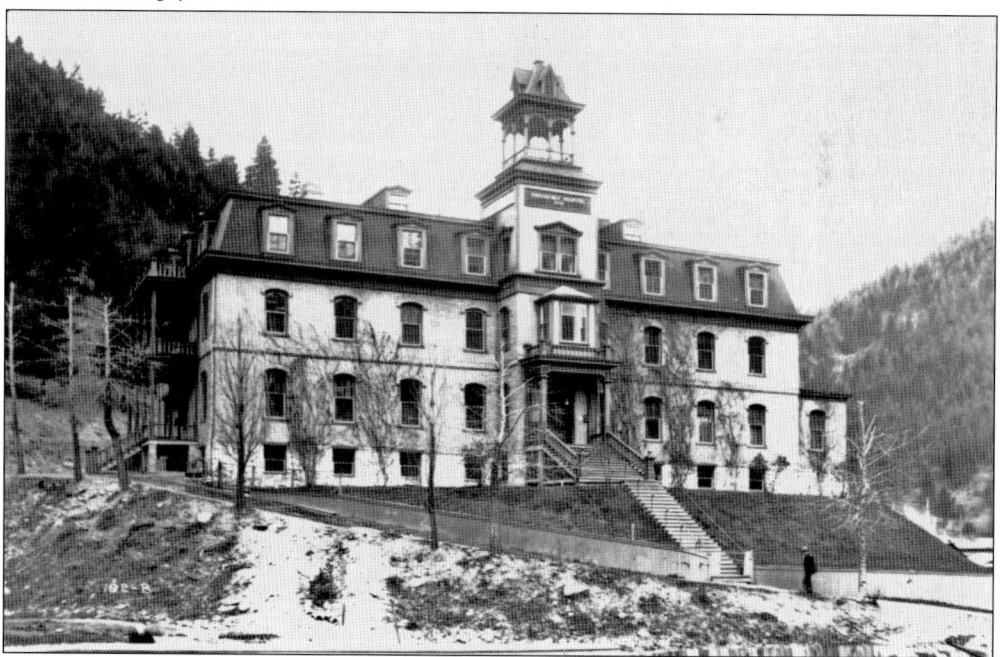

Providence Hospital was built with money contributed from the Central Miner's Union. A. J. Gibson was the architect. The Providence Hospital opened in 1891 under the supervision of two Catholic Sisters, Sister Joseph and Sister Madalene of the Sisters of Providence Order. Providence Hospital was built using the bricks from the Trowbridge Brickyard of Silverton.

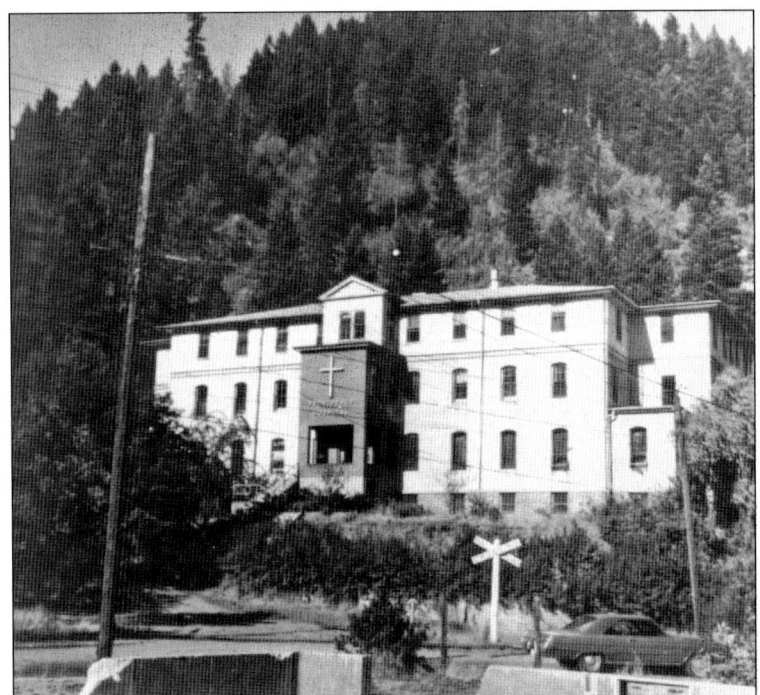

Providence Hospital was closed in 1962 and later condemned and removed by the Department of Transportation when their design for Interstate 90 was to come through Wallace.

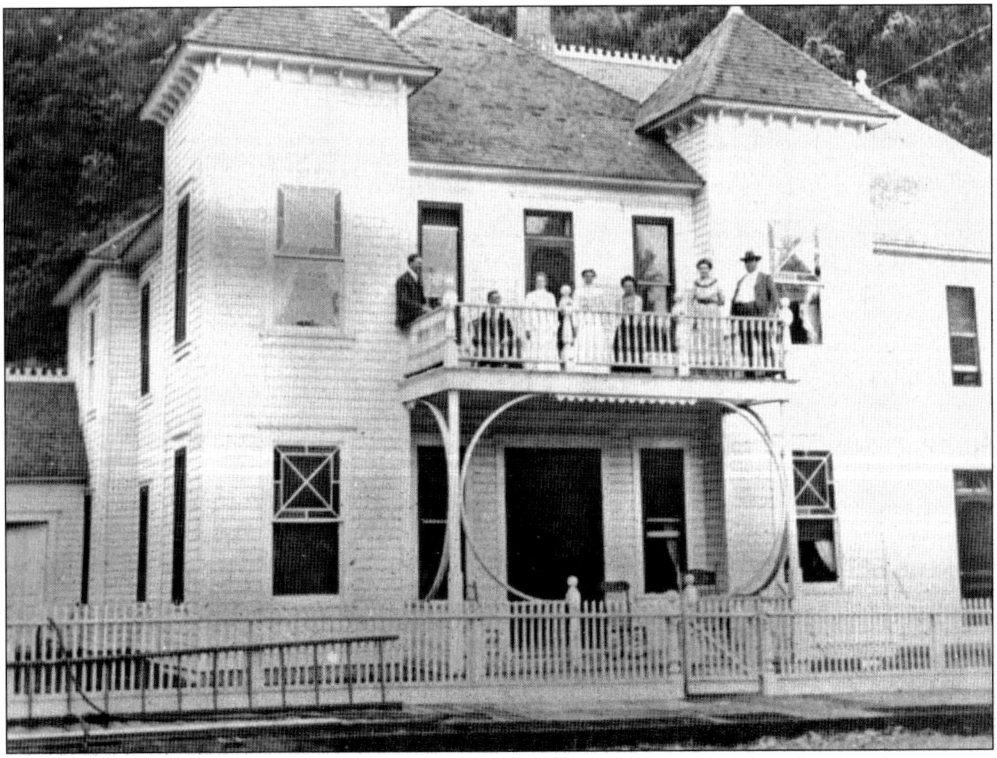

Frances Holland Memorial Hospital at the west end of Cedar Street was the first hospital in Wallace, opening in October 1890. In addition to the money given by Mrs. Holland, donations were taken from the Episcopal Church of Wallace to help build the hospital.

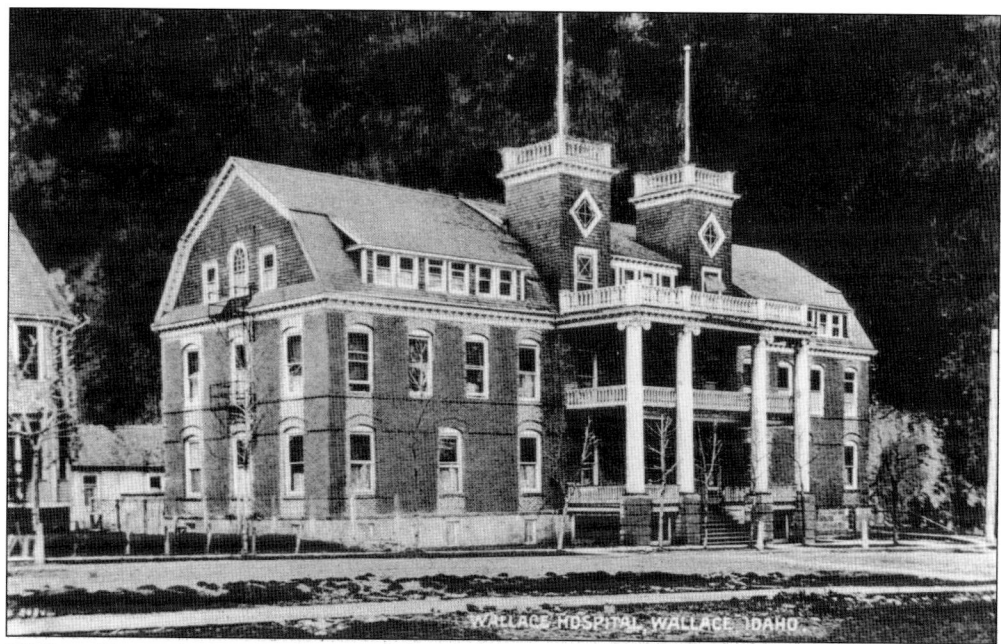

Wallace Hospital after the remodel in 1898. In 1910 this hospital treated the burns on Ranger Edward Pulaski and other firefighters.

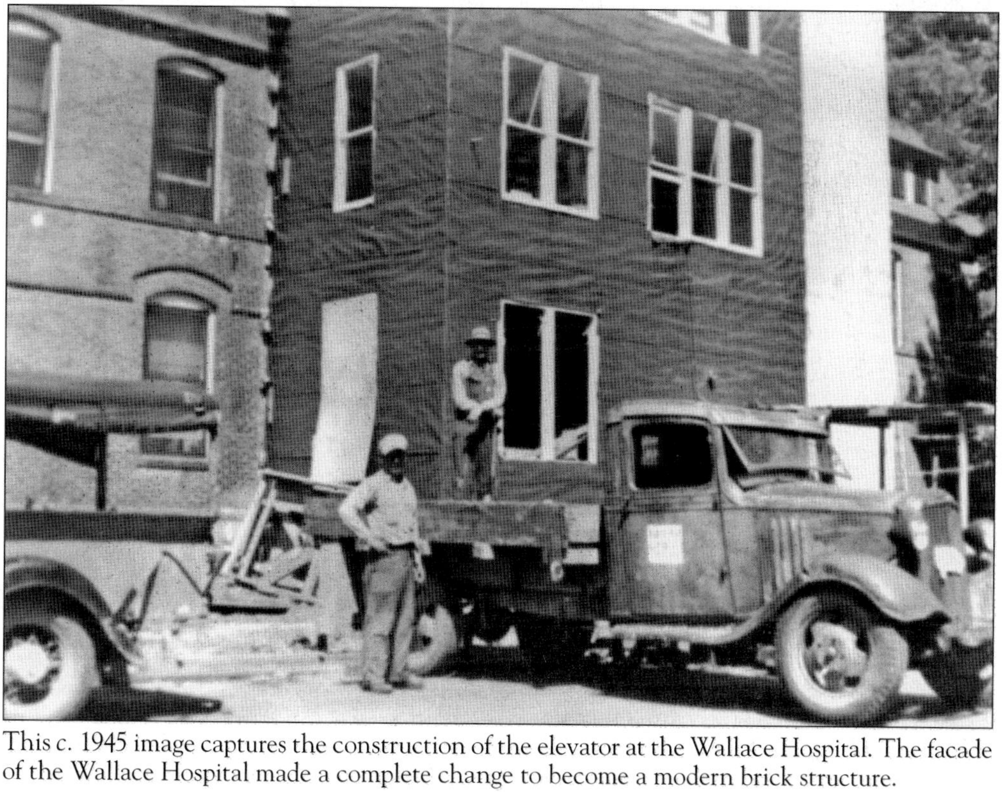

This c. 1945 image captures the construction of the elevator at the Wallace Hospital. The facade of the Wallace Hospital made a complete change to become a modern brick structure.

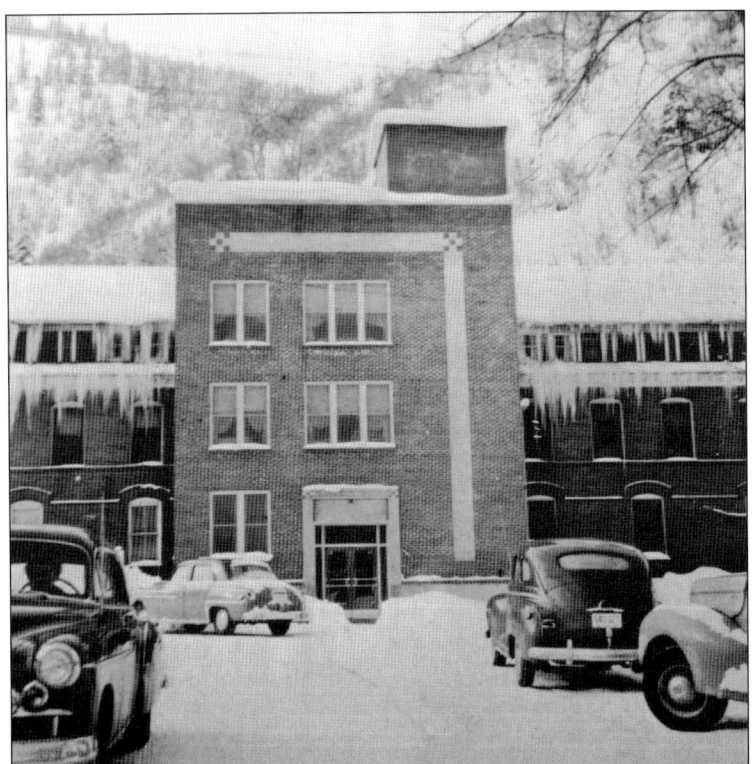

Wallace Hospital is pictured after the final remodeling with the addition of an elevator in 1946. Dr. E. E. "Ned" Gnaedinger was the final owner and administrator. The Wallace Hospital was torn down in 1973 and is now a city park.

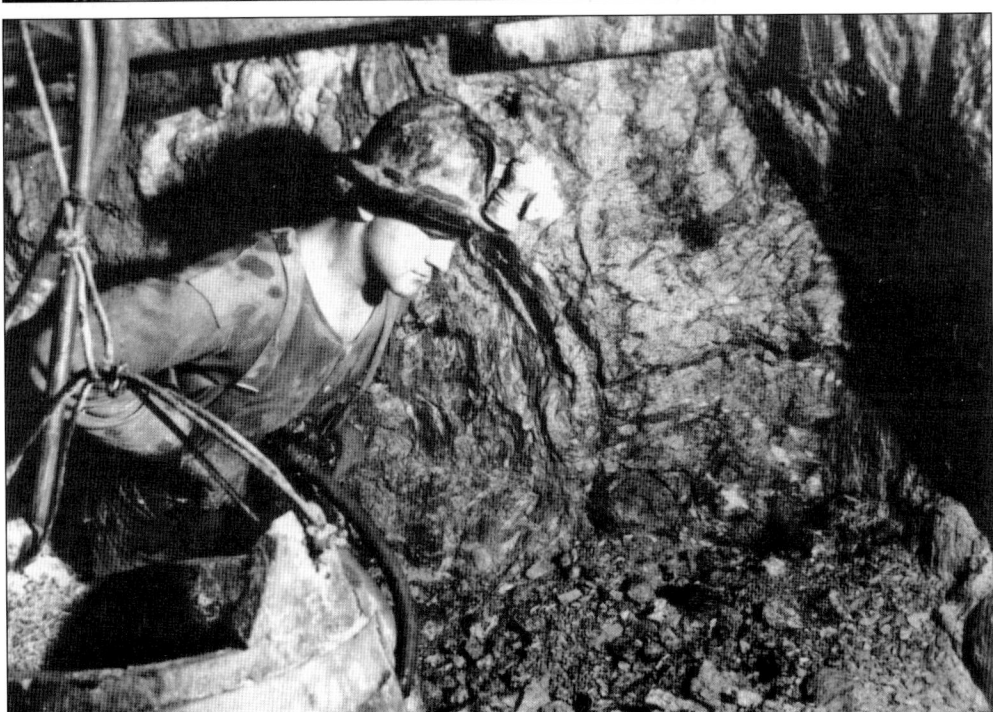

Dr. E. E. Gnaedinger worked his way through medical school with a mine scholarship. This image shows him working at the Silver Dollar Mine.

# Three

# Schools, Churches, and Courthouses

As soon as children arrived to the Silver Valley, so did schools. These schools not only educated their students, but also encouraged them in sports and music. Silver Valley schools have been represented at state events and have excelled. Bands from valley schools have even marched in Oregon's Rose Parade. Two Silver Valley schools have received the Excellence in Education Award from the U.S. Department of Education—an unprecedented feat in a community this size. Mining companies in the Silver Valley hire students to work summers to pay for college and give scholarships, and in the past would make agreements with promising young men to pay for their schooling if they would come back to the valley after college. This commitment to the valley by mining companies blessed it with doctors, judges, and engineers. While mining is considered by many to be mere manual labor, the high caliber of men who founded this valley brought a desire for improving not just their financial lives but also the minds of their children.

Towns that wanted women required churches. According to church records, the first recorded service was Episcopal, held in the fall of 1887 or the beginning of 1888, given by Bishop Talbot. The flyers advised to "Please leave your guns with the usher." While Bishop Talbot's experience was pleasant, Rev. H. W. Ferguson, of the Baptist church, had a less enjoyable stay. His last sermon was reported in the *Idaho Press* on October 24, 1905. His subject was "The Sodom of the Coeur d'Alenes," with Wallace, of course, being that ancient Biblical city. He attributed the lack of sunshine as a curse of God upon Wallace. A dozen times during the sermon, he bluntly appealed to all who wished to live upright lives to get out and stated that he himself "would take the next train."

Shoshone County has had a number of courthouses. Pierce held the designation as the first seat of Shoshone County in the Idaho Territory, as there was a minor gold rush and records needed to be kept close to the location. The Shoshone County seat moved to Murray with the next gold rush. When gold dredging ended, towns like Murray lost their populations overnight, so the seat was moved. Legend says the records were shipped to Osburn, but the people of Wallace, believing that they were the hub of the valley, hijacked the records. Wallace remains the county seat today.

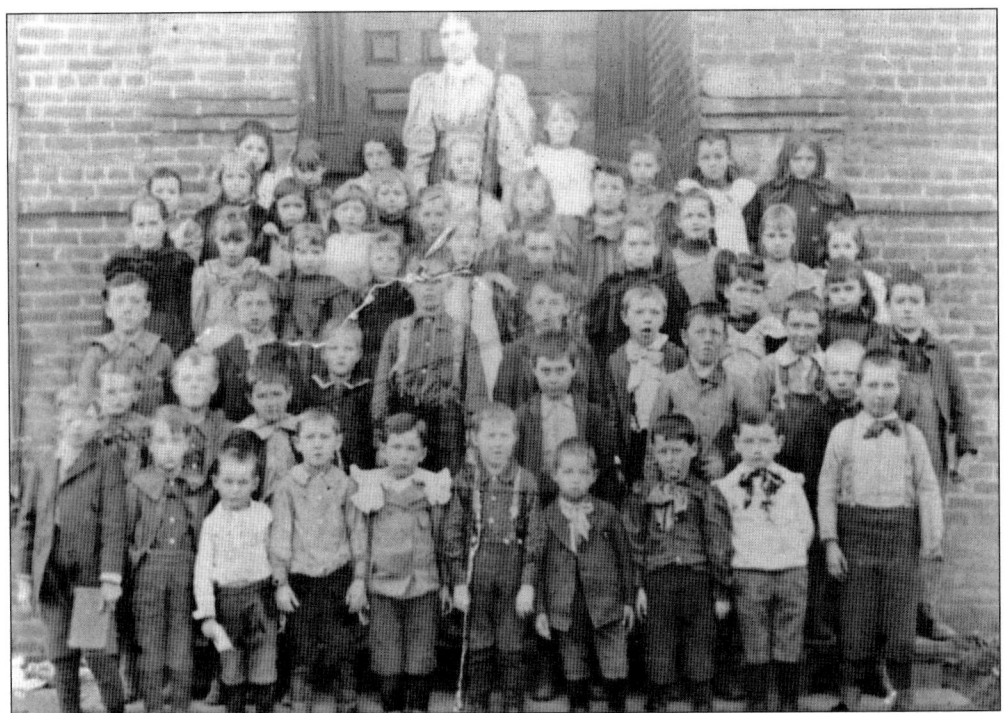

This c. 1860s class photograph was taken on the front steps of either the Mullan School or Burke School.

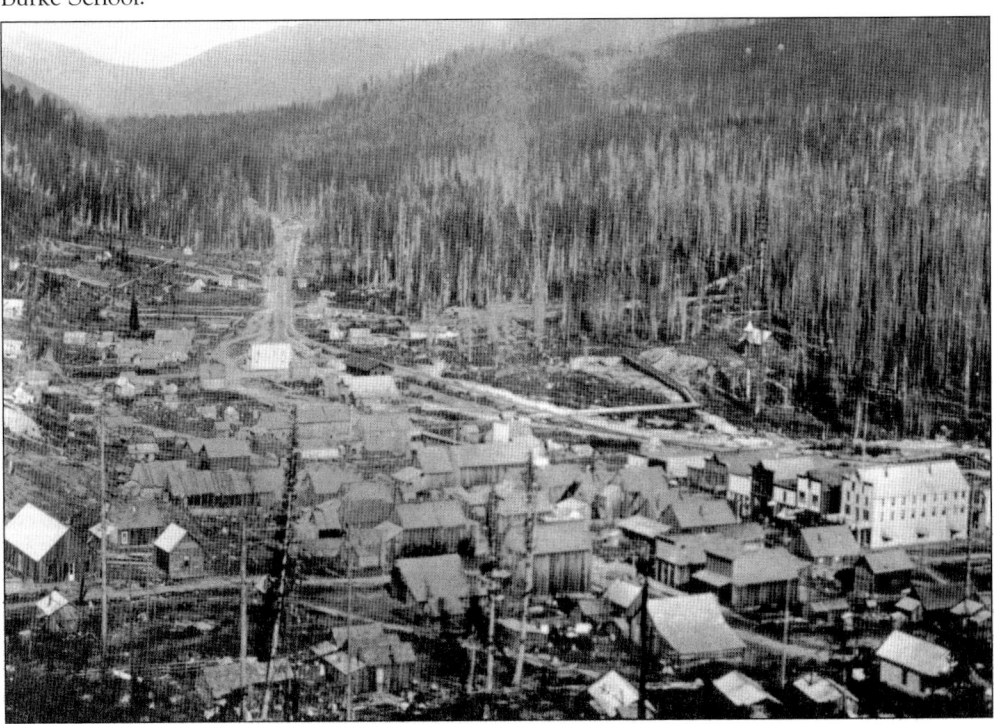

In this c. 1892 photograph, the small white building in the trees to the right is the Mullan schoolhouse.

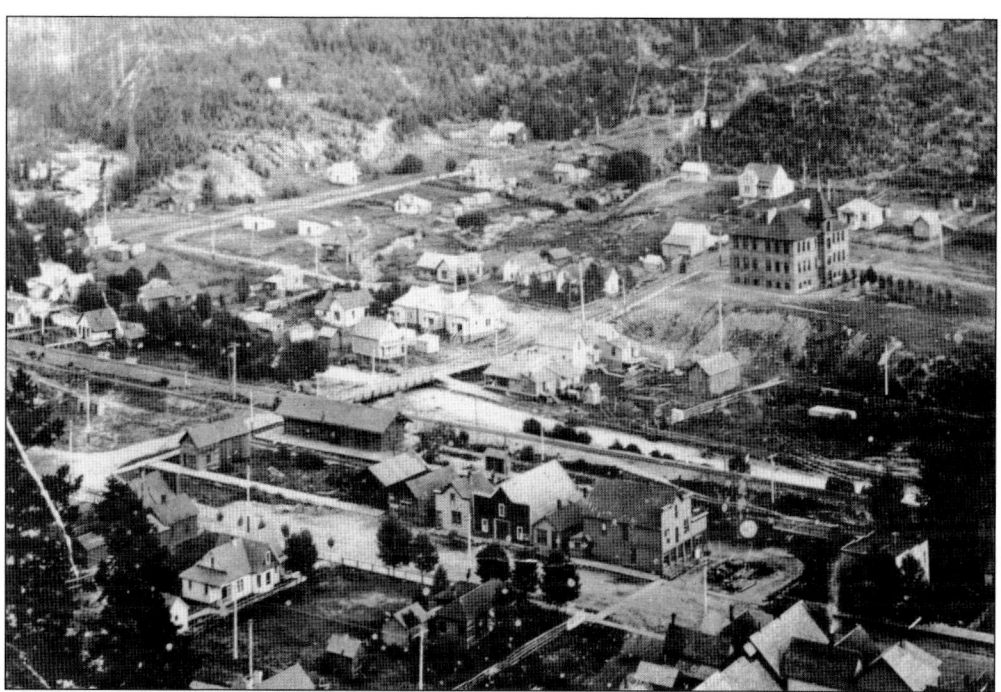

The large building on the hill is the Mullan schoolhouse.

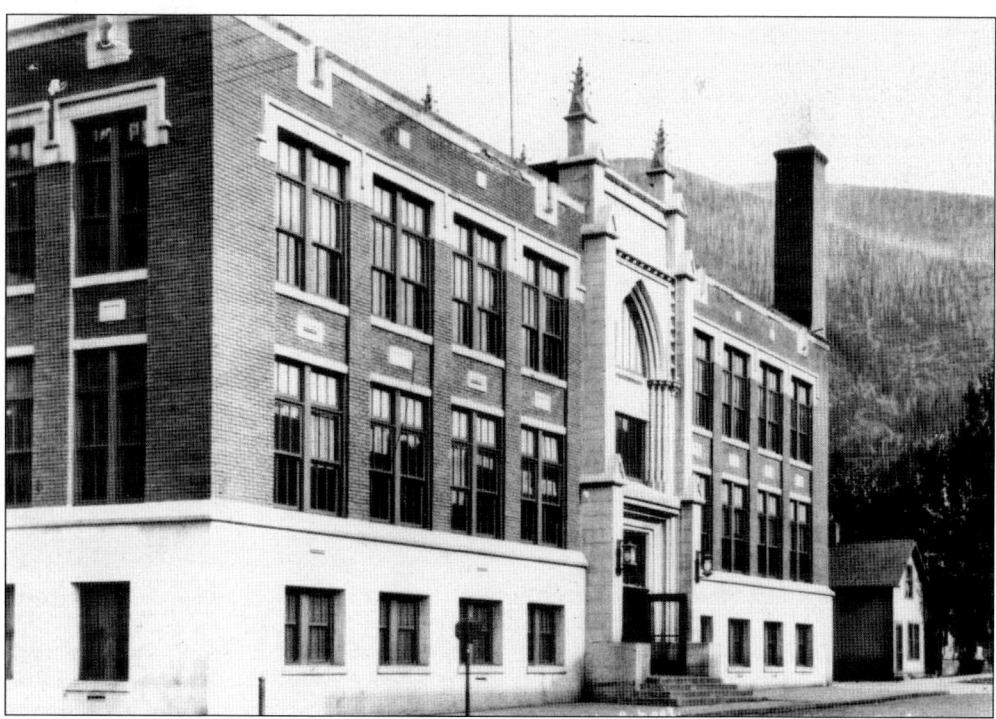

Wallace High School on Third Street is pictured here.

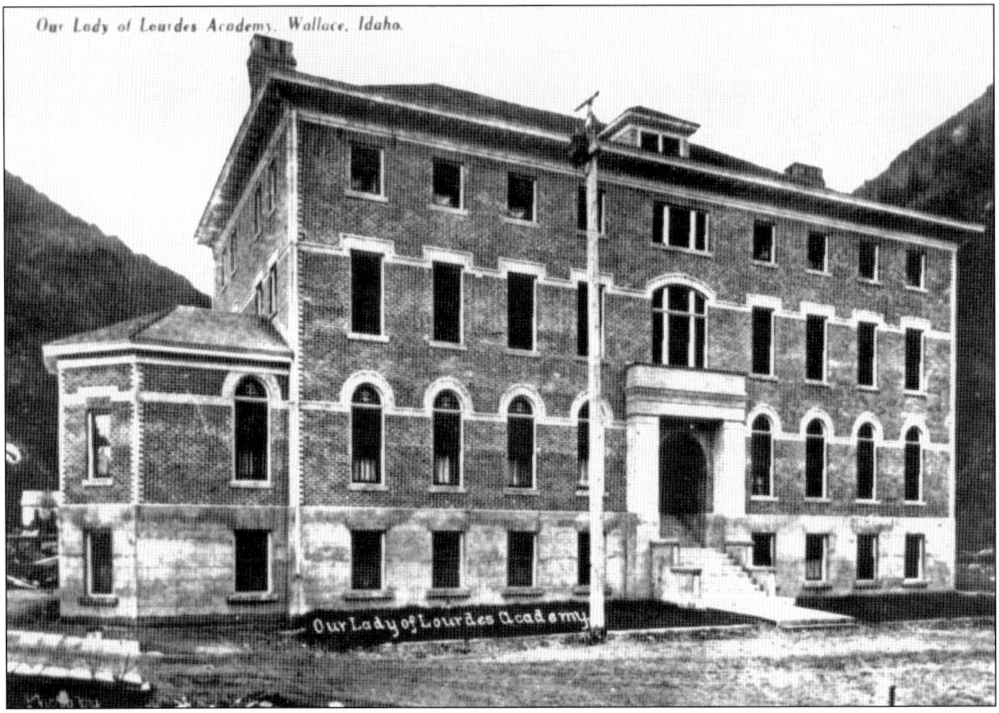

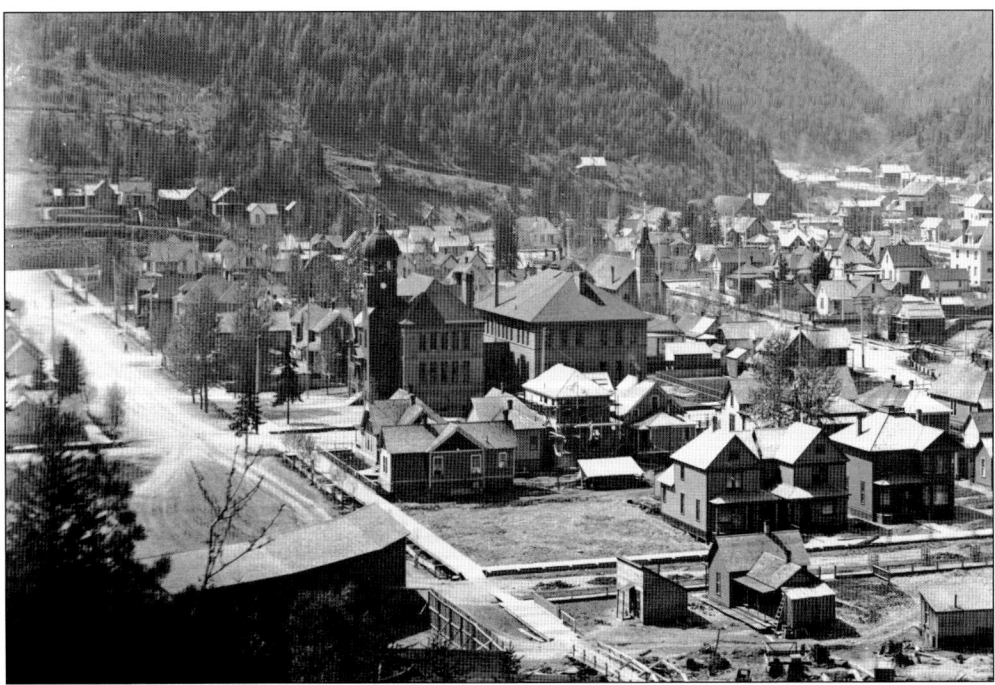

Our Lady of Lourdes Academy, a parochial school, is pictured at the corner of Bank and King Streets in Wallace.

Notice the onion dome on the Wallace school belltower in this photograph taken by Arthur Fay in 1905. Looking south up Placer Creek, the baseball park and grandstand are in the foreground slightly to the left.

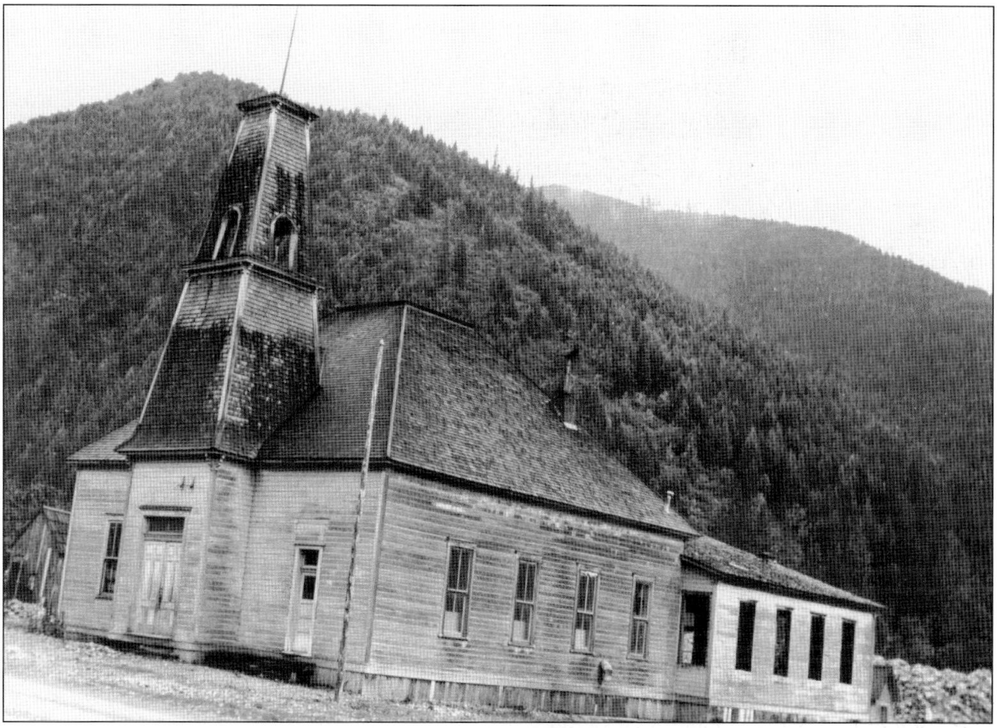

The Murray school is the subject of this c. 1930 photograph.

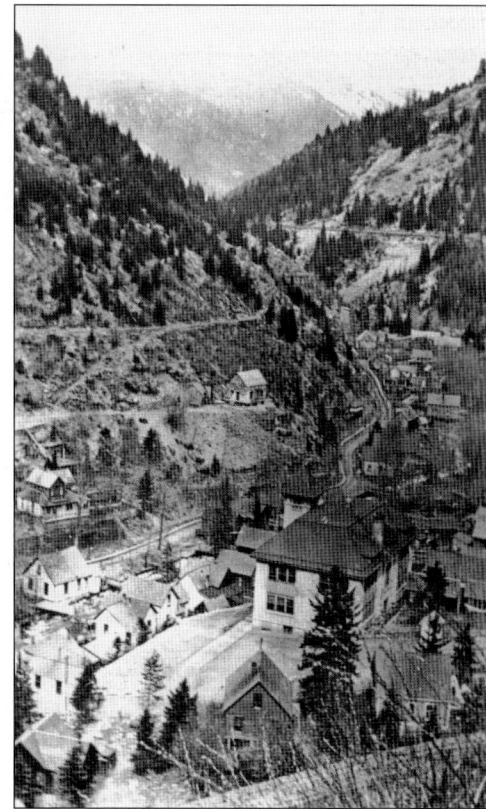

Looking up O'Neil Gulch in this c. 1920s photograph is Burke School. The Never Sweat Mine is across the gulch with a cabin on the mine dump.

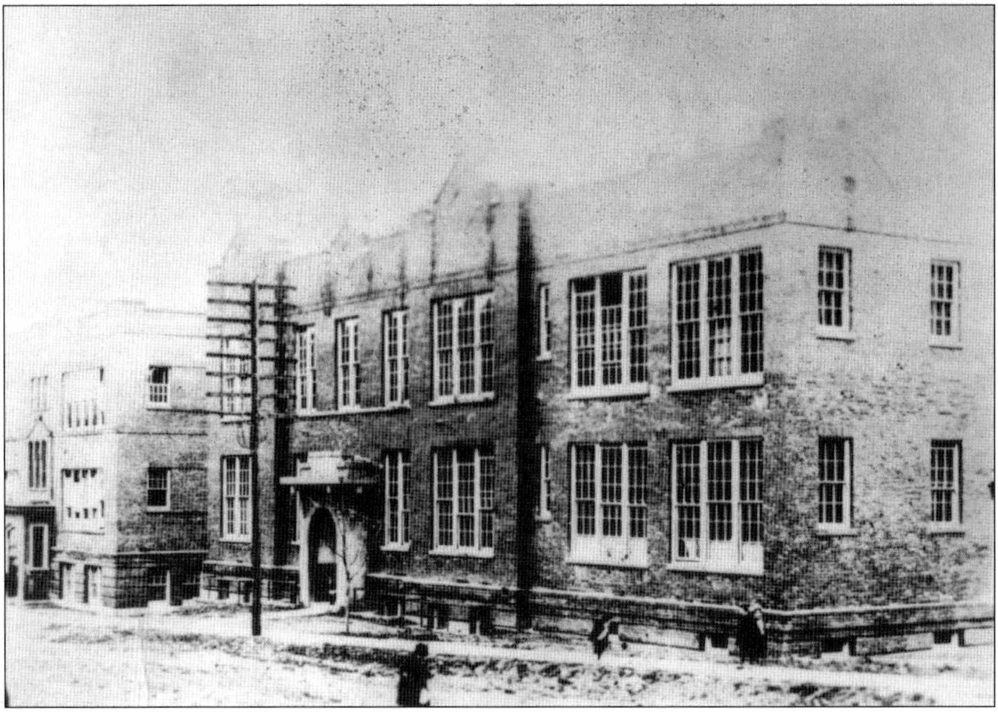

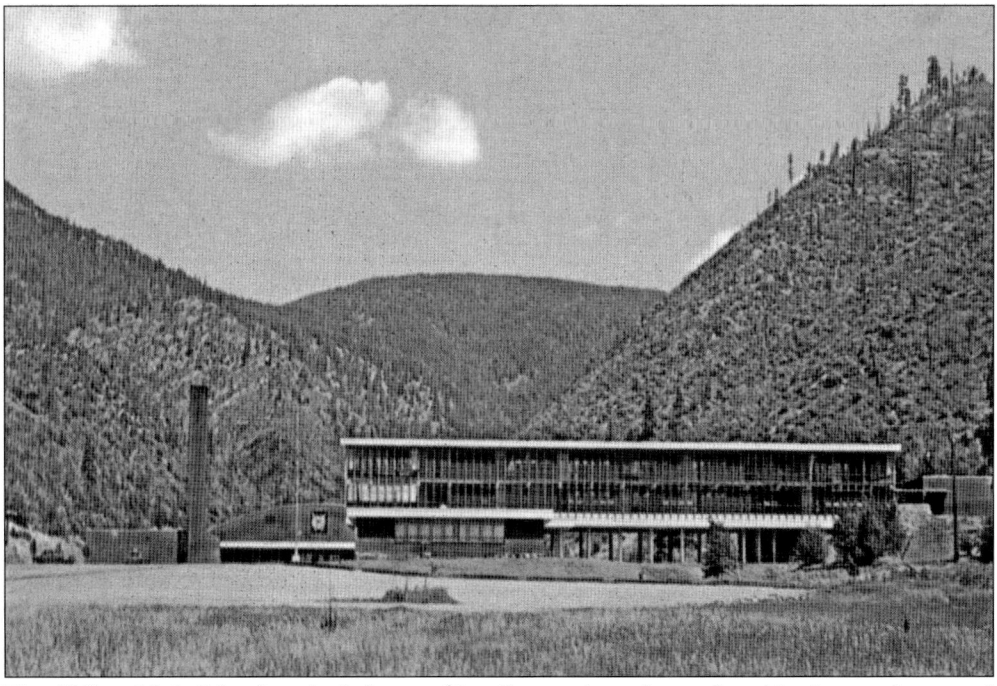

This c. 1930 photograph shows the Kellogg High School and Junior High School.

This Kellogg High School was built for over $1 million and was featured worldwide in architectural magazines. The building was designed so the second floor is above a breezeway and over the creek. The second and third floors have glass walls on both the north and south side of the building in this c. 1960 photograph.

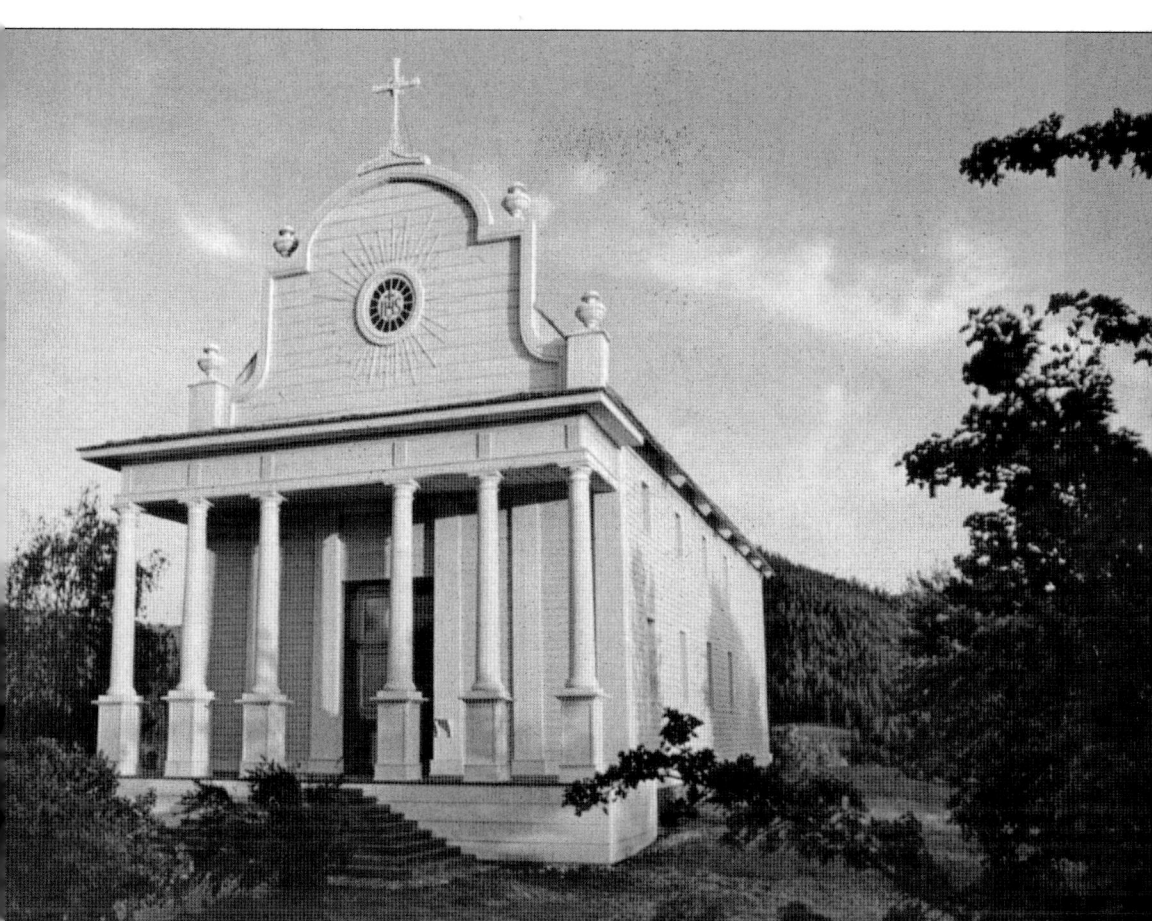

The Cataldo Mission is the oldest building standing in Idaho. It was the first church built in the valley and sits at the west end on the Cataldo flats. This area was named for Father Cataldo, one of the priests that came to the area to teach the Indians of the Coeur d'Alenes. Those who came to work on the building were predominantly Shoshone. Originally designed and built by Father Desmite near St. Maries on the St. Joe River, it was flooded every spring. The problem was solved by moving what they could and rebuilding at the small raised hill on the Coeur d'Alene River in an area now known as Cataldo. The mission is now a state park and a favorite wedding spot for those of all faiths.

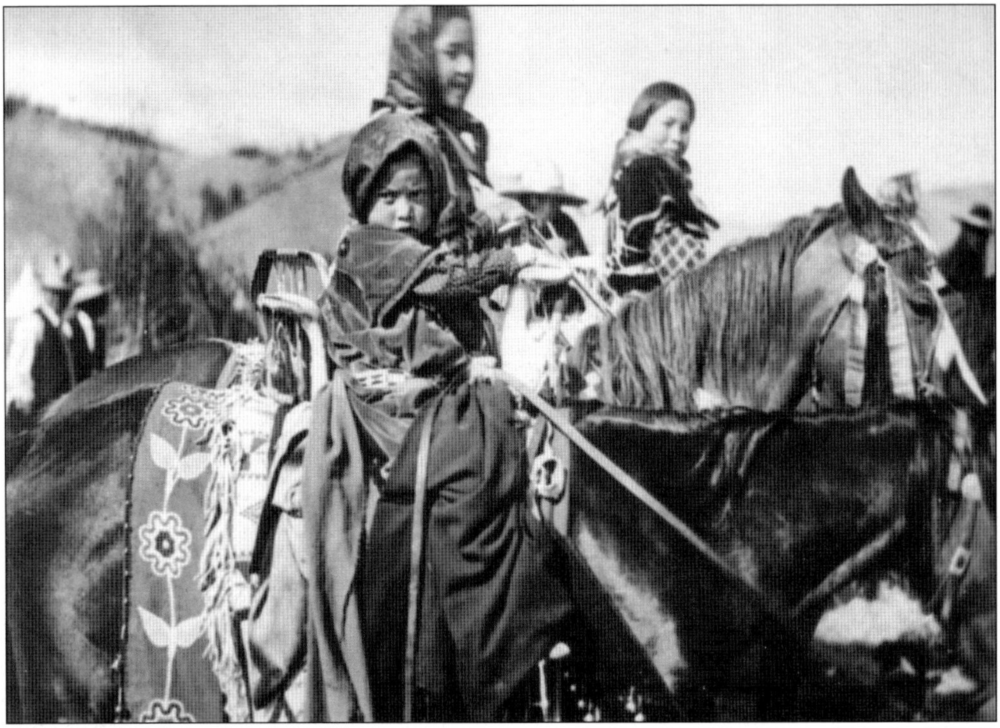

Shoshone children mixed mud and straw together and pressed it between and on the boards covering the walls of the mission.

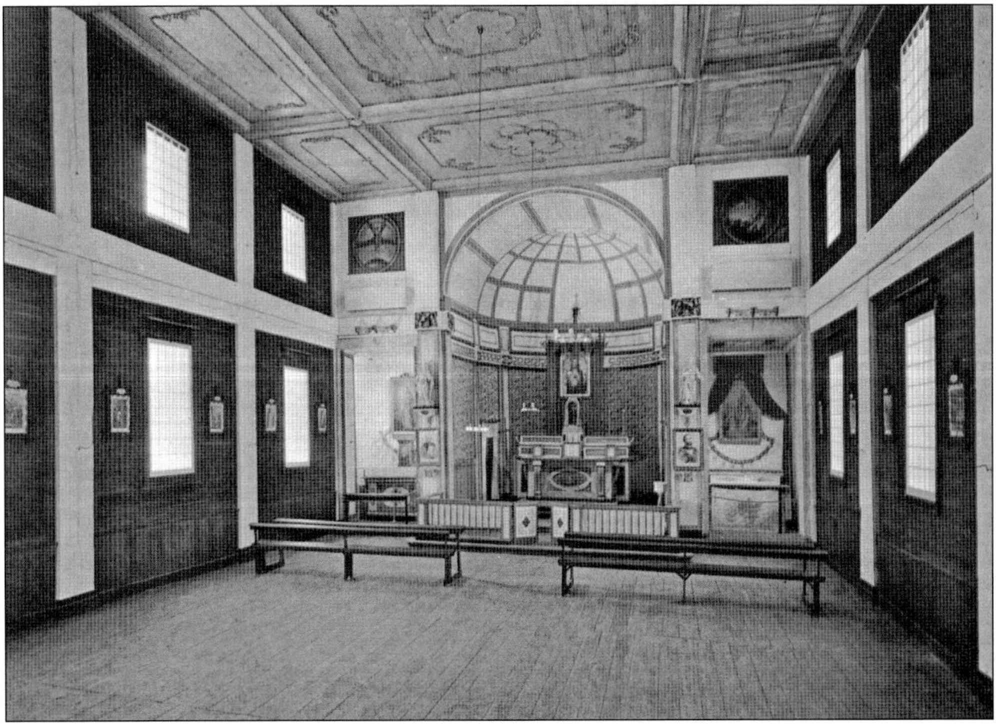

The interior of the mission shows the love and skill of its builders.

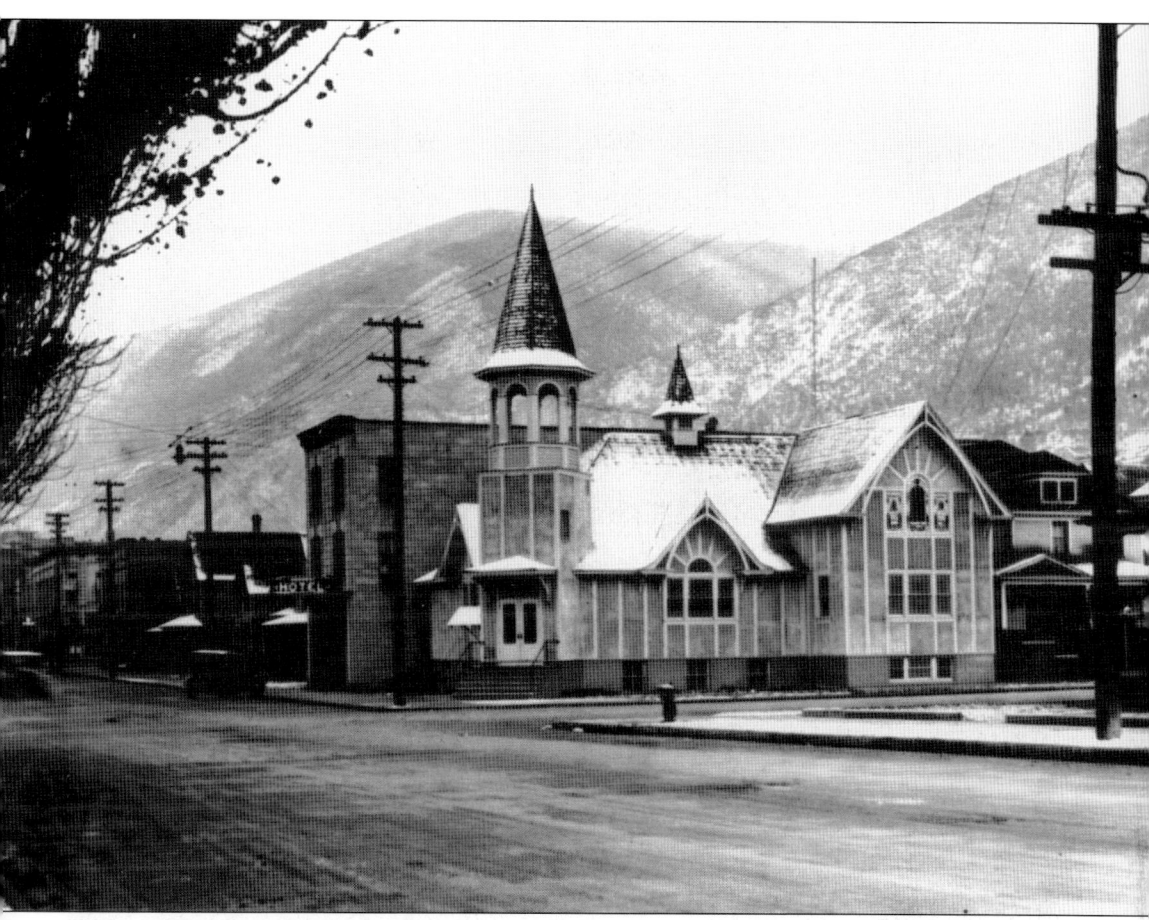

This c. 1923 photograph shows Wallace Congregational Church, located on the corner of Cedar and Fourth Streets. In the early days of the valley, churches were not just places of worship. They were also the center of family entertainment. Parties for young people, teas for the ladies, and family picnics all centered around the church.

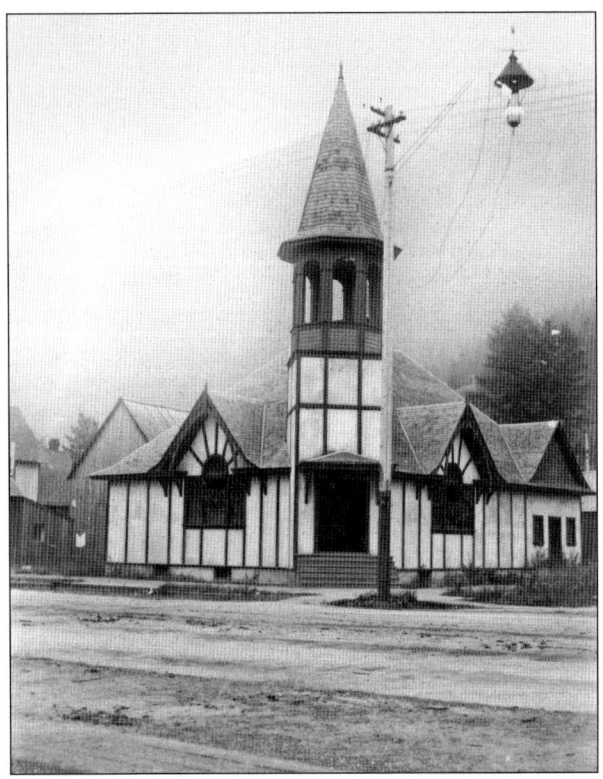

This 1905 photograph by Arthur Fay shows the Congregational Church in Wallace. Notice the streetlight hanging above the street.

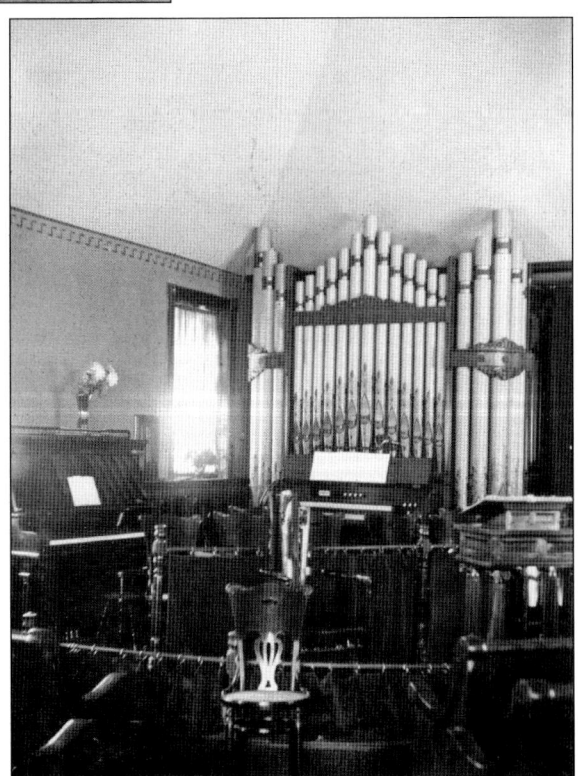

This photograph, taken by Arthur Fay in 1905, shows the interior of the Congregational Church.

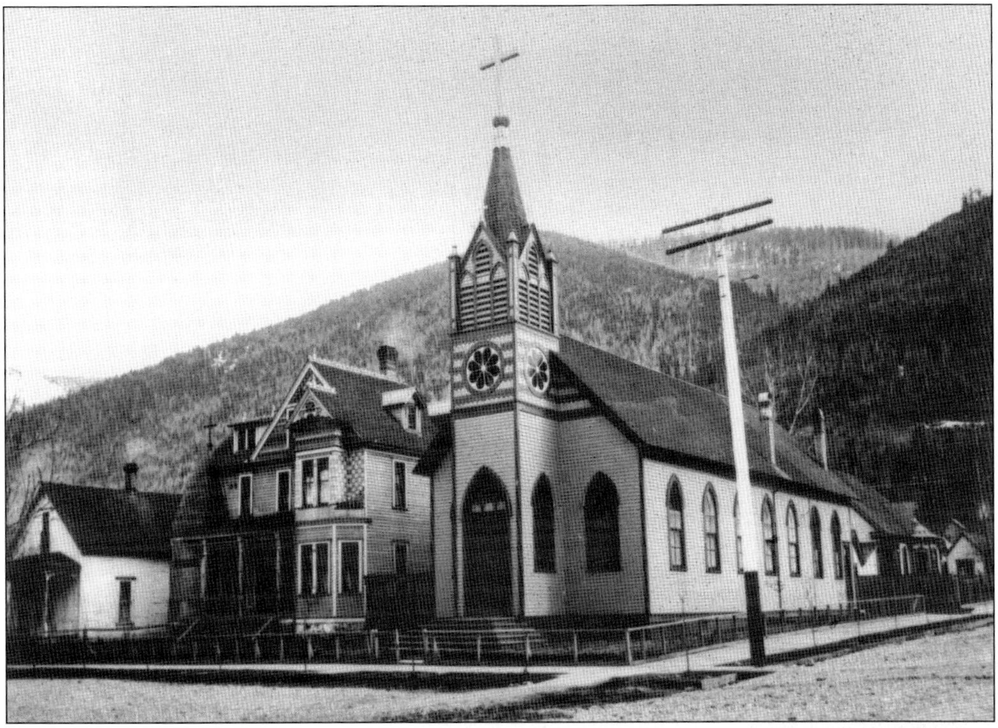

St. Alphonsus Catholic Church, located at Pine and Second Street.

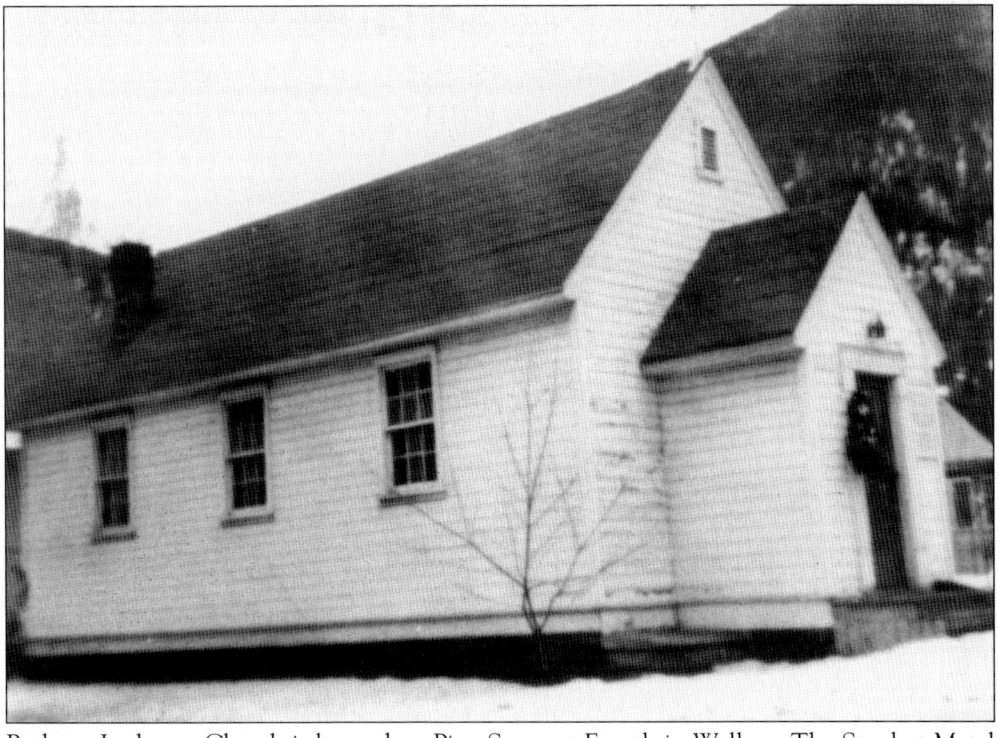

Bethany Lutheran Church is located on Pine Street at Fourth in Wallace. The Stardust Motel is now on this site.

49

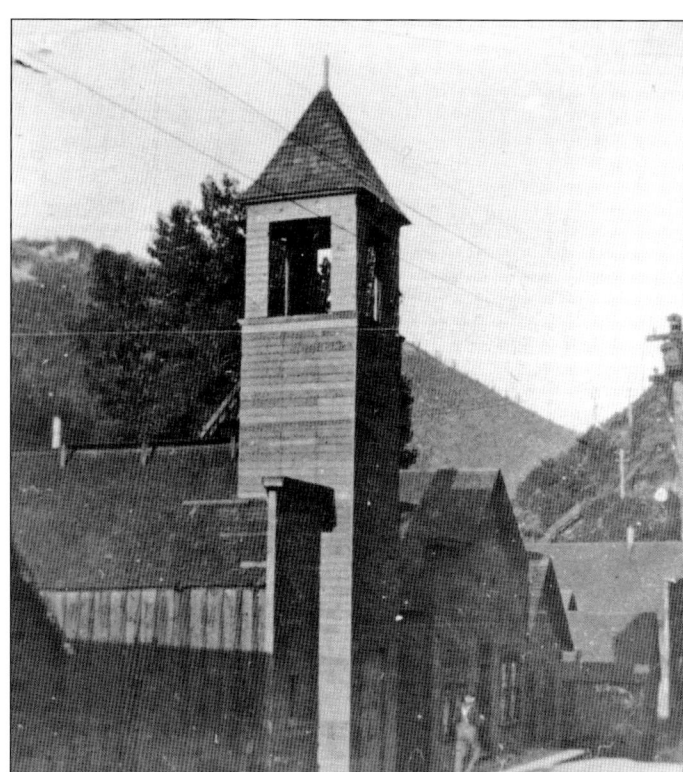

This is Burke Methodist Church.

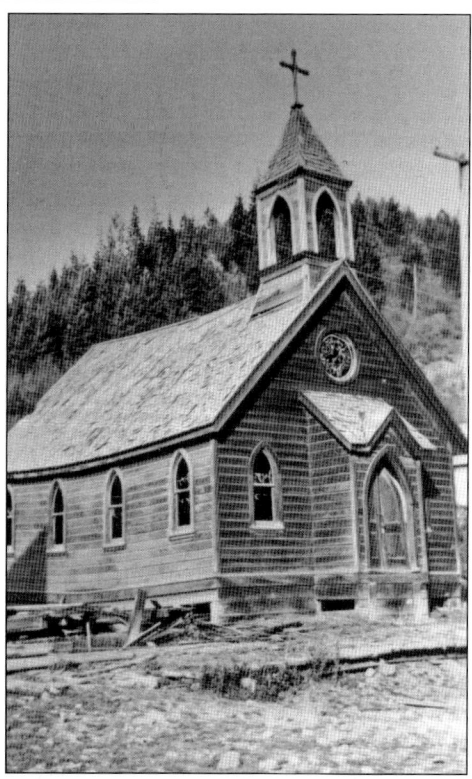

Mullan Catholic Church, recently refurbished, is now known as the "Little White Church." It is available for reunions, weddings, and community functions.

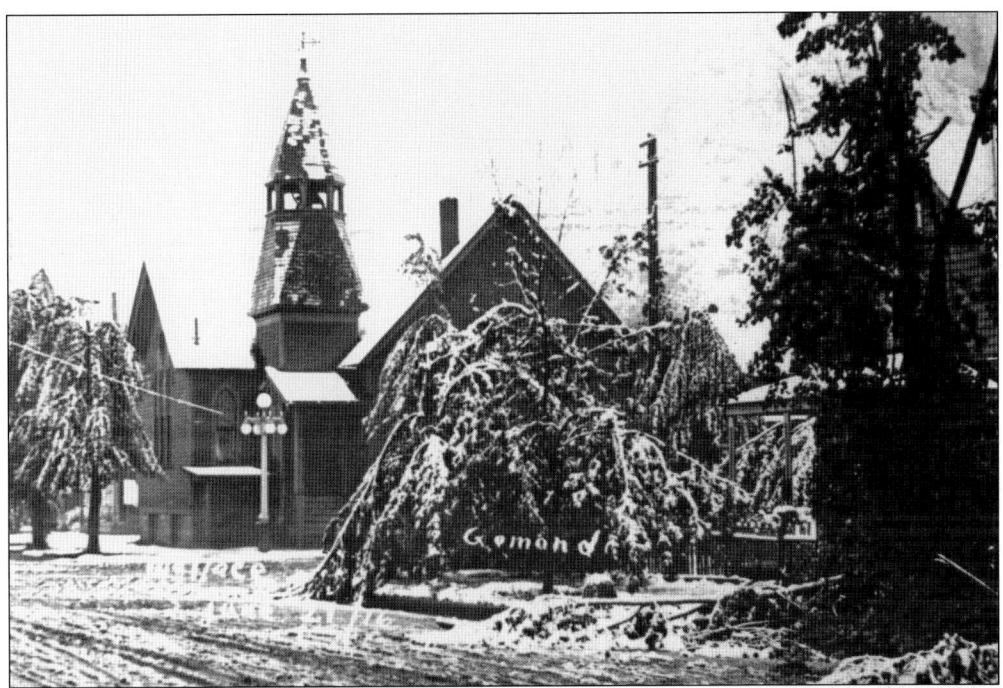

"His wonders to see." This snowstorm in July 1916 was a reminder that God has a strange sense of humor. This is the Wallace United Methodist church located on the corner of Pine and Fourth Streets.

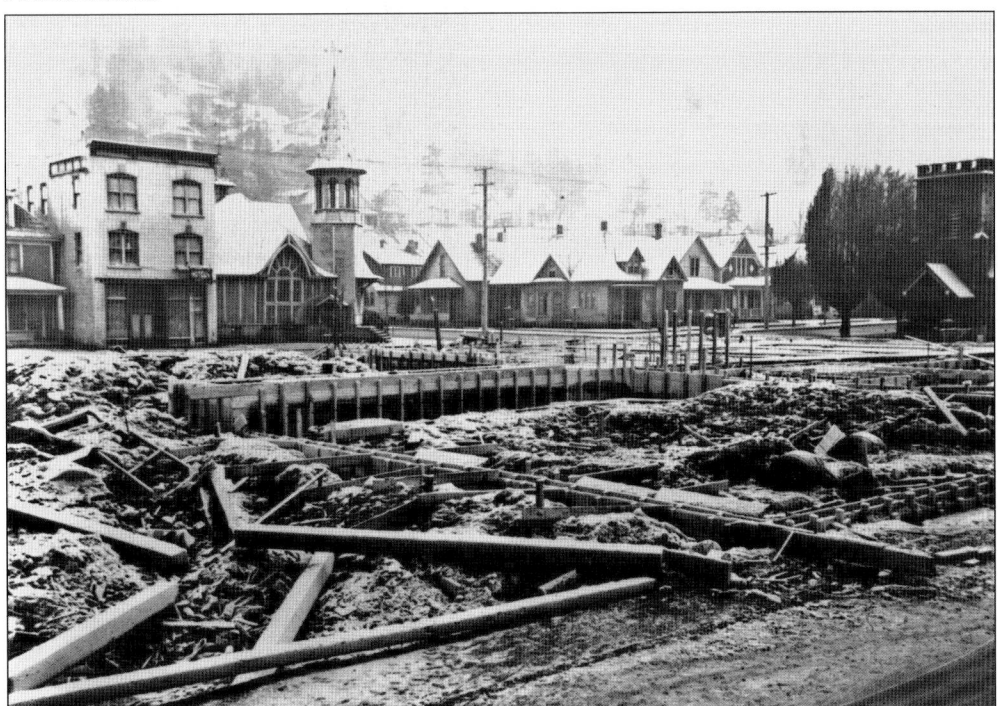

In this *c.* 1930 photograph, the Congregational Church is on the right. At the left is Holy Trinity. The foundation is for the new post office.

The Murray Courthouse is pictured after years of neglect.

This photograph shows the restoration work on the Murray courthouse that is underway.

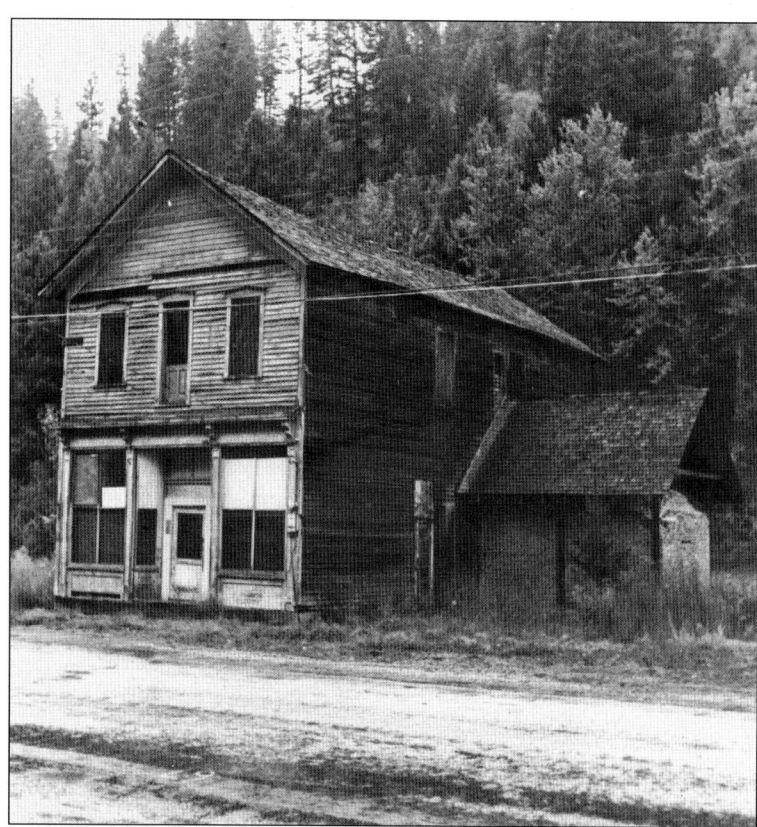

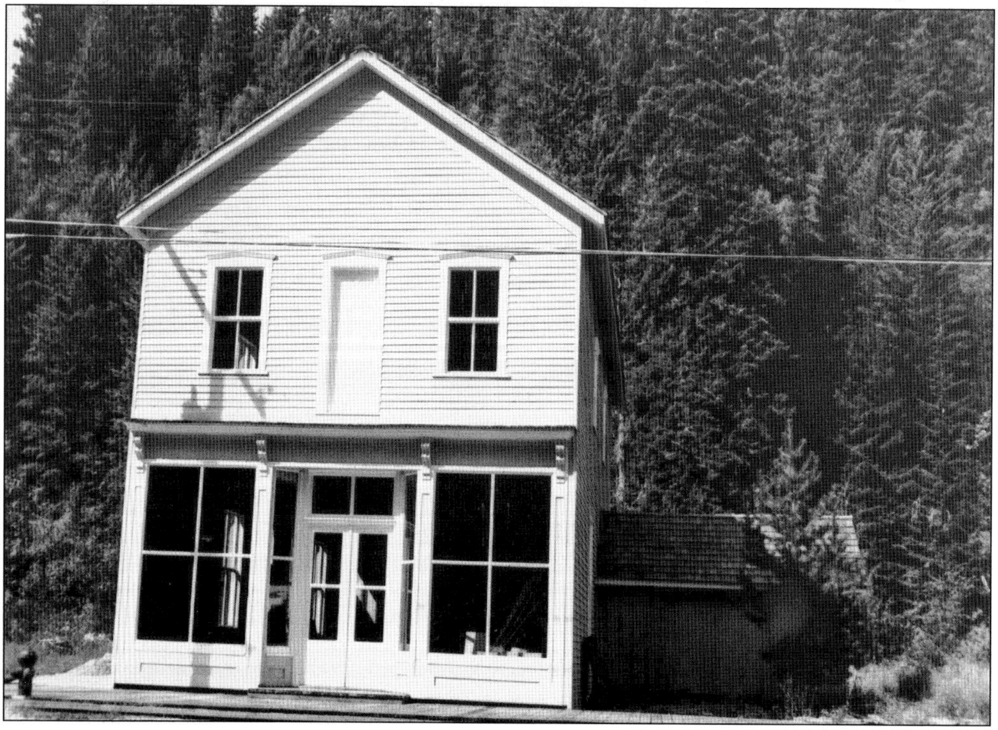

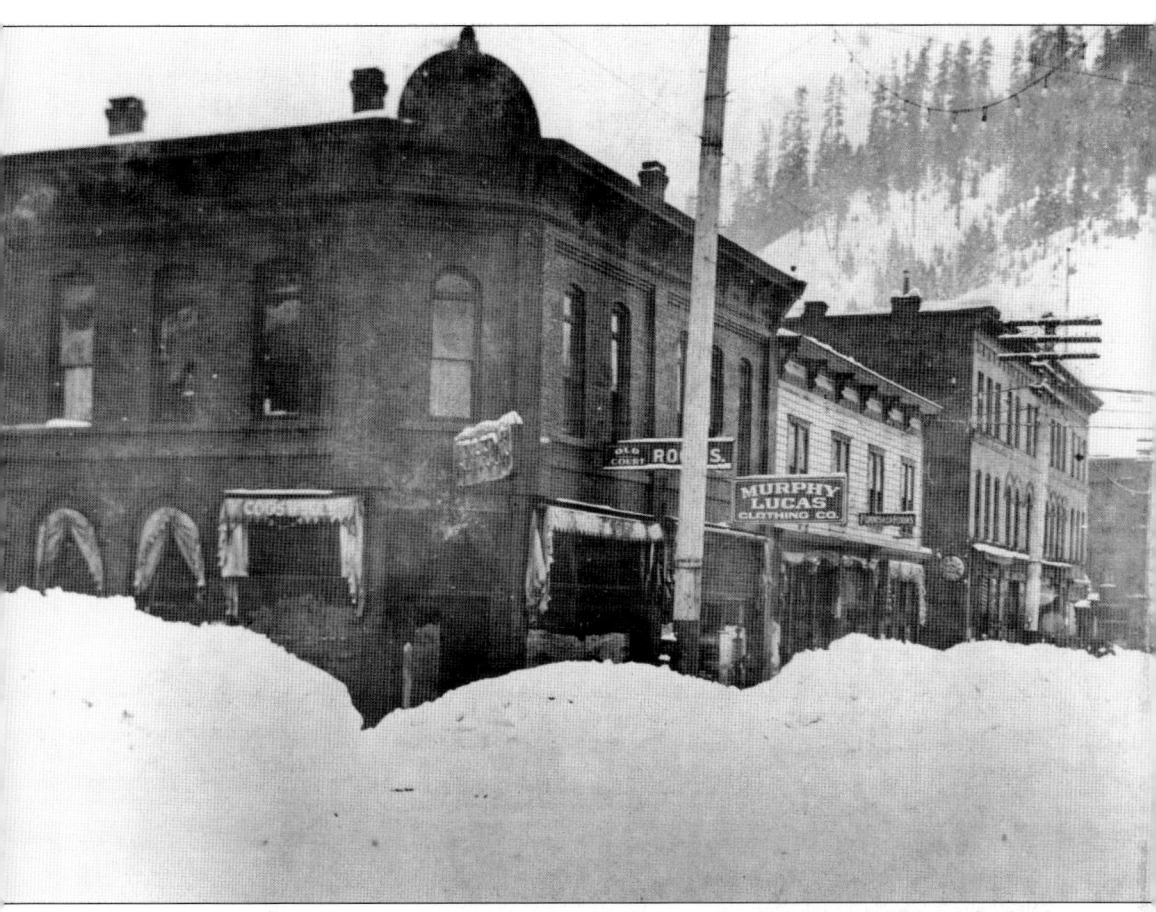

The DeLashmutt Building was constructed in 1890 as the home of the Coeur d'Alene Bank by Van DeLashmutt and George McAnlay. After the bank failed in the spring of 1893, due to shady dealings, Shoshone County purchased the building. From 1898 to 1906, county government's offices were located here. The main floor contained offices for the treasurer and recorder. After moving to the new building, a boardinghouse was operated on the second floor called the Court Rooms. Legend would later say that the Court Rooms were "rooms with ladies." This is doubtful, because those businesses were kept on the south side of Cedar Street and close to the railroad lines.

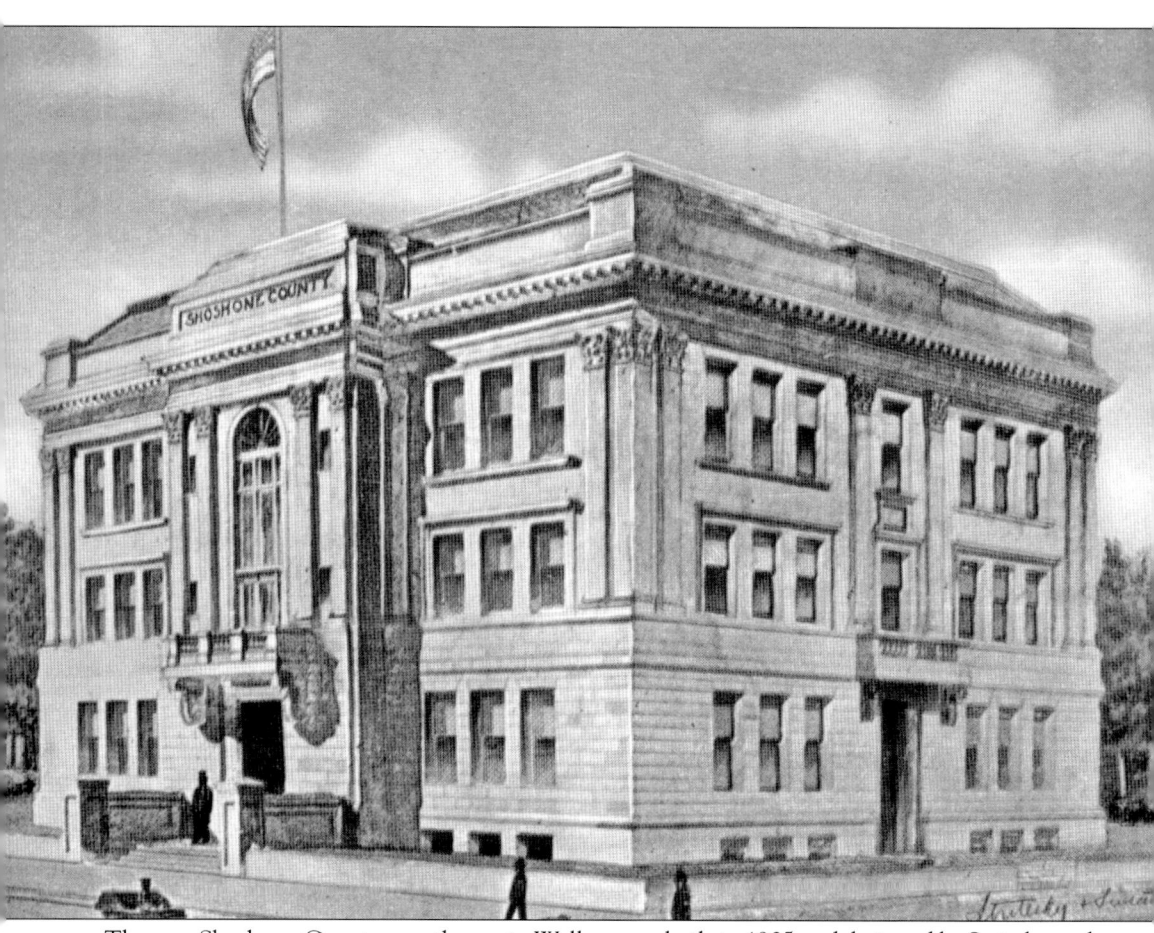

The new Shoshone County courthouse in Wallace was built in 1905 and designed by Striesky and Sweat of Spokane. It is built of locally produced blocks mixed with concrete and mine tailings. Like many public buildings of its day, it has marble floors. Its design was considered of Greek influence, but is actually called Whirling Logs, a North American Indian symbol depicted the cyclic motion of life, seasons, and the four winds and taken from the image of a tree in a whirlwind. This image is also found in Navajo sand paintings. As the cycle of life symbol it reminds us that both good and bad are ever present in our lives; a happy productive life requires both joy and sorrow, as without one you will not recognize the other. Because this symbol was bastardized by Hitler, many public buildings altered the design after World War II. The one in Wallace remains to honor its Whirling Logs meaning. Though local legend says Wallace stole the county seat from Osburn, in truth an election was held to determine where it would be. Whether or not the election was fair . . . is lost in time.

# Four

# VALLEY LIFE

While mining is the reason for the towns in the valley, it is not the only thing the Silver Valley offers. Logging is here as well. From the time they logged with axes and horses men have gone into our forest to eke out a living.

Entertainment is also an important part of day-to-day life. The valley founding fathers realized very early on that entertaining and educating families was important to keeping them safe and create a sustainable community.

Baseball has always been big here. In the early days, mining companies had their own teams. Minor league players from colleges were hired for summer employment in the mines, though their "real" job was to play ball. From Tee Ball to Babe Ruth, and high school to softball leagues, baseball was a staple of valley life.

Wallace's Babe Ruth League outplayed Klamath Falls for the regional title and the opportunity to play in the Babe Ruth World Series in Ann Arbor, Michigan on Aug. 20, 1957. Wallace lost to Stamford, Connecticut in the first round. The team was made up of Terry Kiser, Lee Lundahl, Mike Keller, Gary Fernquist, Jim Thompson, George Vipperman (manager), James Mason, Loreen Solum, LeRoy Viche, Ronald Higgins, George Clapp, Mike Foreman, Larry Clem, Johnny Bordelli, Meredith Stone, Jimmy Bair, and Coach Leonard Olson. By all reports, the well-behaved team enjoyed the trip, a Detroit Tigers baseball game, and a hero's welcome upon returning to Wallace.

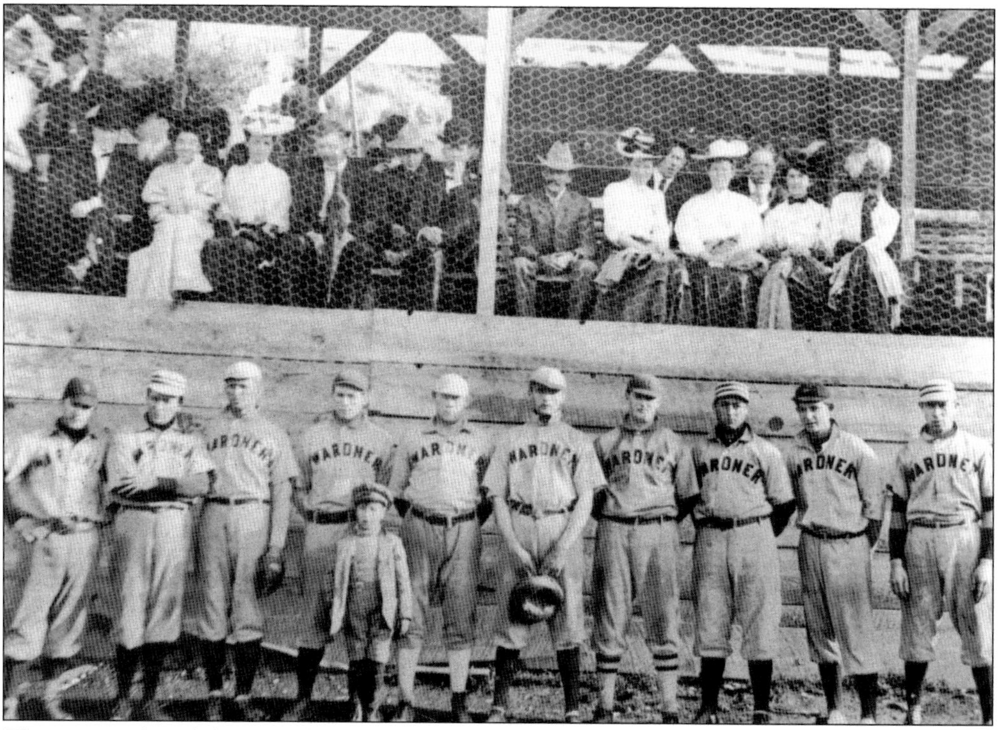

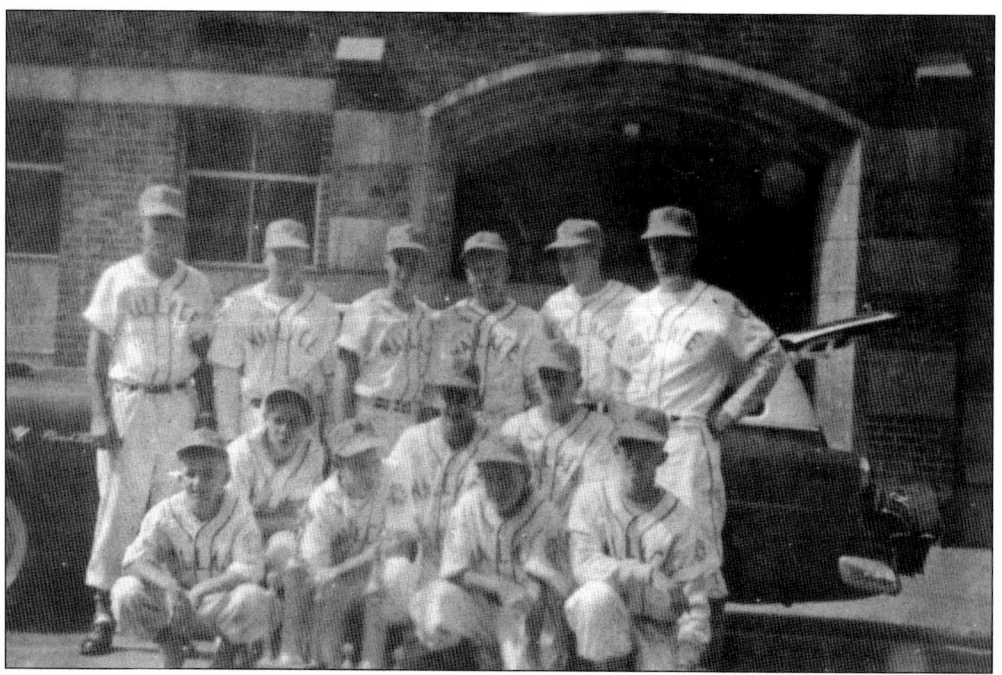

This team played for Wardner. The ladies in the stands have gone all-out dressing for this game.

This is the Babe Ruth team.

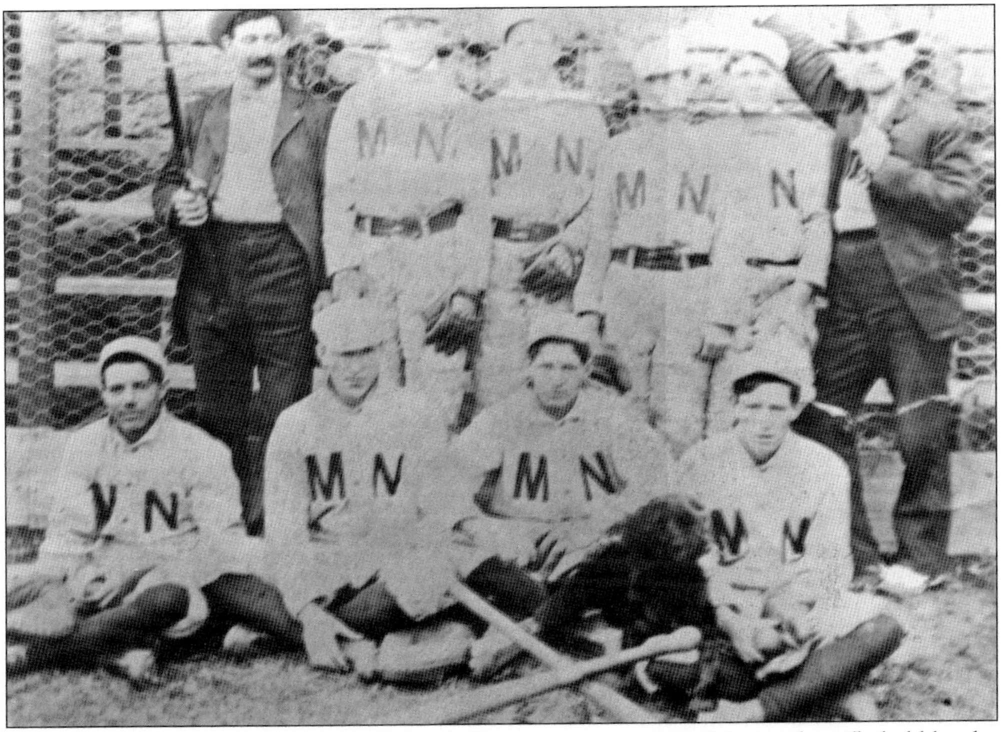

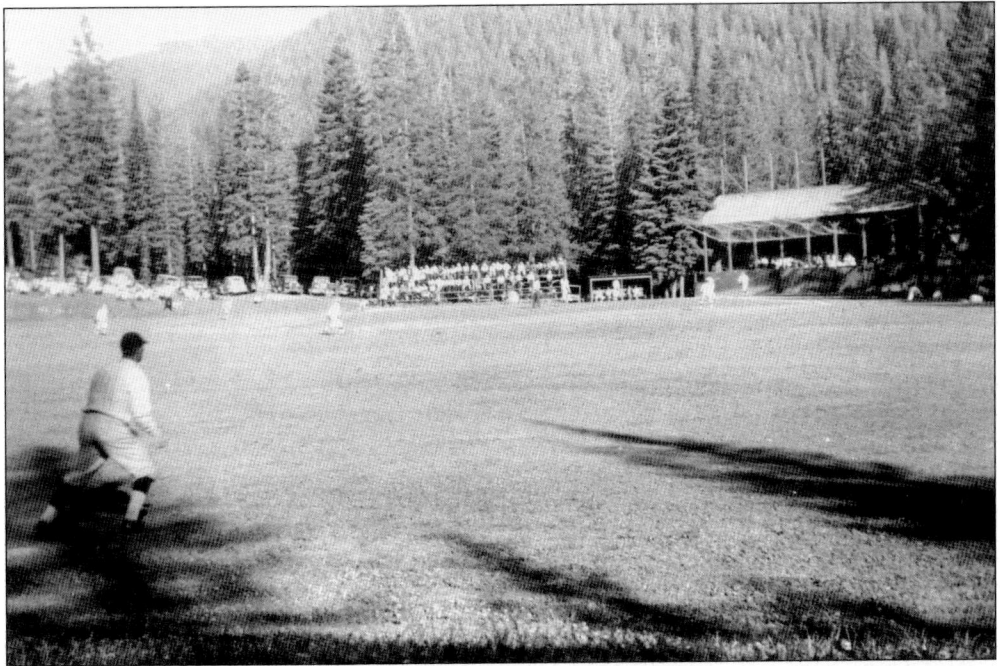

Even during the Mining/Labor Wars, baseball was very important. Notice the rifle held by the guard. The team members in this c. 1898 photograph played for the Mullan Nationals.

This is the Burke baseball field, Hearne Park. "Hap" Smith is running the bases in 1940. Hearne Park was the most difficult of ballparks. There was a steep rise in right field, making it difficult to play the ball in that area.

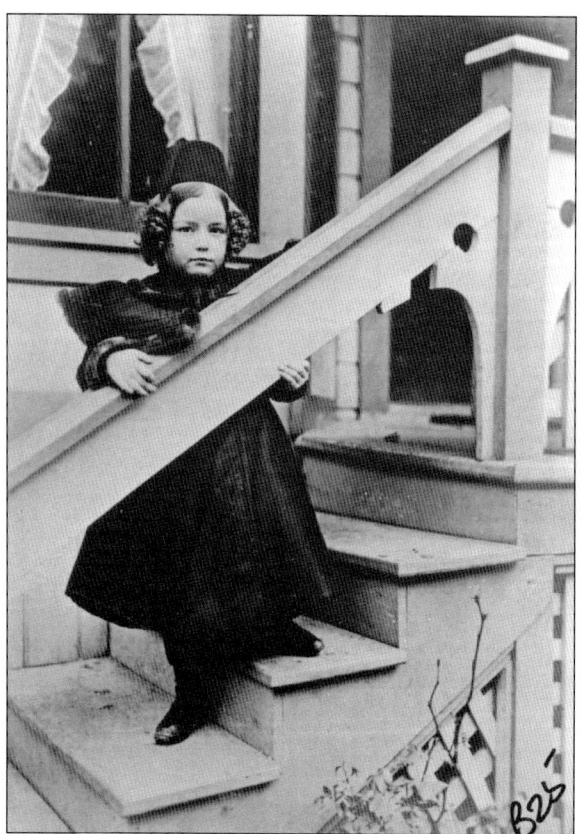

This young lady is believed to be the daughter of Superintendent McDonald of the Helena/Frisco Mine. She is standing on his porch and dressed as a young lady of this family would dress in 1892.

This evening of music was probably a photo op for propaganda during the mining wars. Notice the child holding a firearm in this *c.* 1892 photograph.

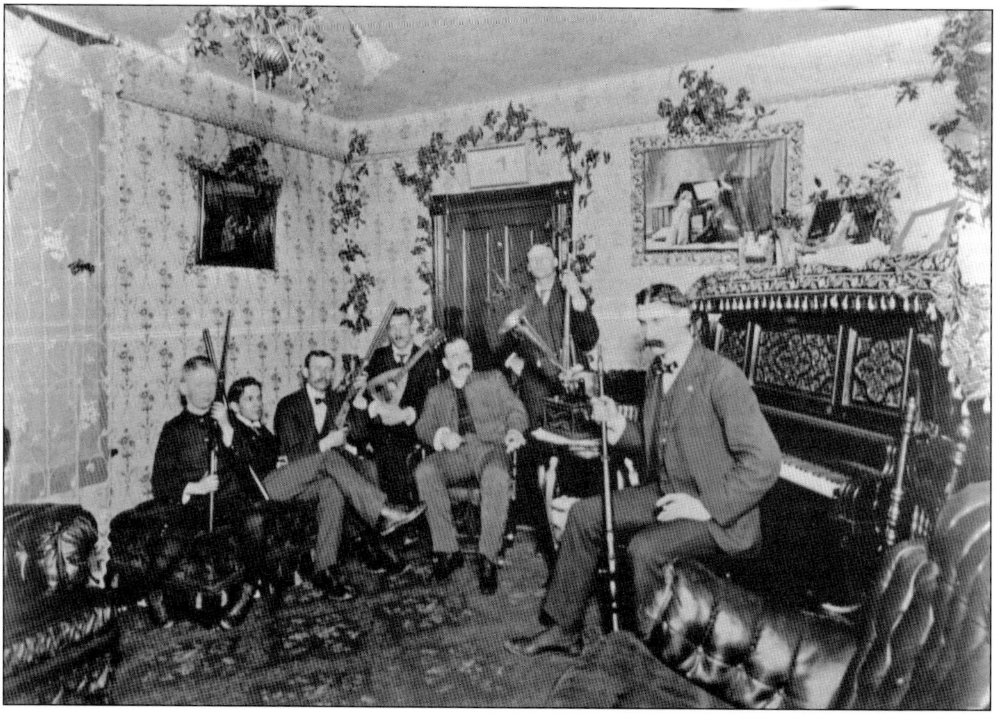

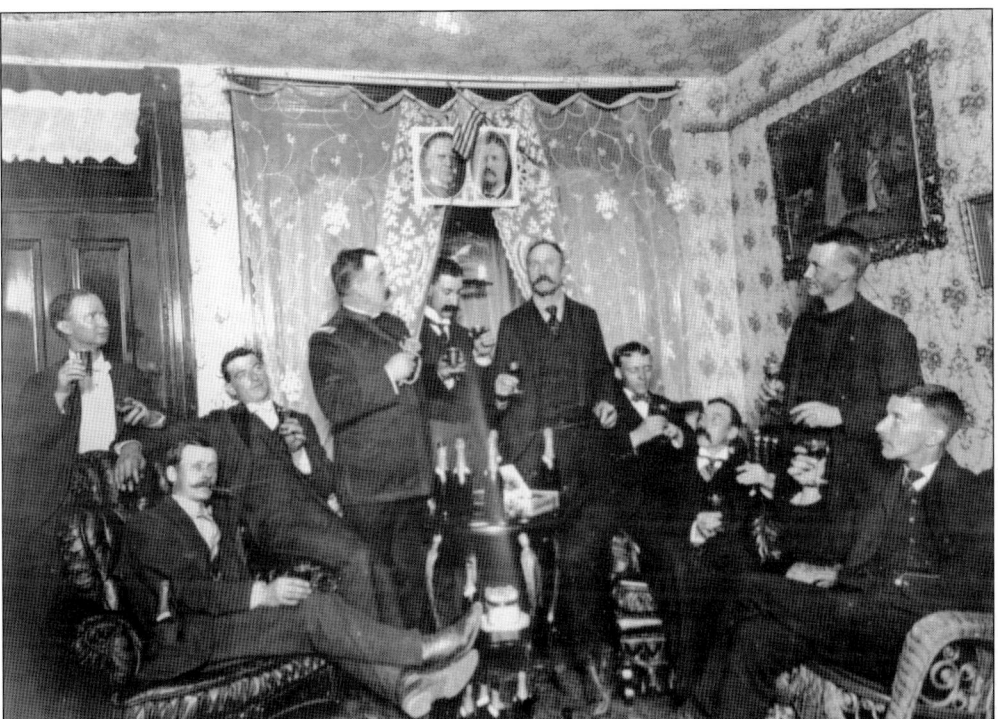

This c. 1900 photograph features what was probably a political gathering, very likely in Gem. Notice the pictures hanging above the doorway on the curtains.

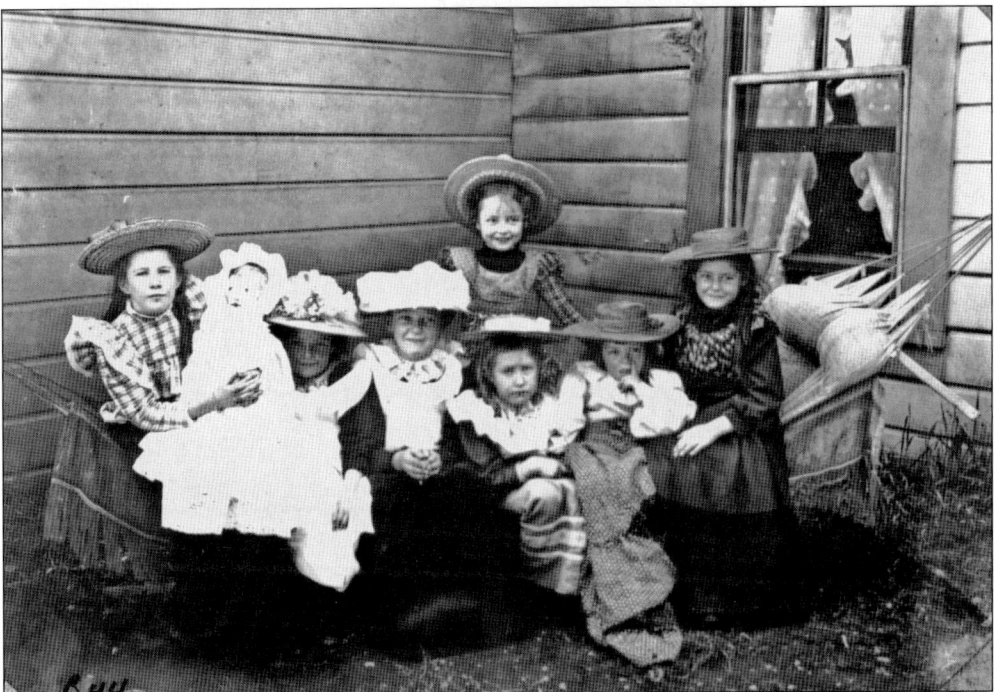

This was perhaps a birthday celebration for the young lady with the new baby doll. The party is at the superintendent's house in Gem, Idaho.

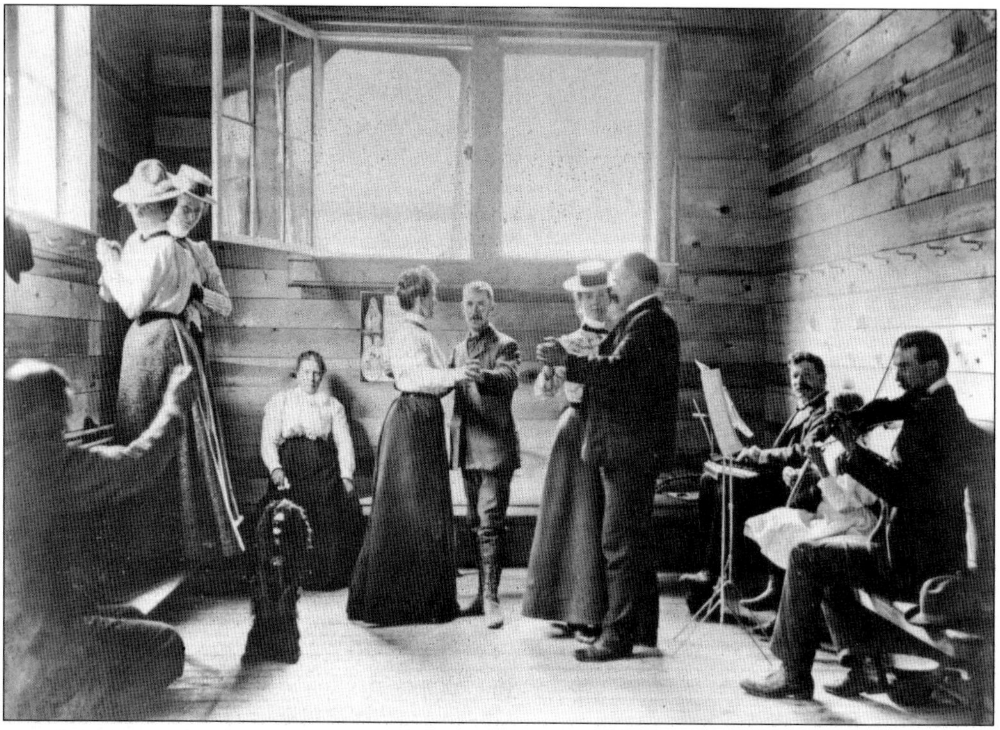

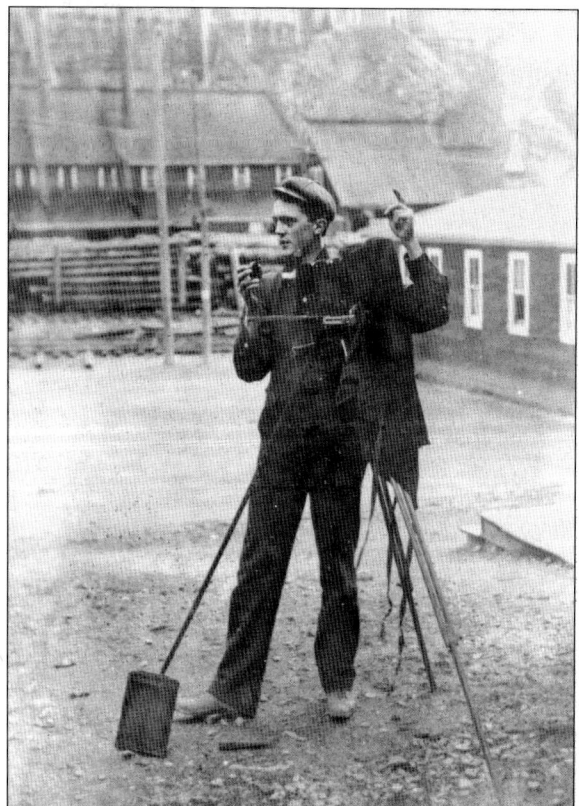

This *c.* 1892 dance must have been the highlight of the week. Note the obedient dog on the left side of the scene.

Photography was a passion at the turn of the century, as evidenced by this unknown photographer, taking pictures at the Helena/Frisco and Gem Mill in 1892. Many people were learning how to take and develop their own photos. Some, like Arthur Fay, used glass-plate negatives. Others used 4x5 negatives. Thanks to all these amateur and professional photographers, we are blessed with images of the past.

This Sunday outing, probably along Placer Creek, was taken by Arthur Fay in 1905. The group includes, from right to left; Minnie Mallon, Sonny Moore, Little Miss Moore, Mrs. Morarity, Mrs. Moores, and Verda Greer. The photographer noted the following: "A nice group of people to associate with. We had many pleasant times together out for hikes in the woods."

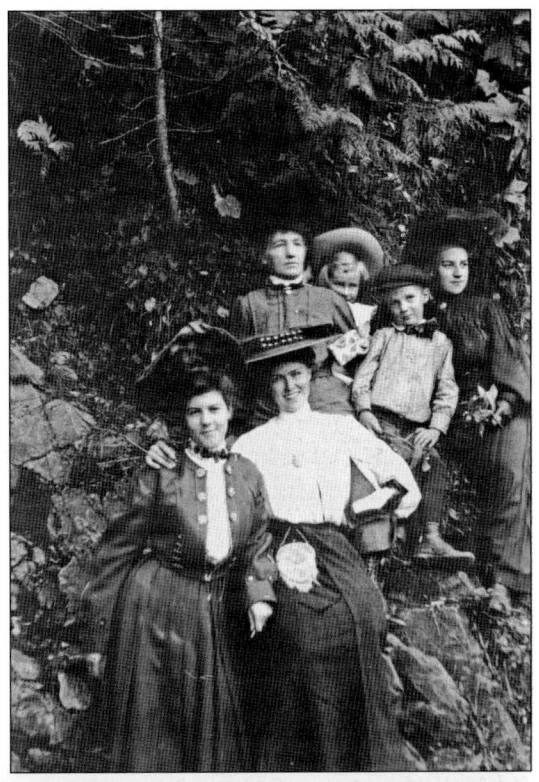

Horseback-riding lessons were something every child had in Gem, Idaho.

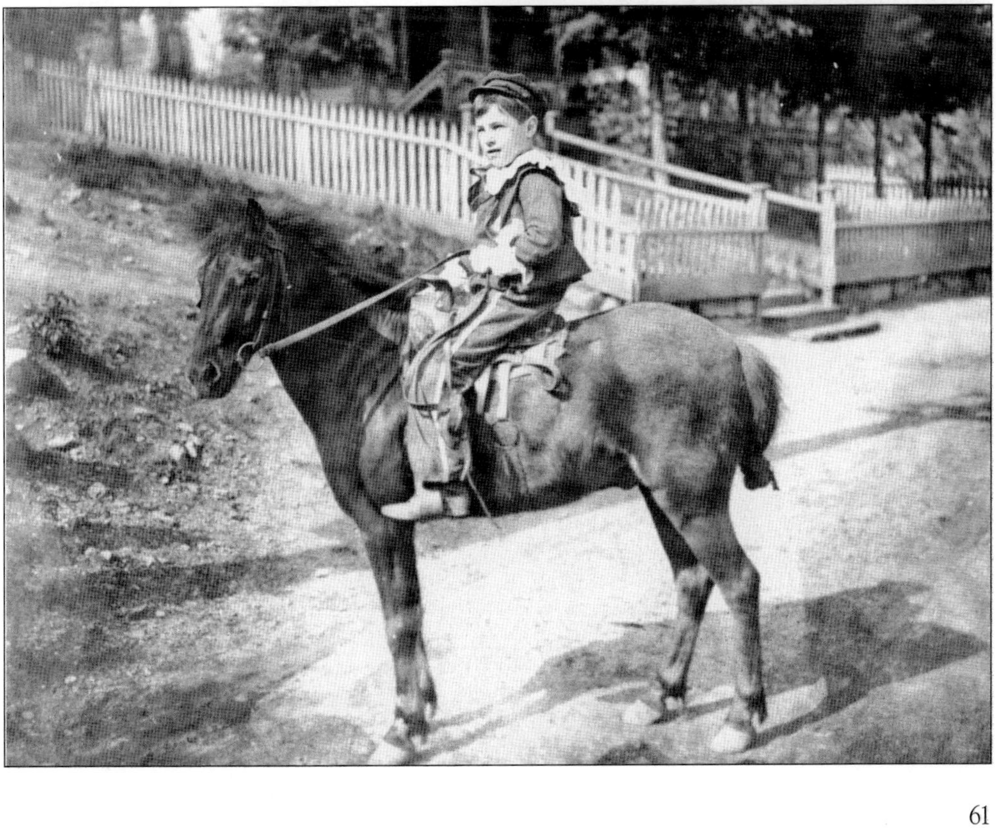

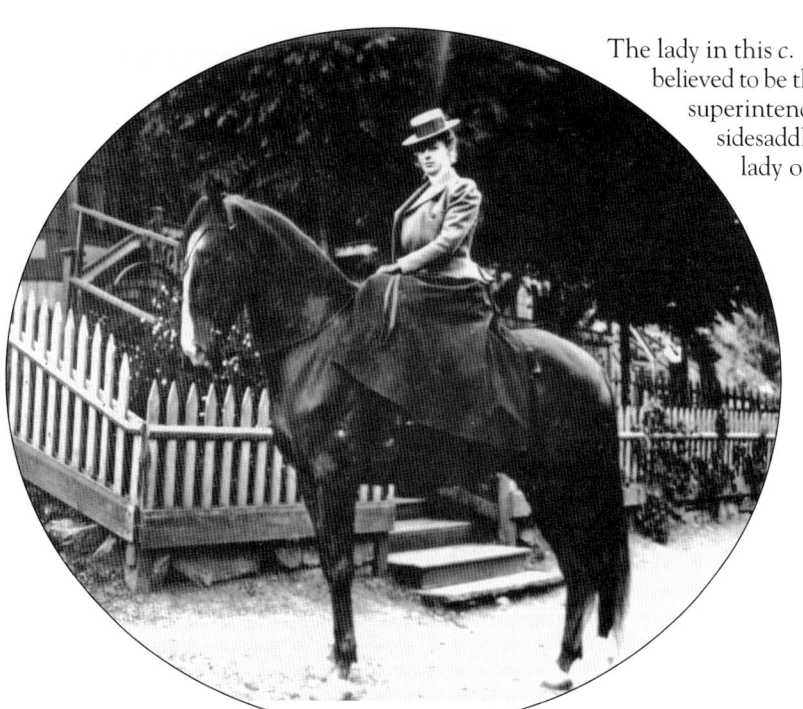

The lady in this *c.* 1892 photograph is believed to be the wife of the Frisco superintendent. She is riding sidesaddle, like every proper lady of the day.

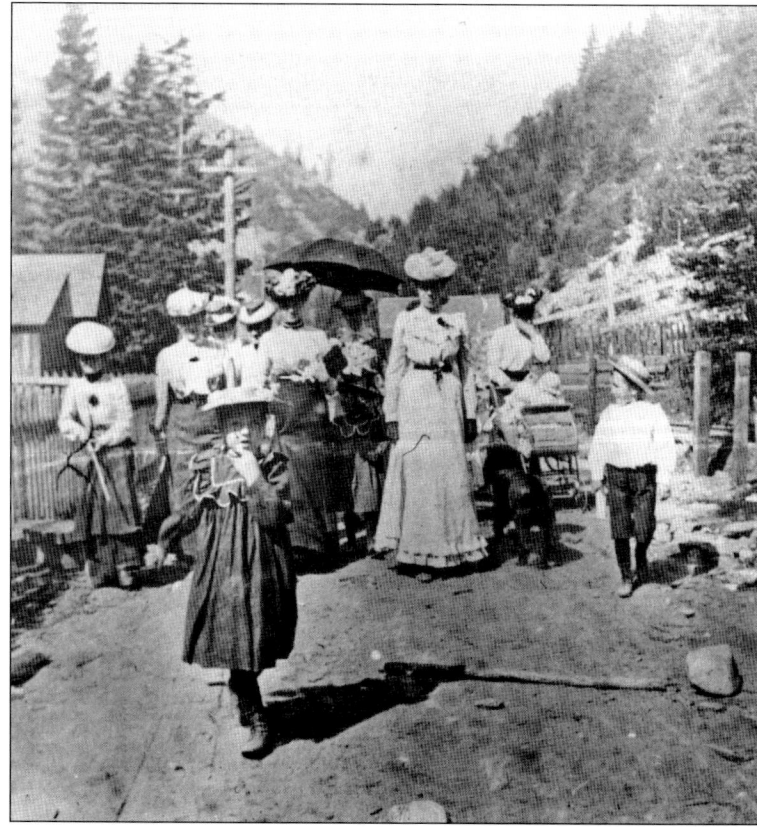

N. Earle Bushnell took this *c.* 1860 photograph of the women of Burke Canyon.

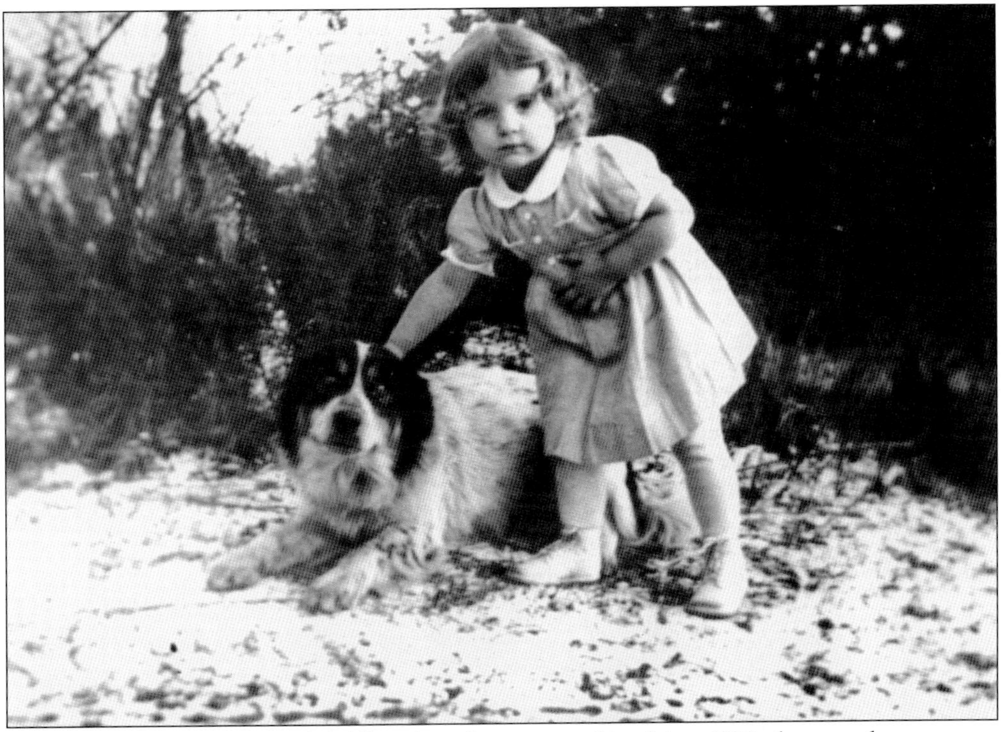

Pets are an important part of childhood, as demonstrated in this c. 1930 photograph.

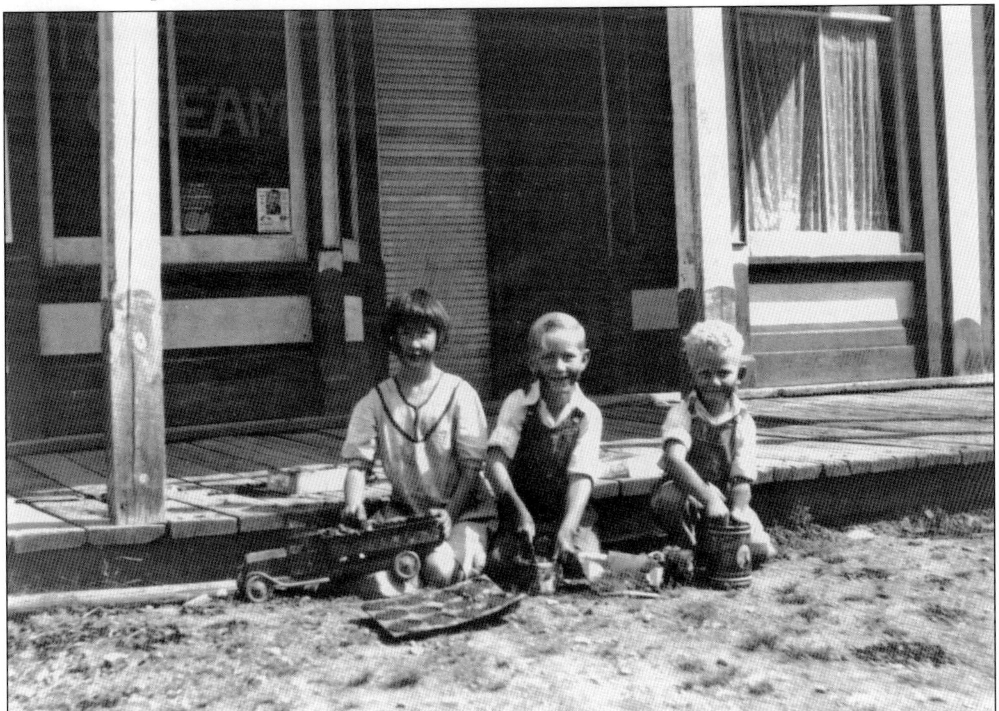

Children in Murray, like children everywhere, can entertain themselves for hours with a couple of trucks.

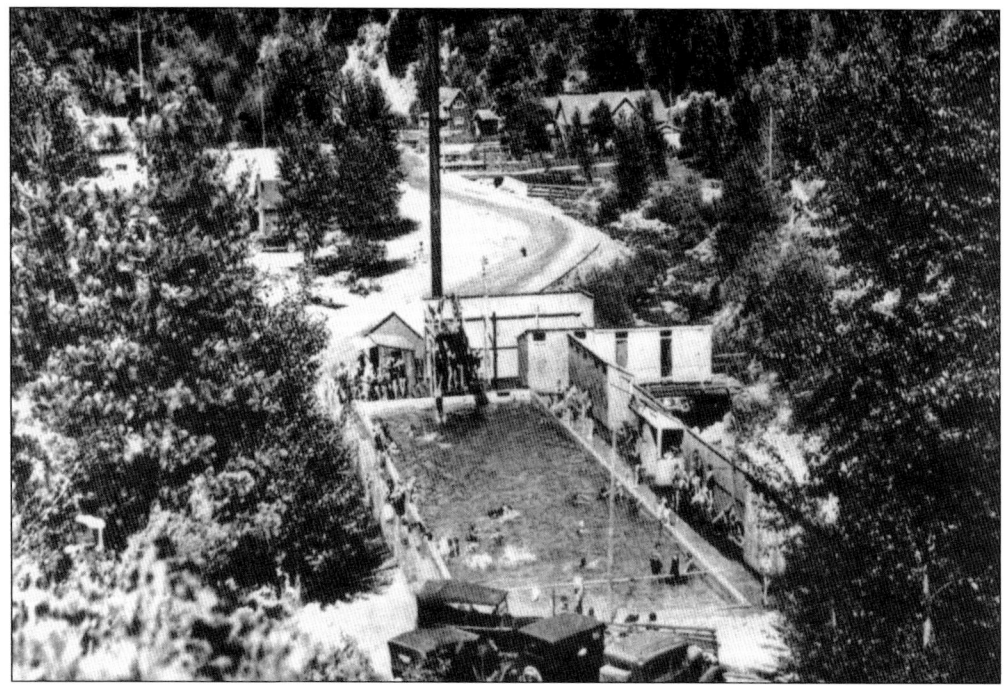

This is the Wallace swimming pool on King Street. The pool was filled with fresh water from Placer Creek. During the flood of 1933, Placer Creek filled the pool with sediment. With the help of the CCC, Wallace built a community swimming pool on Hotel Street.

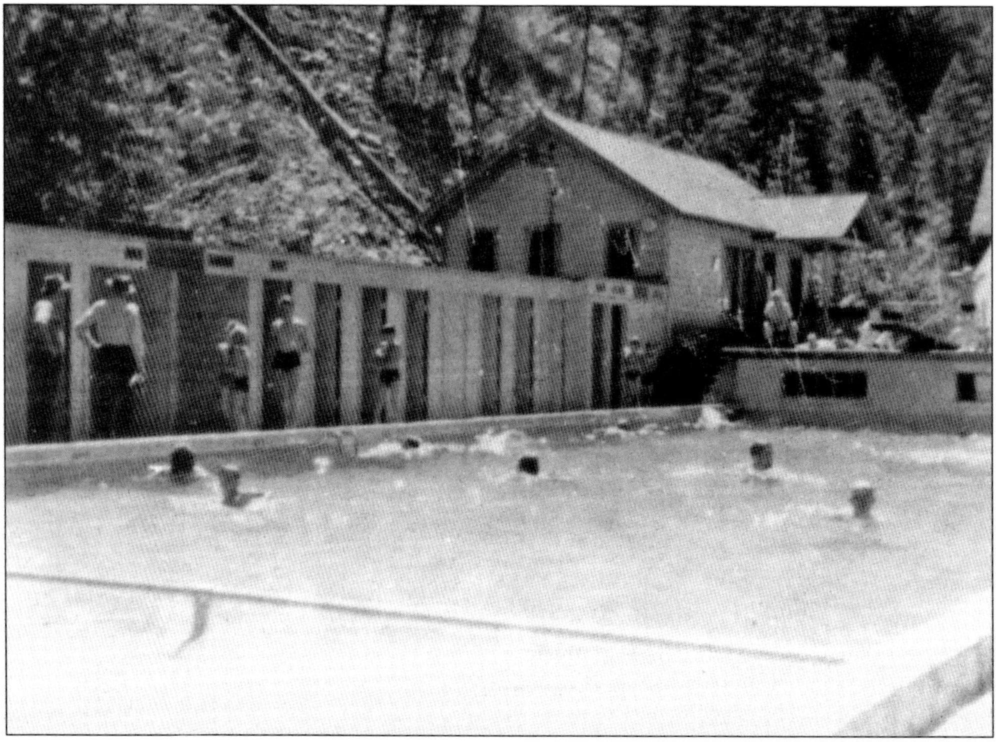

Burke Canyon pool is pictured here with changing rooms along the side.

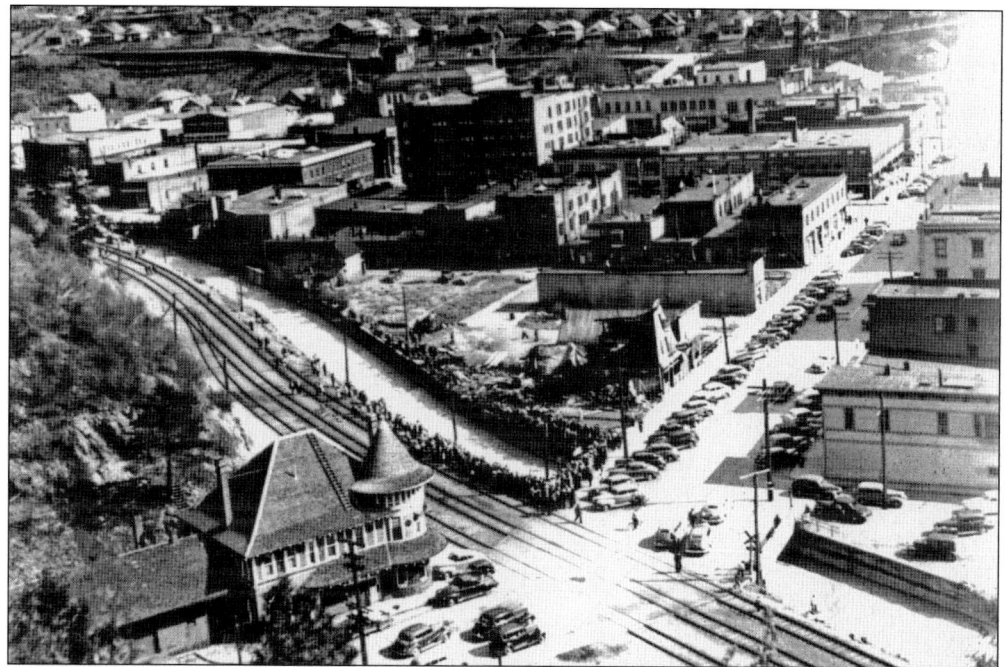

One of the most fun weekends is Gyro Days and the Lead Creek Derby. On this weekend each June, the Gyro Club sponsors a carnival in Wallace. This photograph is believed to have been taken at the first Lead Creek Derby, 1942. This event requires a big beach ball being dropped into the river at Mullan and timed until it reaches the Sixth Street Bridge in Wallace. In the beginning people would buy tickets and guess the time it would take the ball to make the trip. The winner received 1,000 silver dollars. In recent years, the tickets are numbered and synchronized with the times calculated by a computer. The winner these days wins 100 fine silver (.999) centennial rounds weighing 1 troy ounce each.

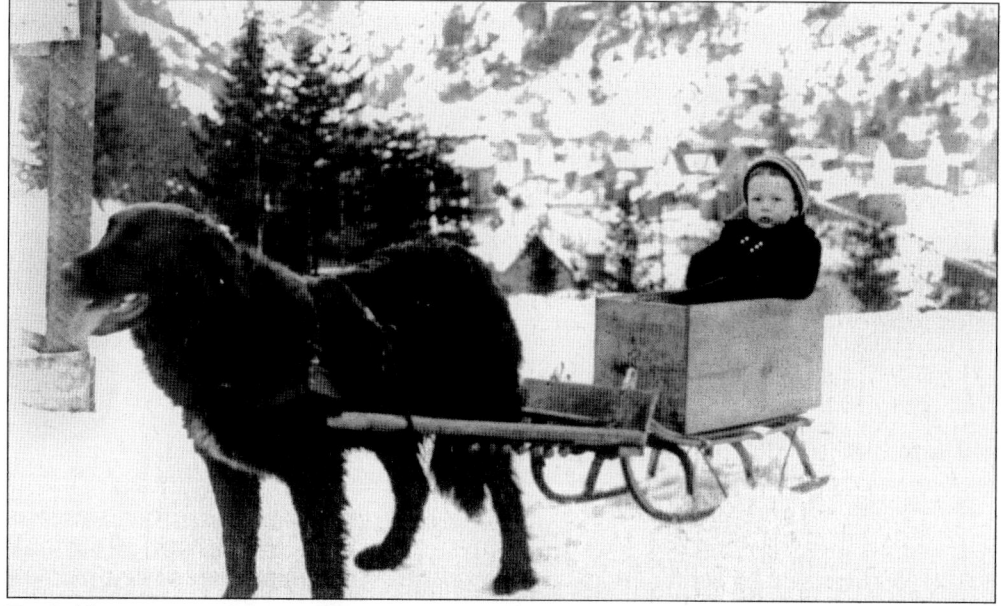

To children, winter and pets can always make for a fun day.

Pictured here is a ski-jumping competition on Fifth Street at the corner of Bank Street in 1898. The large building is the Hope Hospital.

Miners play as hard as they work, and a chance to show off their skills to others can't be passed up. These fellows are driving a hand steel with a double jack at the Labor Day competition in Murray, 1907.

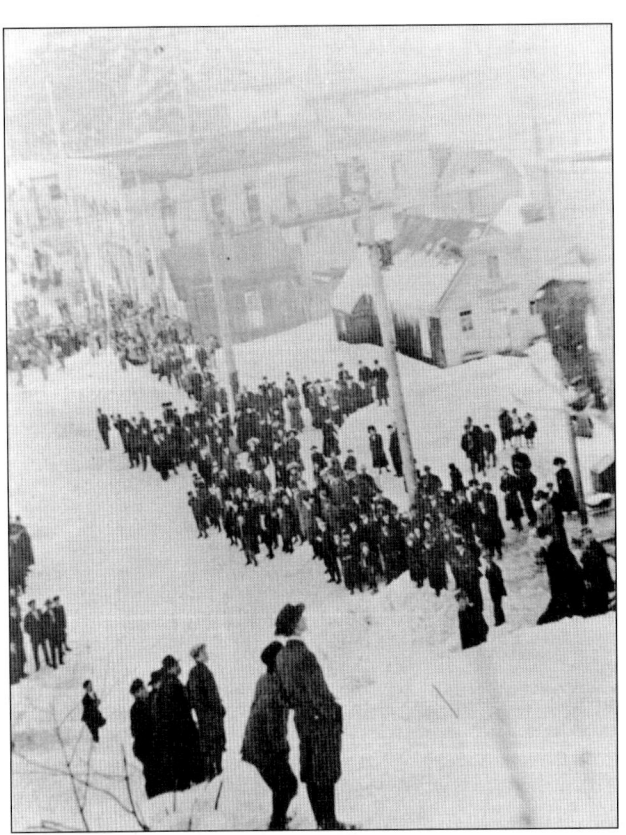

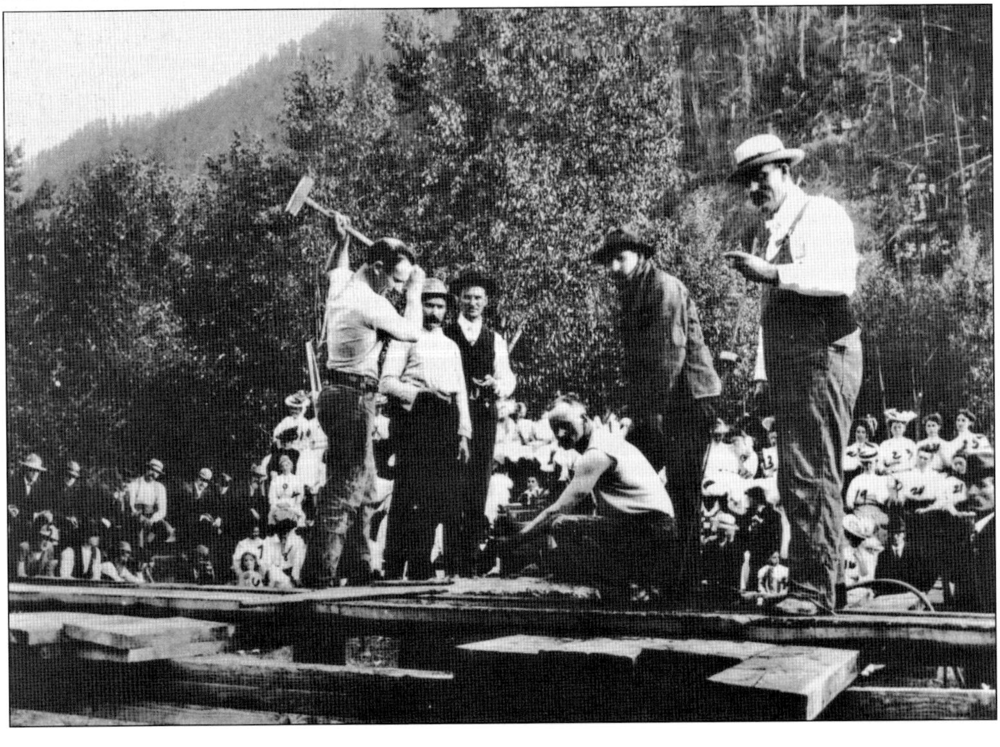

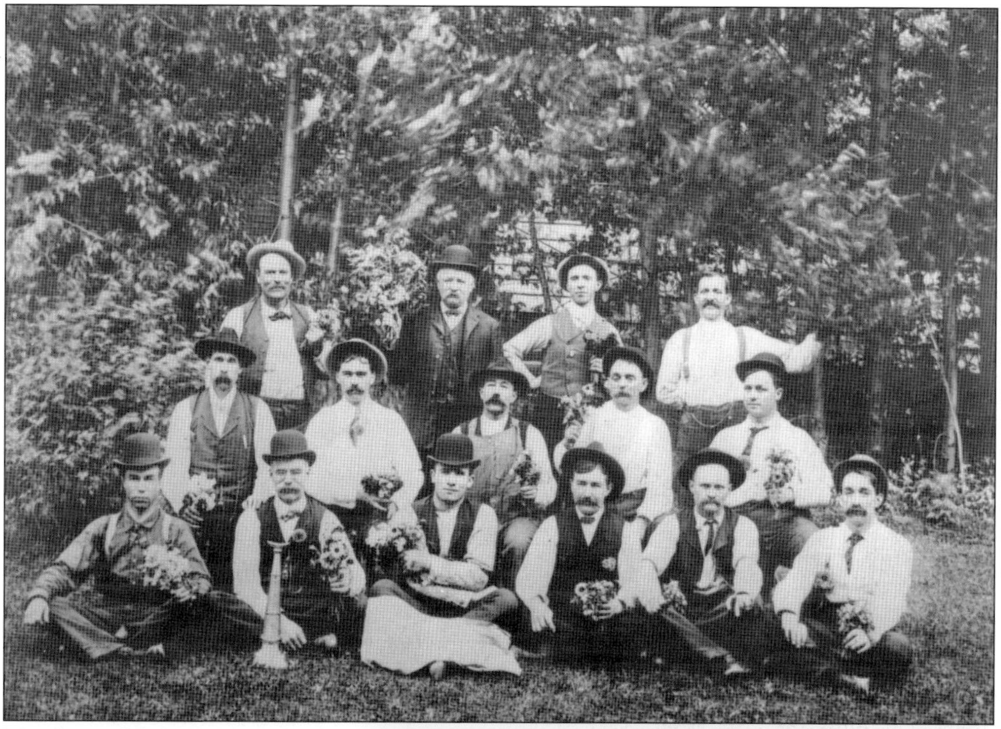

Members of the Murray Labor Day Celebration Committee posed for this c. 1907 photograph. From left to right are (first row) Jess Cochran, Chas. Melroy, Walter Jay, Walter Keister, Jess Kerr, and Ed Smith; (second row) Sam Ferguson, Johnny Williams, Frank Savage, Ed Smith, and Ed Harper; (third row) Ed Collagin, Adam Aulbach, Calence Landis, and Jay Burton.

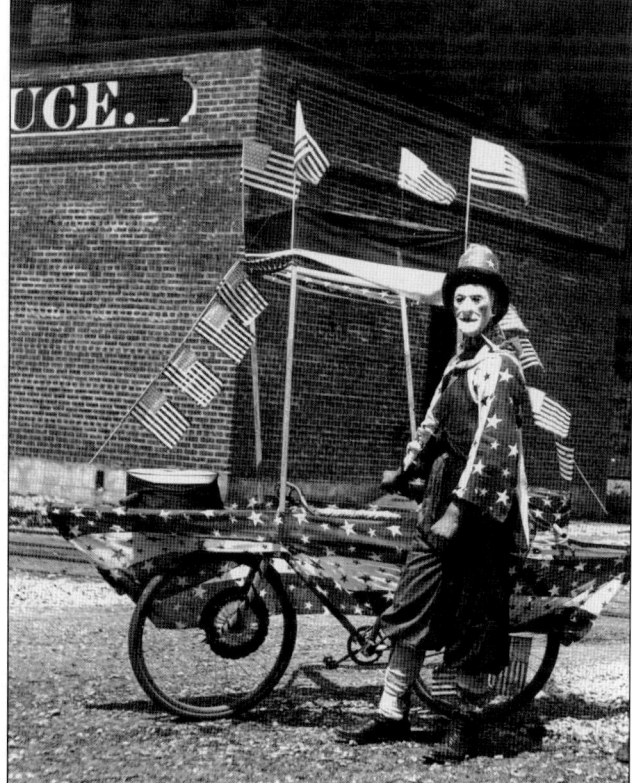

This photograph taken by Arthur Fay shows a float he built for the parade of July 4, 1904, representing good old Uncle Sam. It won the second prize of $10.

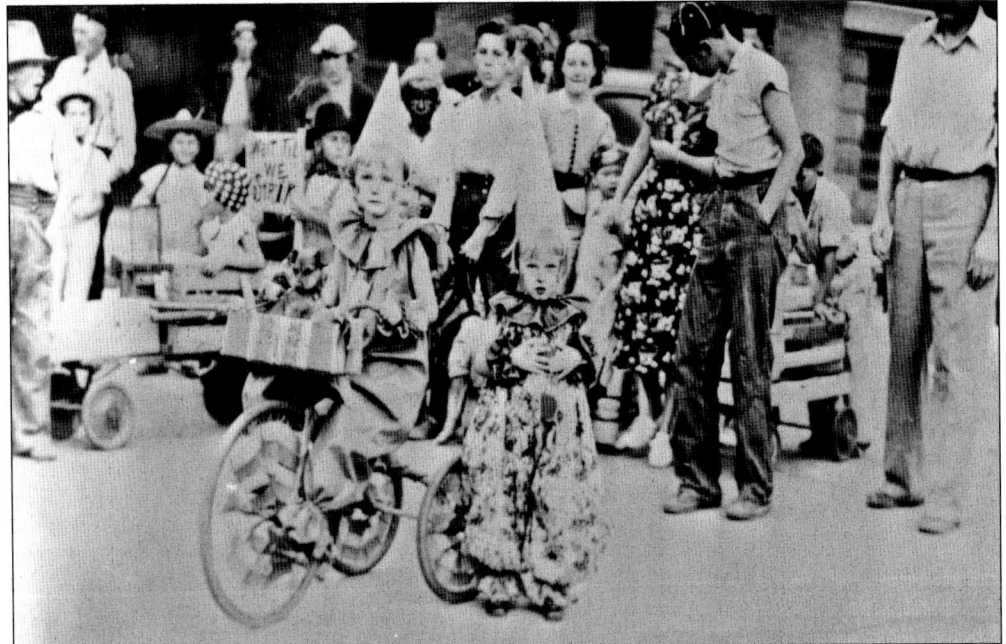

Parades, such as the one featured in this c. 1956 photograph in Kellogg, celebrated many different occasions and groups: holidays, clubs, and fraternal organizations, and welcomed home winning sports teams and returning soldiers. But no matter the reason for the parade, the kids play the most important part.

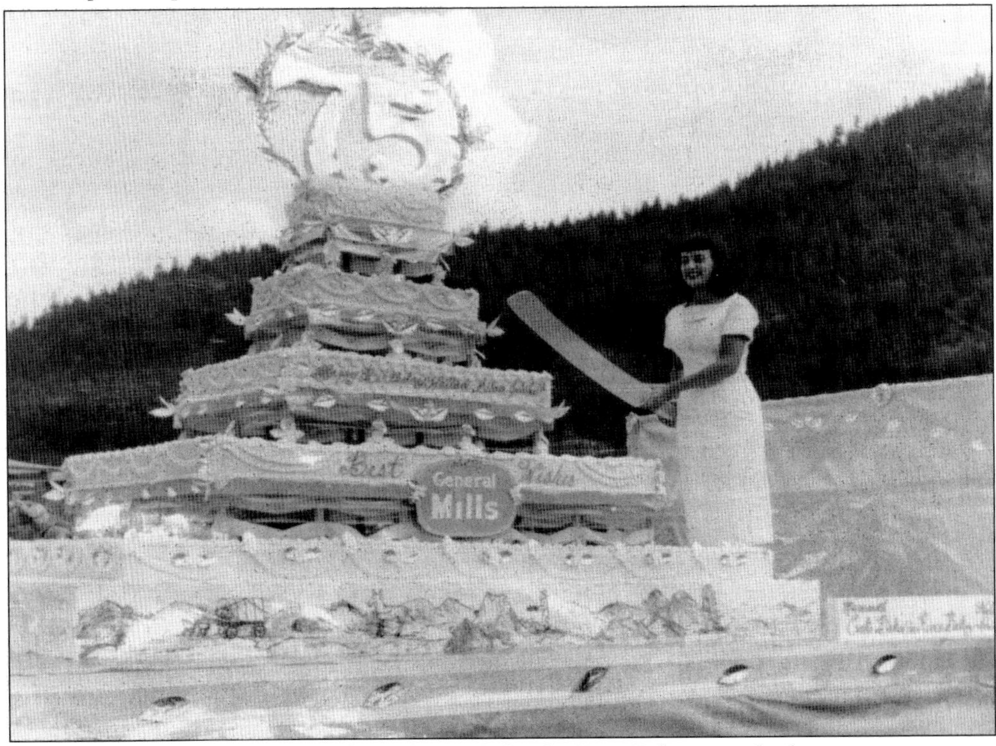

Happy 75th Birthday, Wallace! This cake made by the Rice Bakery weighed in at a ton.

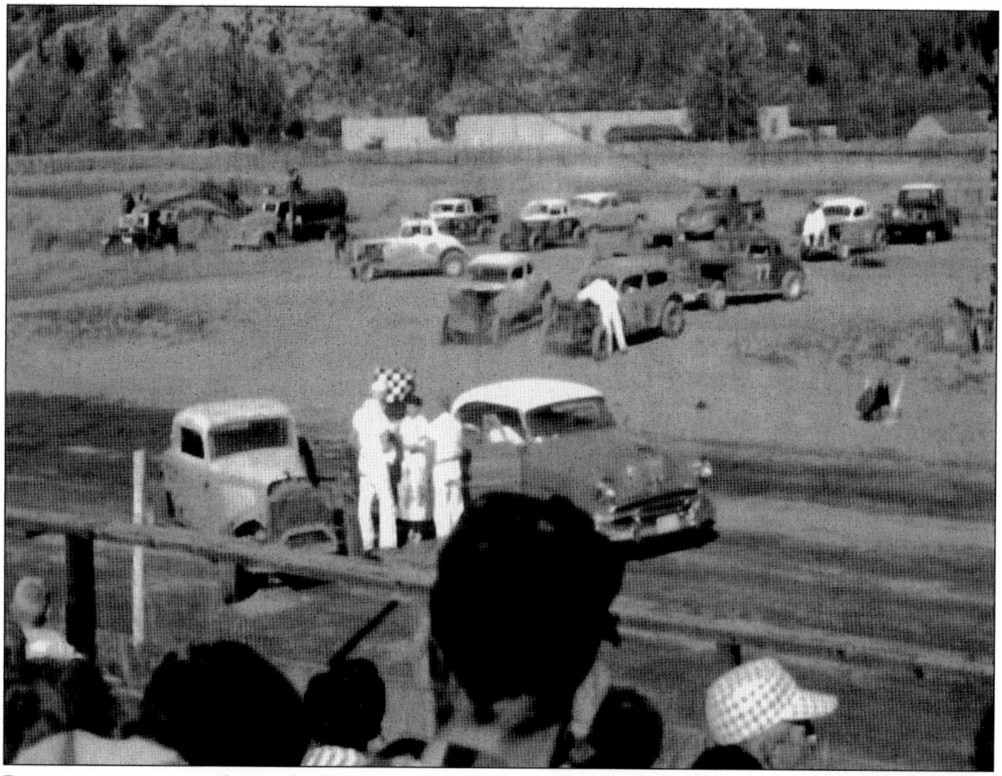

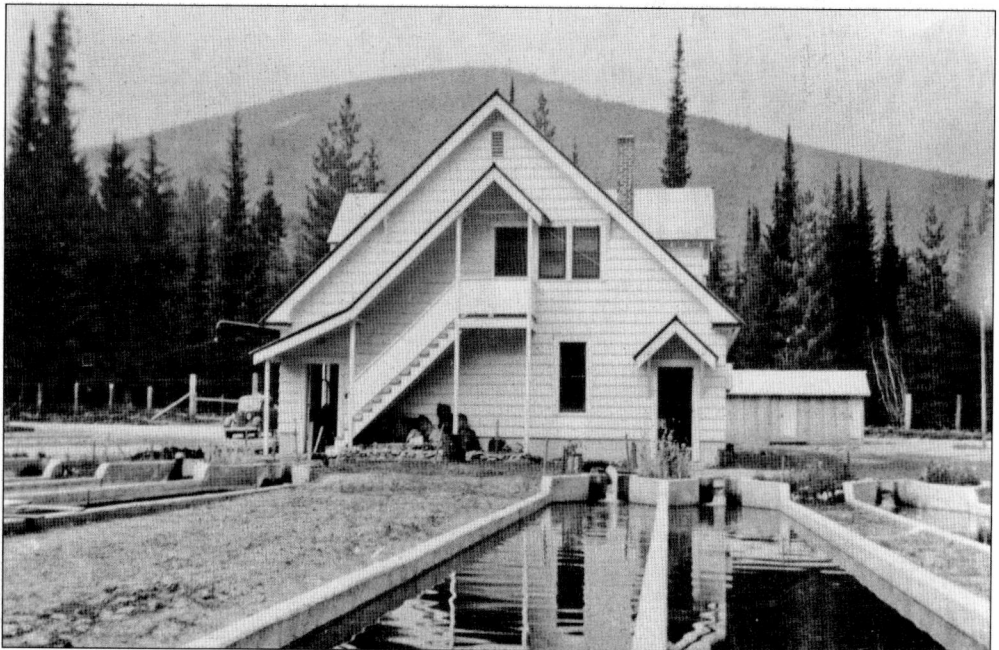

Racing cars was popular in the Silver Valley. This c. 1943 photograph taken at the Pinehurst dirt track located behind the Tee Off bar, was just one of the tracks. Smelterville had a demolition derby track.

The fish hatchery north of Mullan is pictured here.

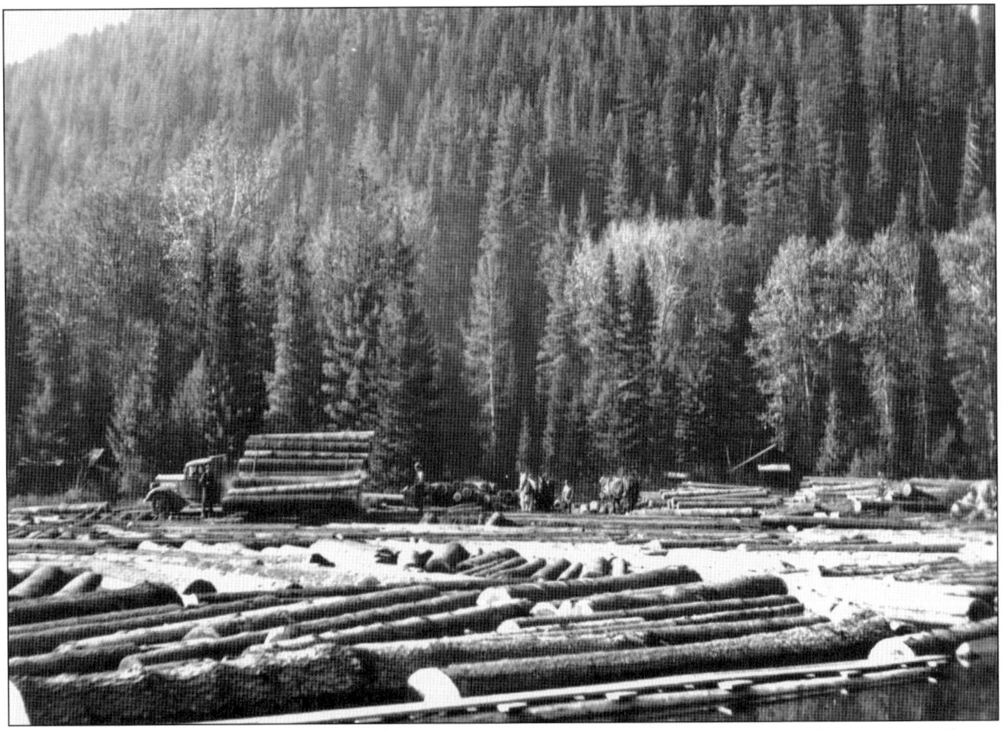

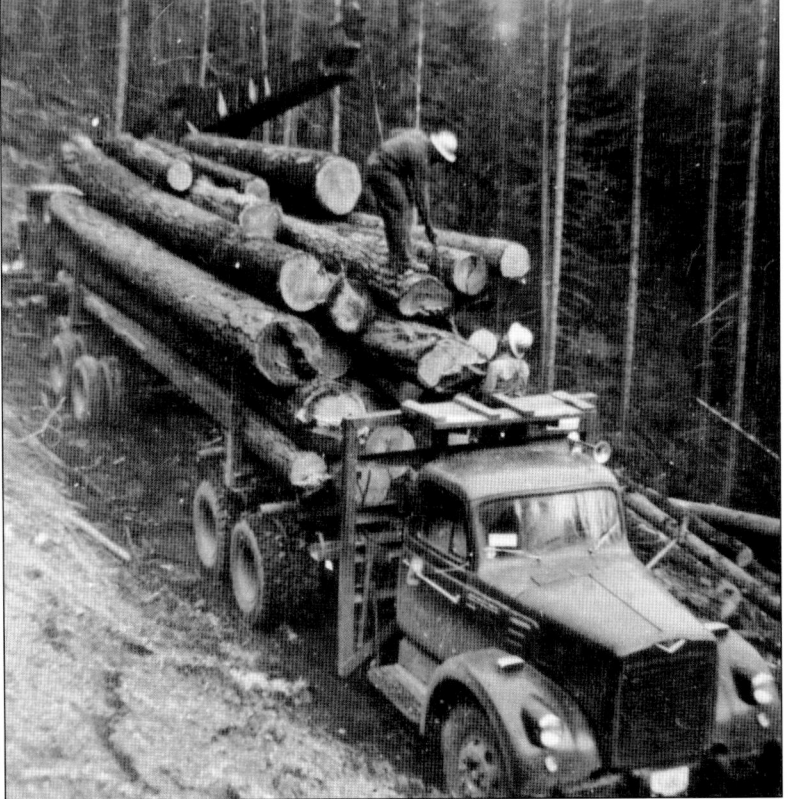

Logging trucks are common on mountain roads. This truck is carrying a very large load of trees. The Silver Valley is home to White Pine, Red Fir, and Western Larch. Most of the timber went to service the mining industry.

This 1954 photograph shows Bud Whipps, Em Hall, Carl Hoiland and Peanuts Hojem logging up the North Fork at Magee.

# Five

# BARS AND FURNISHED ROOMS

Mining camps have always been known for their large consumption of liquid refreshments. The exact count of the number of bars in the Silver Valley at its highest will probably never be known. But in the years after a license to serve was required in the four blocks that make up the business district in Wallace, there were over 30 places to buy a drink. Like the names of mines, the names of bars often tell of the hopes, fears, or experiences of their owners. Places like the Stein Club, 1313 Club (the original bar was 13 feet long, with a 13-foot ceiling and 13 bar stools), The Metals, The Mint, The Turf, Babe and Ted's Billiards, El Rey, Mascot, Comet, Sweets, and The Jameson. Sweets and The Jameson were considered to be in the rough part of Wallace. Amazing that a town of only four blocks could have a good and bad side. Whether you were a miner, logger, cowboy, or railway worker, there was a saloon that would make you feel at home.

In the early days, when a woman lost the support of a man due to death or abandonment, she was left on her own to keep a roof over her children's heads. There were little opportunities out there. Taking in laundry or cleaning other people's homes would hardly pay for food. Along the railroad tracks in Kellogg and Wallace, places offering comfort to workingmen would hire them. In a few weeks of work, they could earn enough to pay the mortgage and provide for their families in the coming year. In Wallace, the ladies remained a part of the fabric of the community until the last house closed in 1988. Delores, Wallace's favorite madam, made sure that schoolchildren had sports and band supplies and that the county had police cars and snowplows.

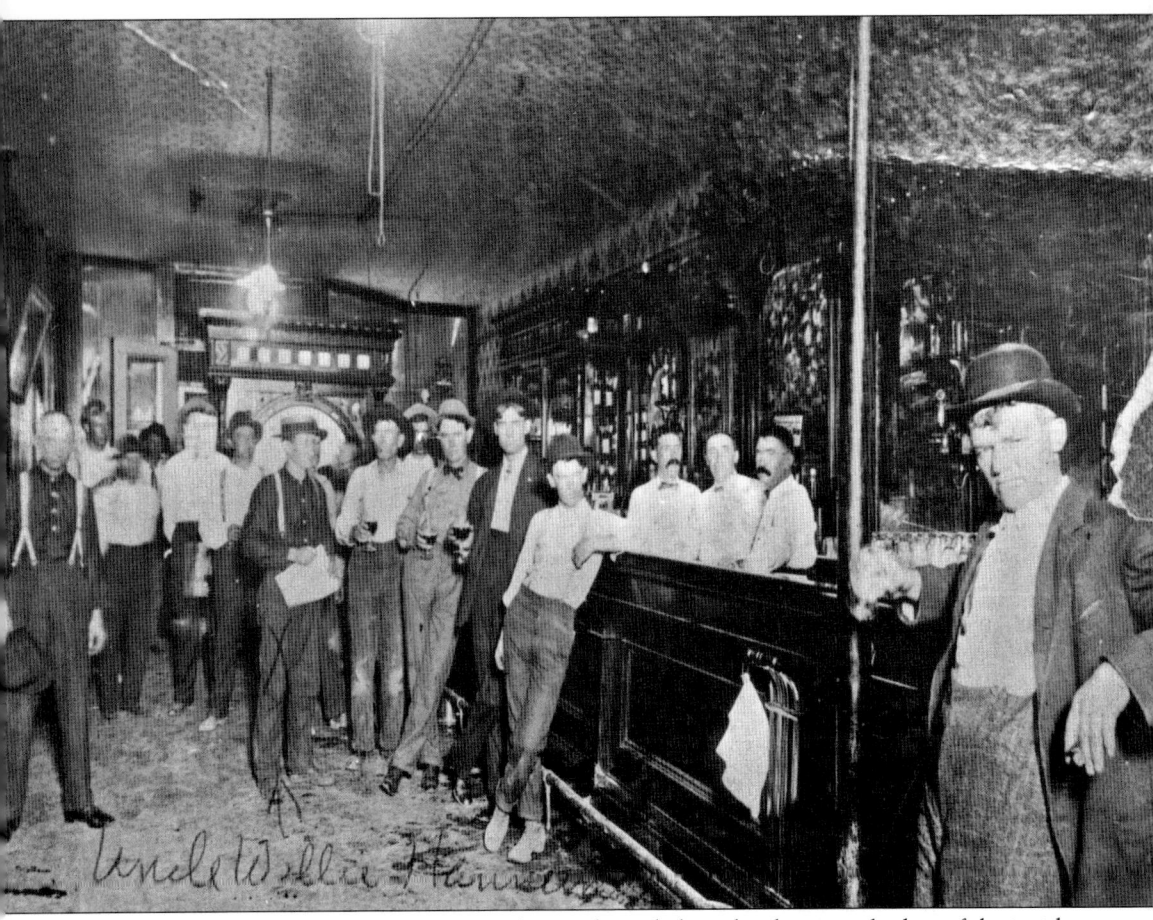

This is the typical inside of the average saloon. This is believed to be an early shot of the inside of The Jameson, which was later The Mint and is now The Jameson again. Built in 1907 for Theodore Jameson, it is now the home of "Maggie," the ghost that has been haunting the joint for as long as locals can remember. She is a lady who makes her presence known—in polite ways that get your attention. Stop in, and if you're lucky . . . Maggie may visit with you. In 1970, The Jameson was restored for the movie *Heaven's Gate* starring Kris Kristofferson.

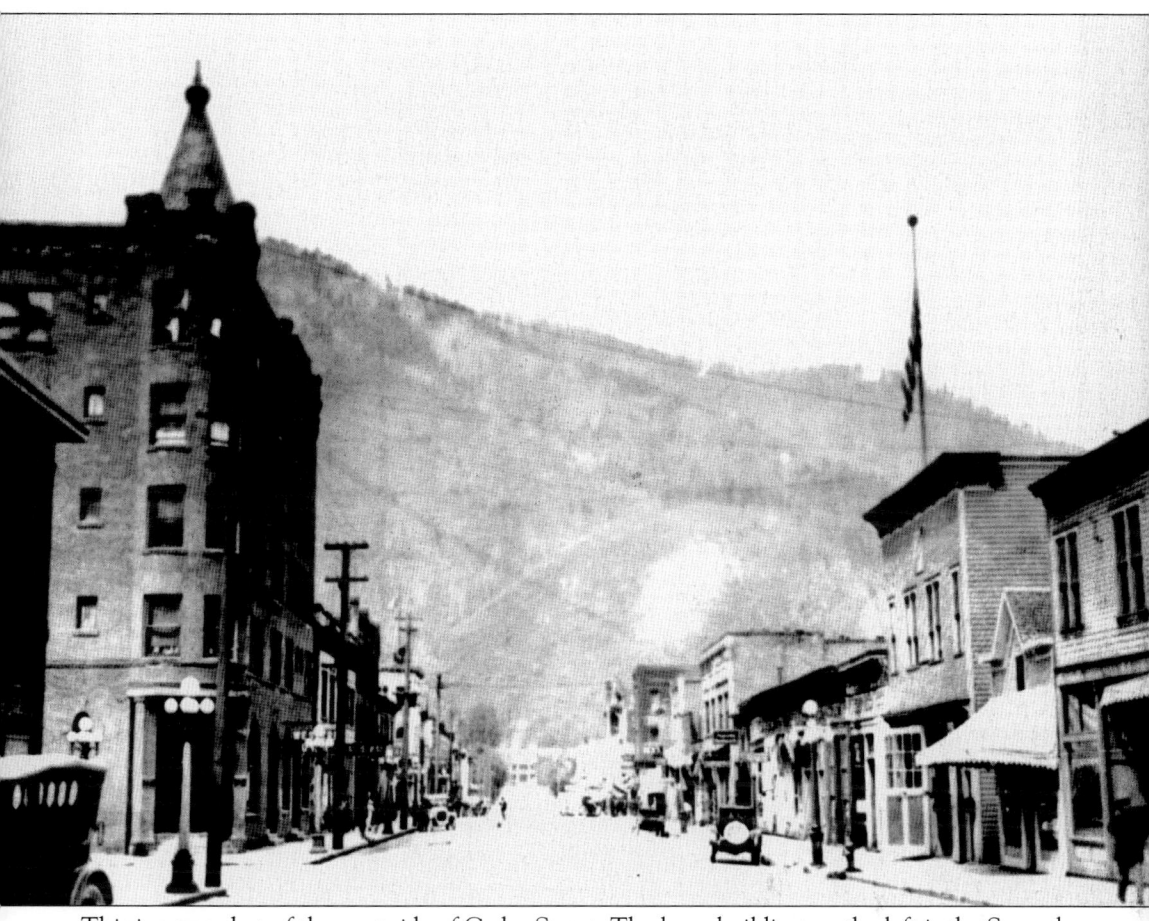
This is a rare shot of the west side of Cedar Street. The large building on the left is the Samuels Hotel. On the right with the flag are city hall and the fire department. Continuing up the street on the right are The Jade Rooms and The Oasis. For many years, a lonely miner could rent a "furnished room" for the evening. Establishments with exotic names like The Jade Rooms, Lux, The Luxette, The Oasis, and the Arment Rooms offered accommodations that came with a "girl."

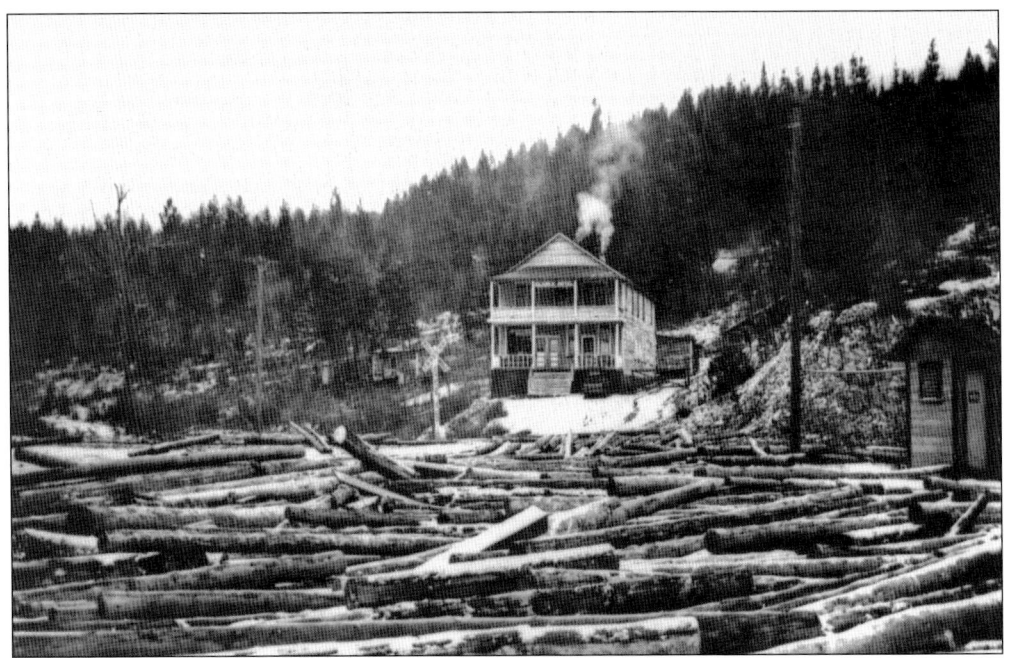

This is the Enaville Resort, better known to locals as the Snake Pit, at Enaville on the Coeur d'Alene River. The logjam in the foreground is the result of a flood.

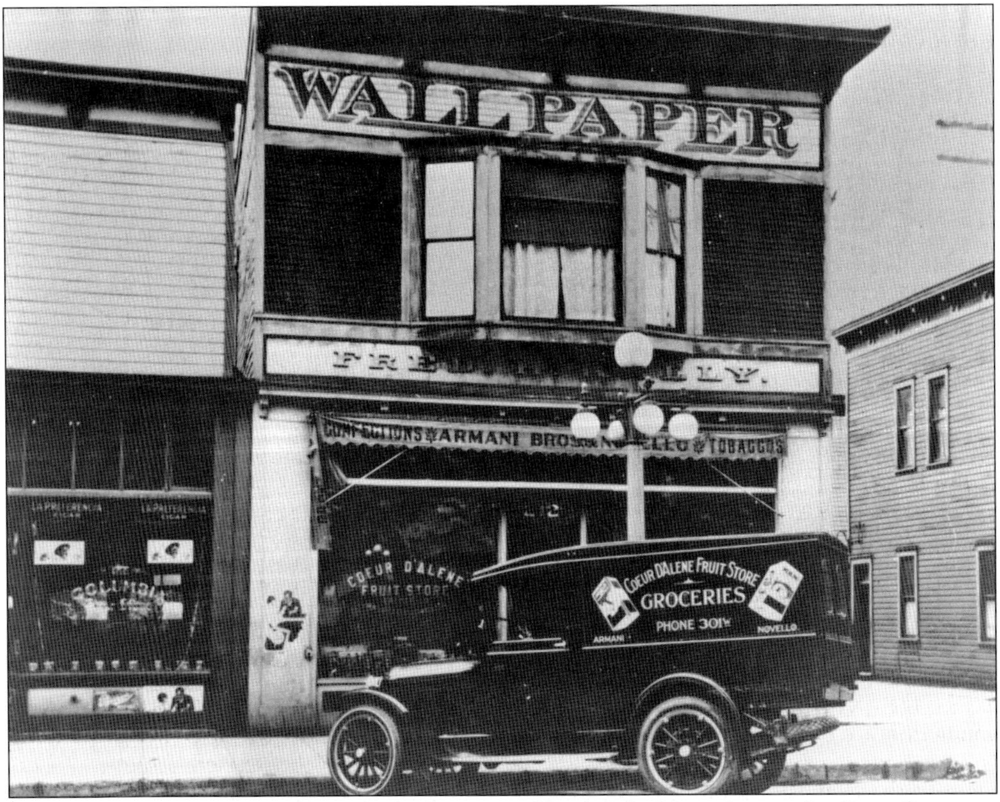

The Lux Rooms were located above the business of Fred Kelly. Next-door is the Cigar Store.

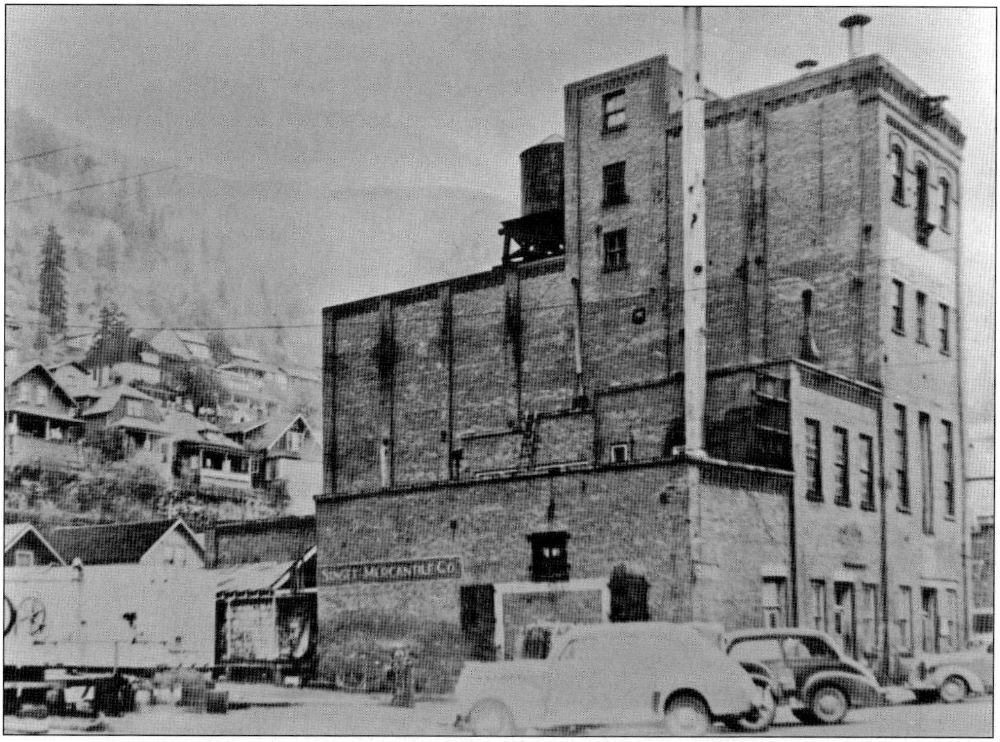

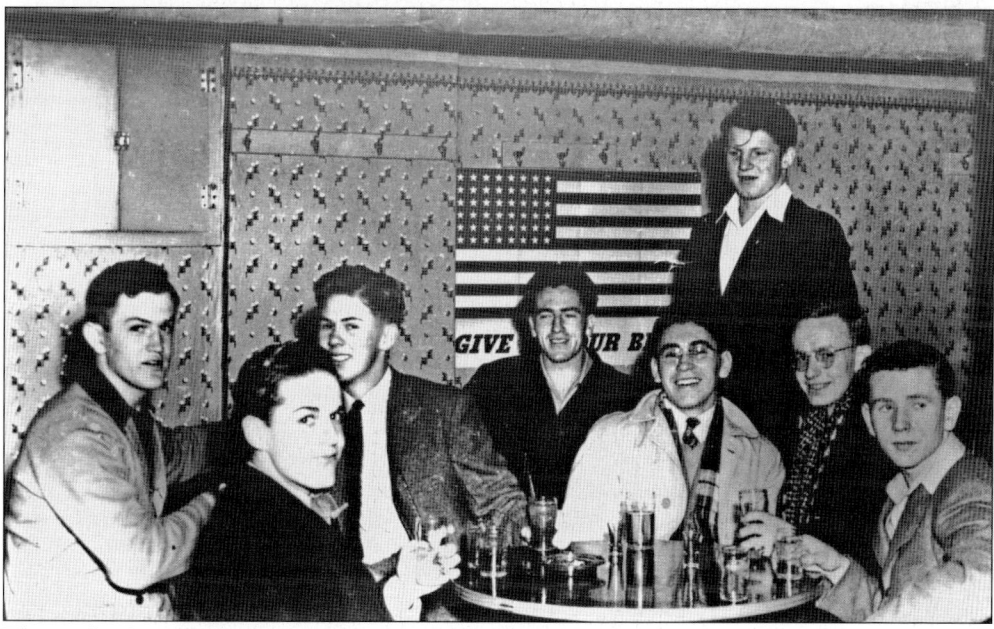

This is the Sunset Brewery, on Hotel Street.

This is the Stein Club, downstairs in the Hales building. World War II was in full swing. These young men are having one last party together before they head off for basic training. Standing is Rusty Larson, who enlisted during World War II. From left to right are Herb Arnett, "Dinky" Duncan (he became a doctor), Bruce Berg, John Brunelle, Joe Espinosa, Paul Wickward, and Bob Young.

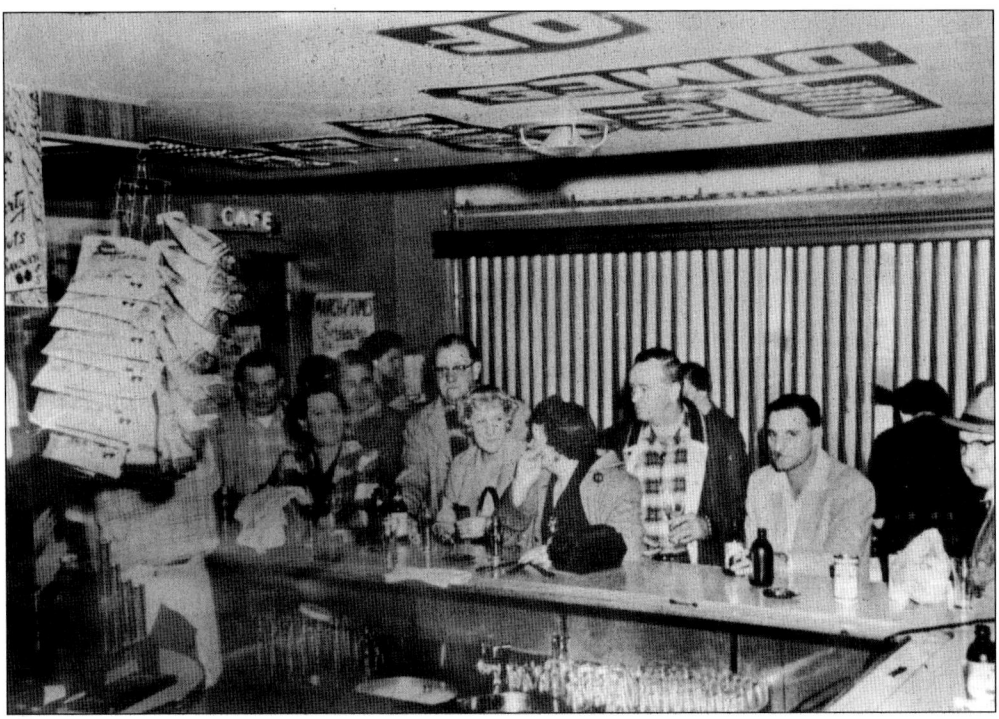

The March of Dimes committee celebrates at Albis Gem Bar at Sixth and Pine.

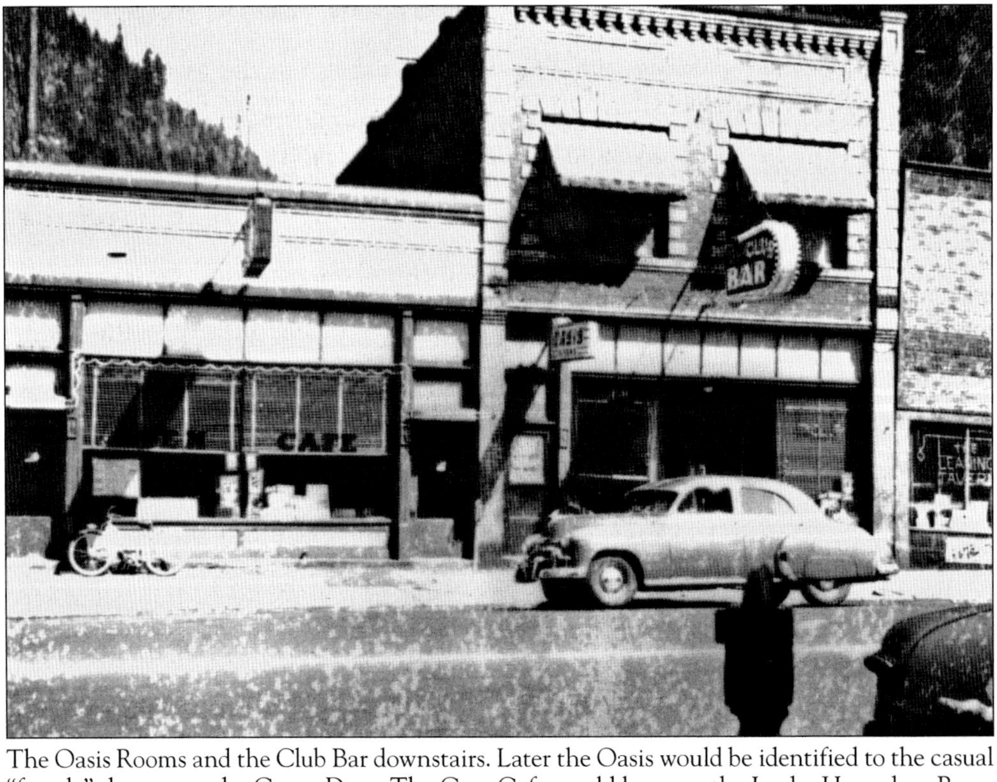

The Oasis Rooms and the Club Bar downstairs. Later the Oasis would be identified to the casual "female" shopper as the Green Door. The Gem Cafe would become the Lucky Horseshoe Bar.

# Six

# TRAINS

The railroad arrived in the Silver Valley in 1876 and left in 1993. In the intervening 117 years, they would haul tons of ore, countless goods, and human cargo. Building a railroad in the mountains is never an easy job, and the train system serving the valley took its toll in lives as well as finances.

The 1800s were a time when men left families behind in hopes of striking it rich. They would work for a few days, pick up their pay and move on. Some would be killed for their pay, others in accidents, without their families ever knowing what happened to them. The builders of the railways would overcome weather and geography to lay track. They would tunnel through mountains and build trestles over deep gorges. Through the rail construction, the towns of Taft, Montana, and The Loop Saloon boomed. Now gone, much of the line has become bike trails, giving riders the chance to see the mountains in much the same way as did our ancestors.

In 1887, a narrow-gauge line, the Coeur d'Alene Railway and Navigational Company, dropped passengers at the Cataldo Mission where travelers bound for Coeur d'Alene would board steamboats on the Coeur d'Alene River. They would then go down-river to Harrison, up the St. Joe River to St. Maries, or head north on Coeur d'Alene Lake to Coeur d'Alene. From Harrison one could board The Northern Pacific for the coast. By 1889, the Oregon Railroad and Navigation Company had made it here. This standard-gauge rail connection was highly competitive with the less efficient narrow-gauge and steamboat route. The Northern Pacific tracks reached Wallace from the east in August 1891.

The Northern Pacific is probably the best known of the lines to come to the valley and had depots in Wallace, Kellogg and Mullan. On May 20, 1902, Wallace's Northern Pacific Depot opened. Built in the Chateau style, it is two stories tall with a cupola. Mine tailing were mixed with the concrete for the aggregate. The bricks were imported from China as ship ballast and were also used in the railroad-owned Hotel Olympic in Tacoma.

The cost in 1902 for its construction was $9,368.21. In 1986, the NP Depot was moved across the river to protect it when the new freeway came through. This move and restoration would cost $588,056. Talk about inflation! It now houses the Depot Museum.

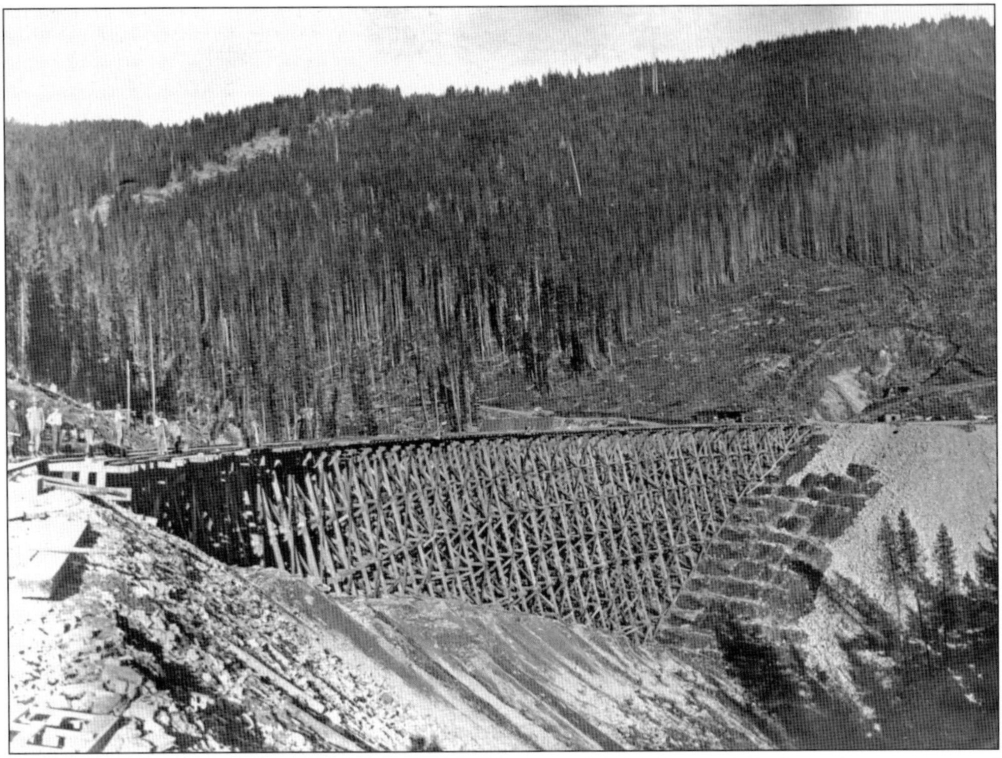

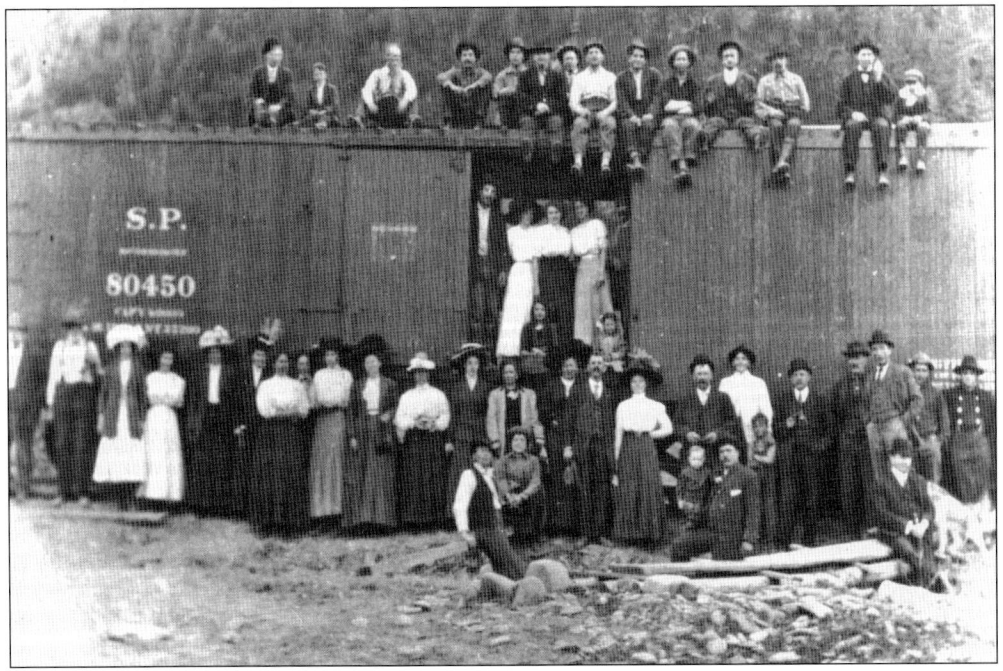

This photograph by Harry English shows the Chicago, Milwaukee, and St. Paul Railway route of the Hiawatha, Burn's and Jordon Camp No. 1–Bridge No. 3—East Portal Tunnel No. 22.

Pictured here are employees and their families from the Gold Hunter on Union Pacific Rail car, west of Mullan.

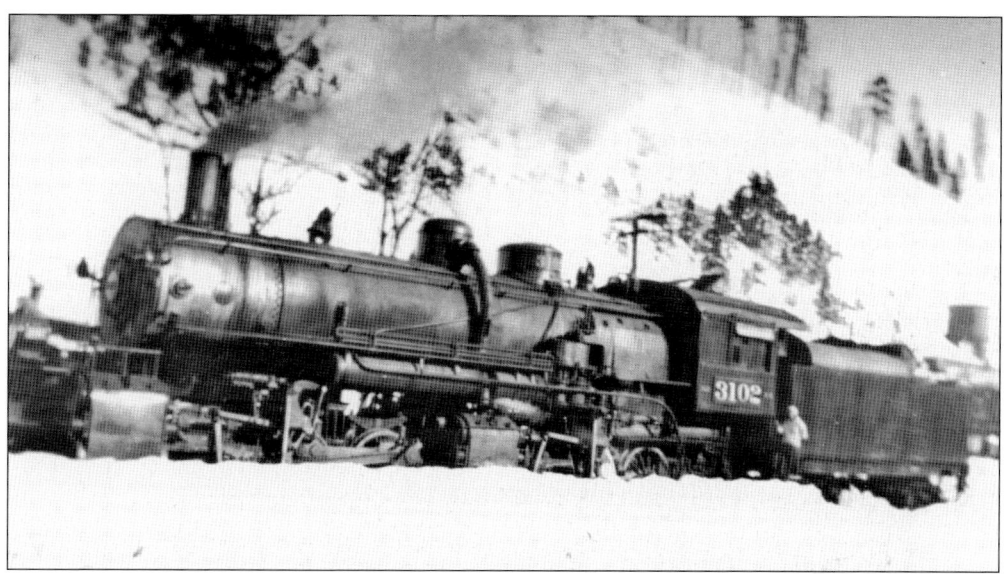

This c. 1930s photograph from the Leroy Thomas Collection shows his mother, Hilda Adams Thomas, posing with Engine No. 3102, west of the Wallace Railway Depot.

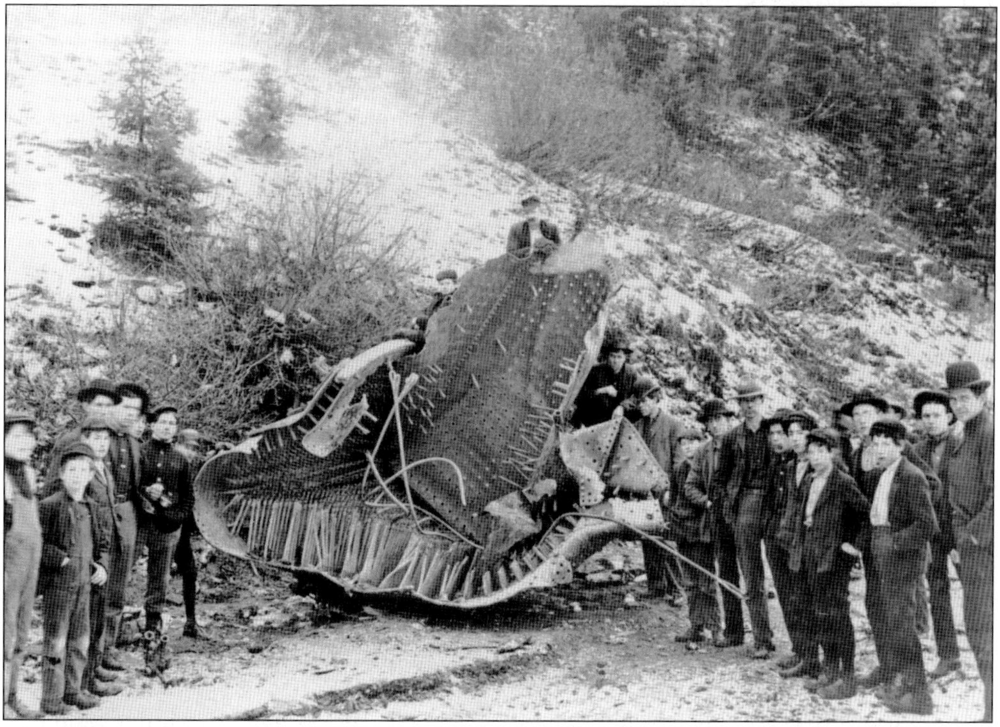

This photograph remained a mystery until the donation of a 1907 newspaper story was made to the Historic Wallace Preservation Society, featuring images of the explosion of a train engine in the Burke Canyon.

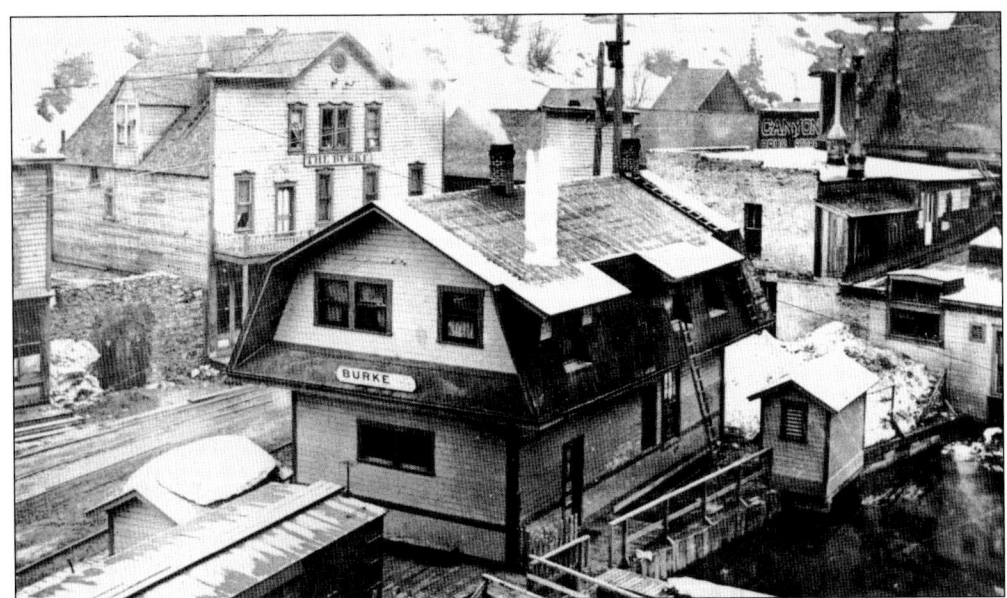

In this c. 1889 photograph is the Union Pacific Railroad Depot in Burke, Idaho, with the business district in the background. The small building by the creek is the outhouse.

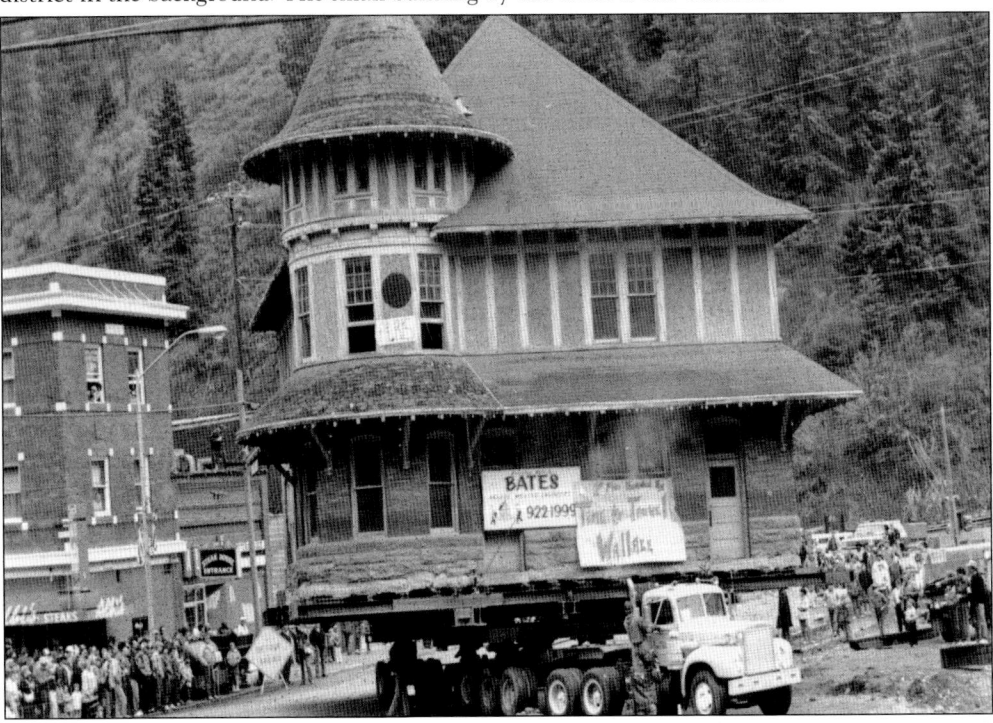

The Northern Pacific Railroad Depot is moved by the Bates Moving Company on May 10, 1986. The bridge of the south fork of the Coeur d'Alene River was reinforced to handle the extreme weight. A crowd of about 2,500 people turned out to watch the depot move to a new location south of the river and existing tracks. The NP Depot Foundation was formed. Depot Day is celebrated on the second Saturday in May with an antique car show and a raffle for 100 ounces of .999 fine silver medallions.

The finial is placed on the Northern Pacific Railroad Depot cupola—a true Depot Derby!

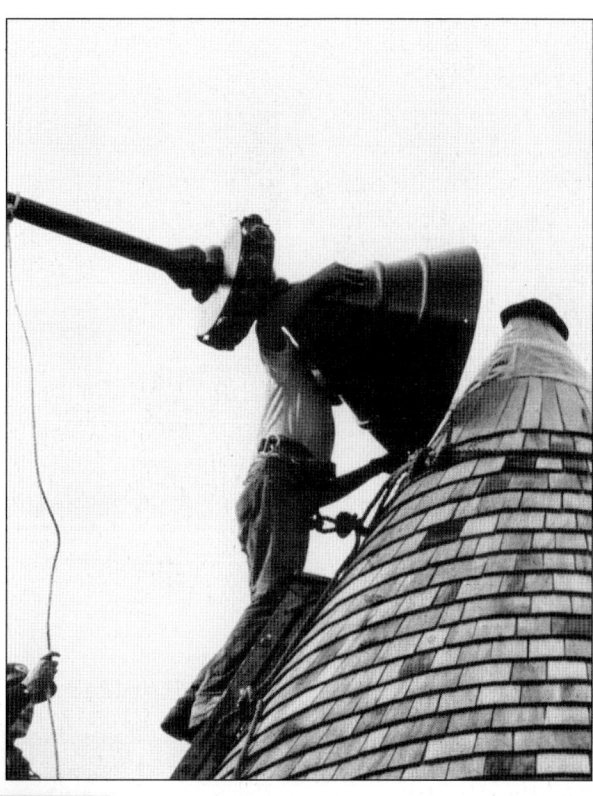

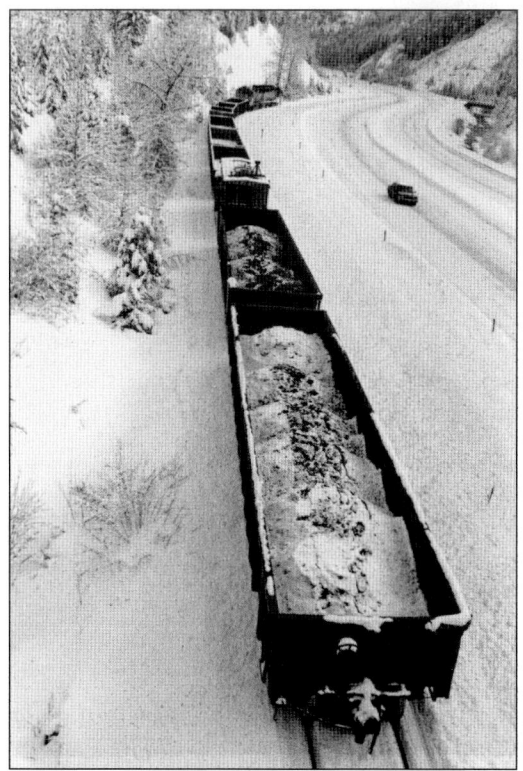

The train is headed up to the Lucky Friday Mine in Mullan to pick up ore. This ore is from the Galena/Coeur complex at Wallace. (ASARCO property is now owned by U.S. Silver Corporation.)

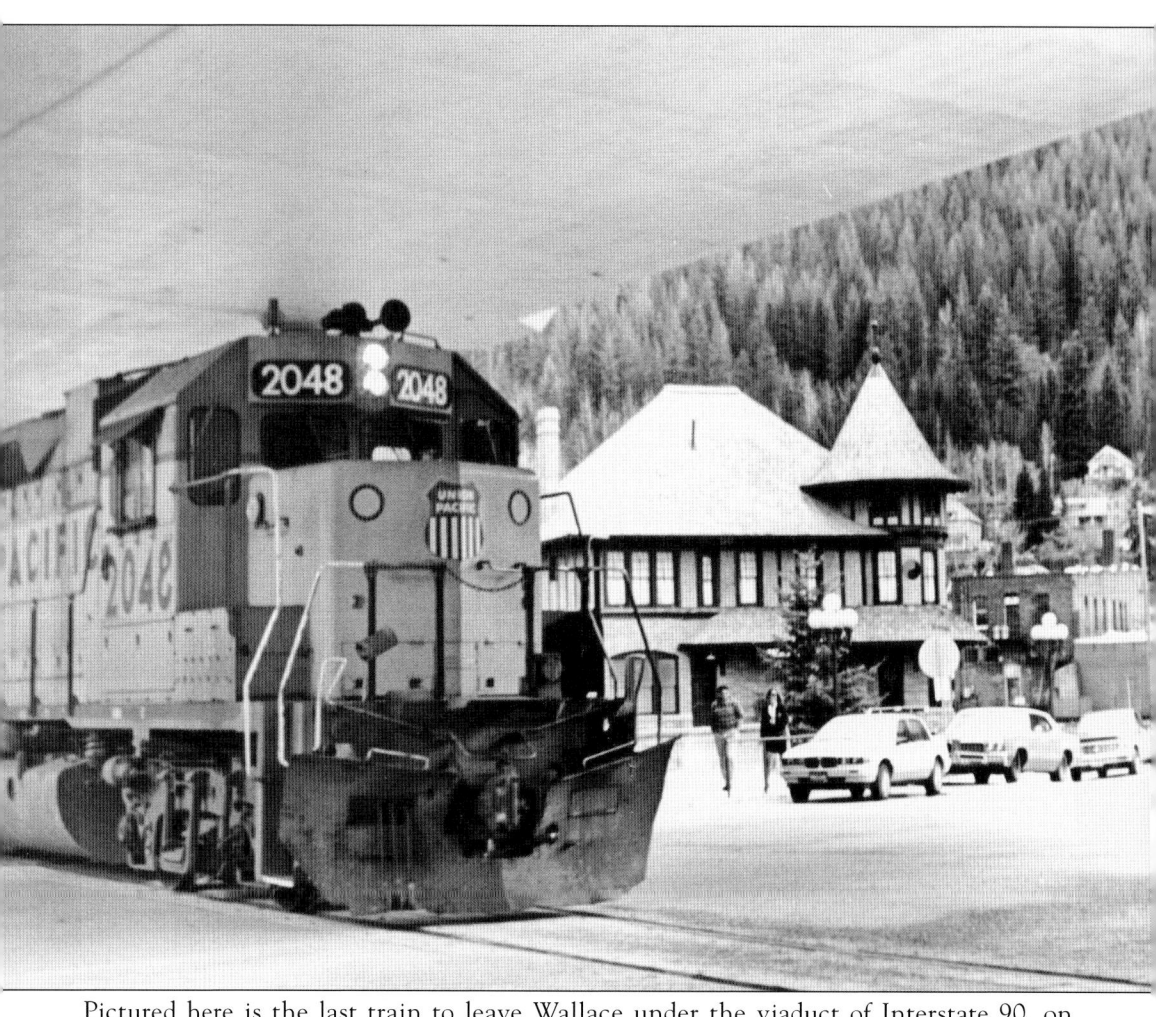

Pictured here is the last train to leave Wallace under the viaduct of Interstate 90, on April 23, 1993.

# Seven
# MOTHER NATURE AT WORK

While she has blessed the area with rich ore deposits, abundant wildlife, and beautiful scenery, Mother Nature also shows that she is in charge with floods, fires, and snow. The climate in 1910 had been very dry, with small fires scattered around the western states. As the summer wore on, these small fires began to join together. The bigger and hotter they got, the more wind they produced, which sped them on. By August 19, the fire was fast approaching Wallace. Women, children, and hospital patients were sent to safety on trains. Between fear and smoke, breathing was becoming impossible. Soon the fire would burn the tracks and trestles, leaving no escape. As the fire moved along the south hill people buried their valuables in their yards and prayed. With a fire this big, many believed the world was ending. By August 20, as it roared along the hillsides, fire brands were landing in town. Soon the east end warehouse district was in flames.

Meanwhile, on the mountains, men fighting the fire were being caught by the flames. Some would survive by covering their heads with wet blankets and laying face down in water. The best-known group was held by Ranger Edward Pulaski at gunpoint in the Nicholson Adit while the fire raced over them. The adit (a mine tunnel) was deep enough to hold them and a few horses. Ranger "Big Ed" Pulaski held wet blankets over the opening to keep out as much of the smoke possible. Between heat, smoke, and lack of oxygen, they lost consciousness, but 45 men survived. Ranger Pulaski's eyesight was badly damaged, and though he never completely recovered, he would go on to invent a tool still used by firefighters everywhere; the Pulaski—a combination axe and hoe. While the exact number of lives lost will never be known because it was a time when many men were on the move looking for their fortune, 87 firefighters were recorded lost.

With the trees gone from the mountains there was nothing to hold back the snow and water, so for the next 40 years floods and snow slides would come to call.

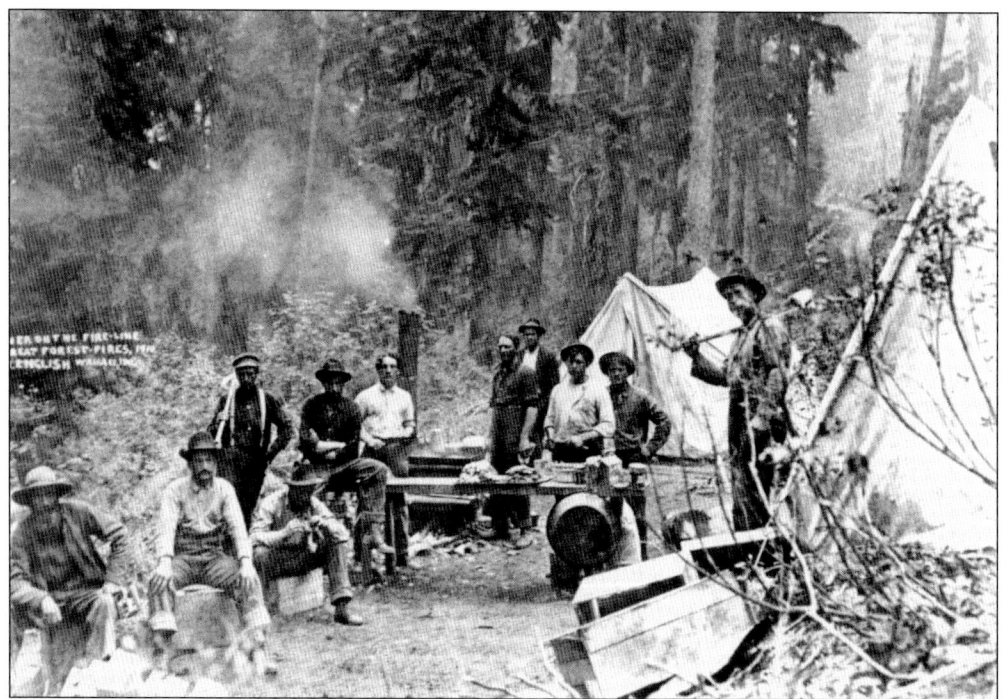

This photograph was taken by Harry English while he was documenting the building of the Chicago, Milwaukee, and St. Paul Railroad along the North Fork of the St. Joe River at Bullion Creek. As the 1910 fire approached the area, English continued photographing the fire and the forest. This was a camp where firefighters could get a meal.

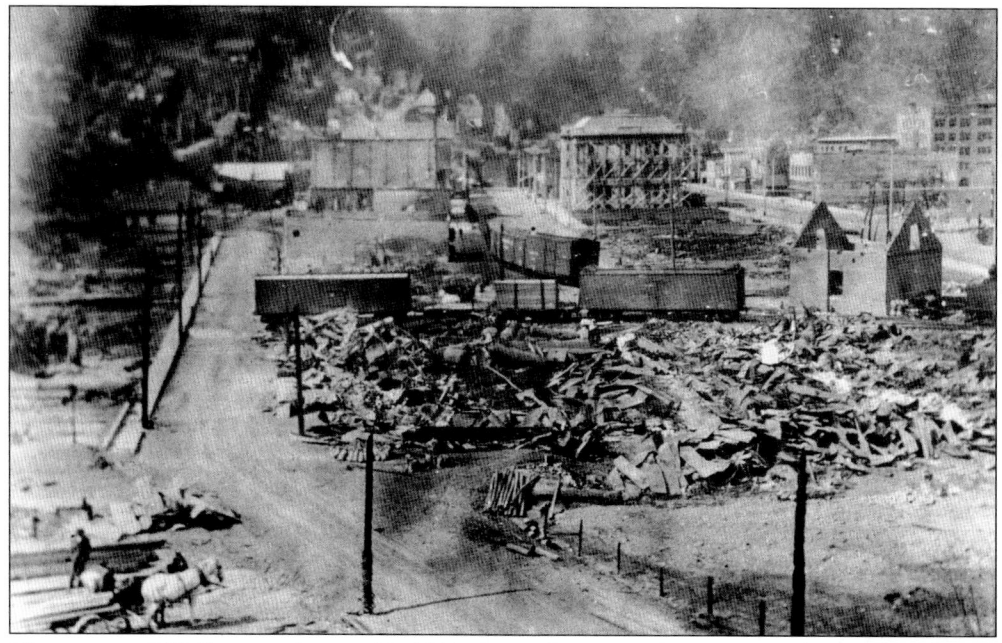

This image of Wallace on August 22, 1910, shows that everything east of the courthouse has been burned. Warehouses and the Union Pacific Railroad Depot were in this part of town. Most structures were still wooden at the time.

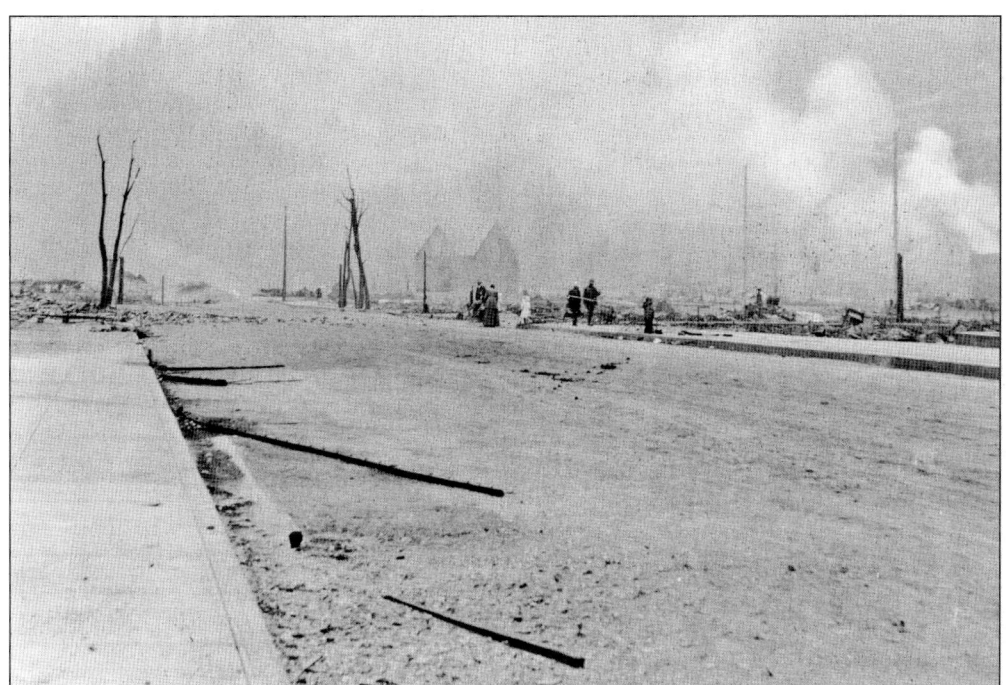

In this photograph of Wallace's east end, buildings are still smoking, but those who survived are already out assessing the damage.

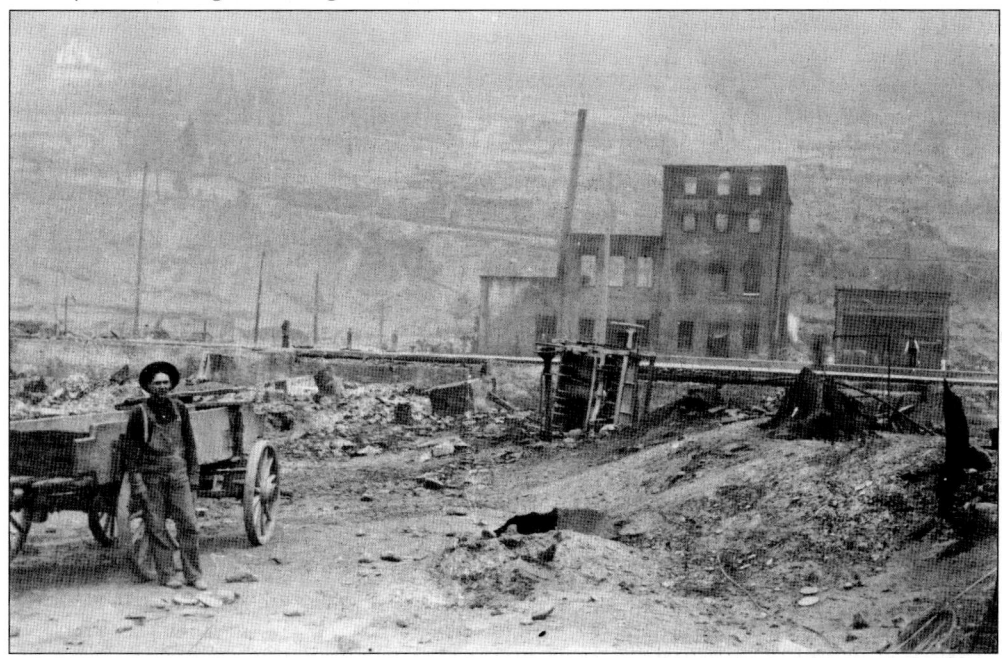

This photograph was taken by Arthur Fay on August 22, 1910. The white house on the hill is the only house to survive the fire on the south hill. The large building is the Sunset Brewery. It was gutted but would be rebuilt. There were exclamations of "wall of beer" flowing through the streets of Wallace as the brewery burned. The man with his wagon is not waiting for someone else to clean up the mess.

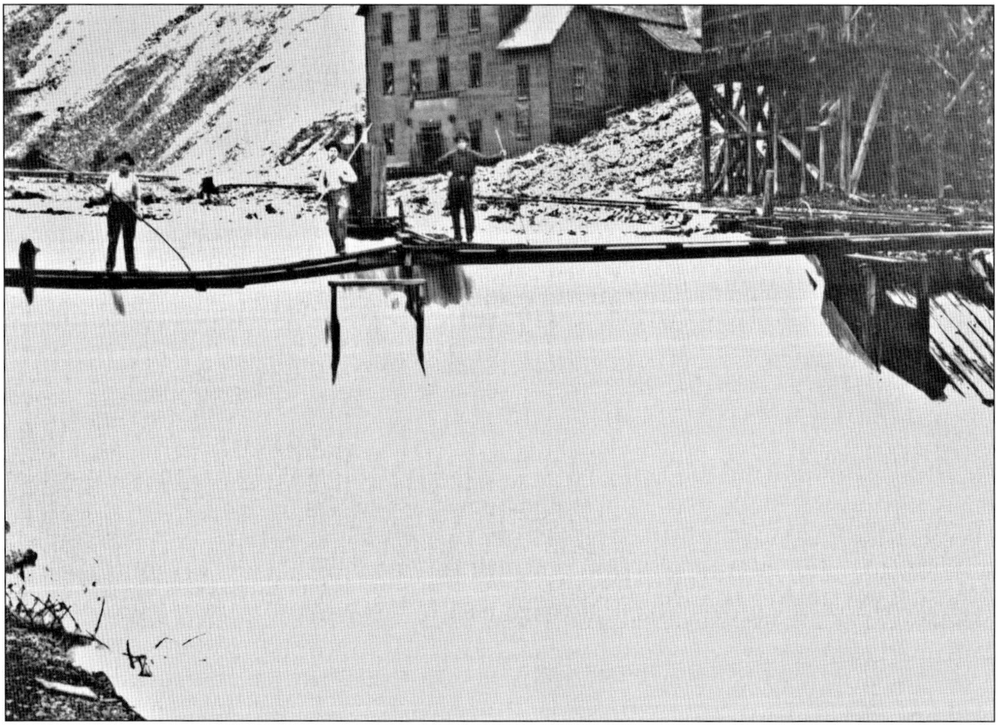

Because of the narrowness of the Burke canyon, flooding is inevitable.

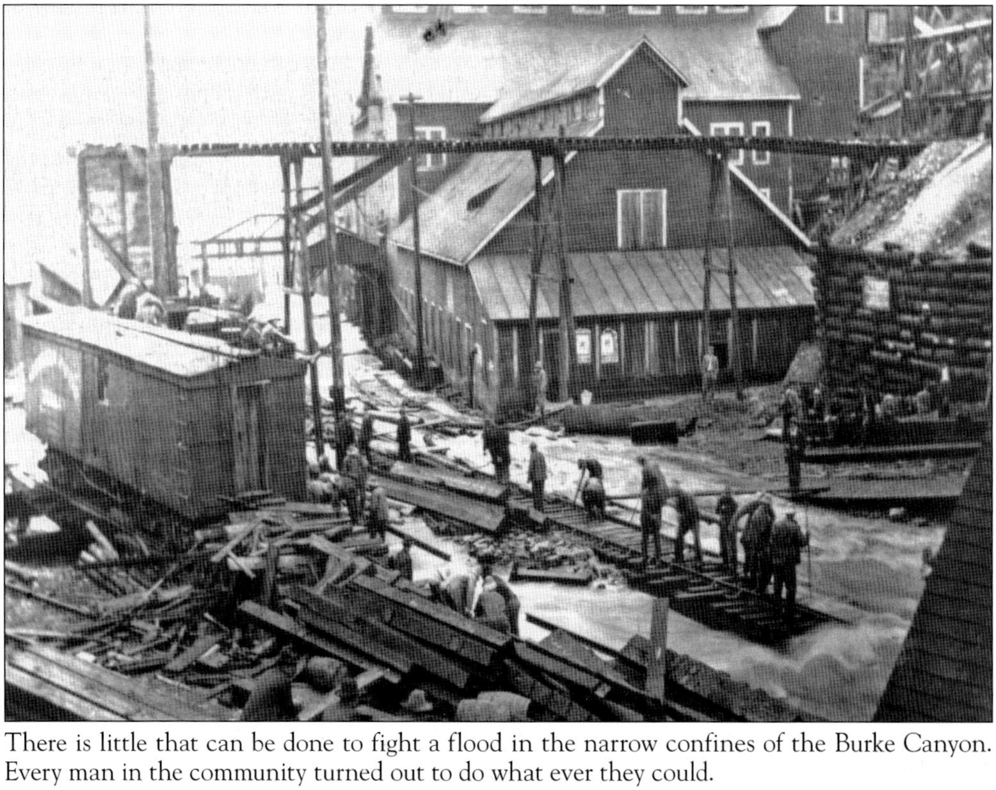

There is little that can be done to fight a flood in the narrow confines of the Burke Canyon. Every man in the community turned out to do what ever they could.

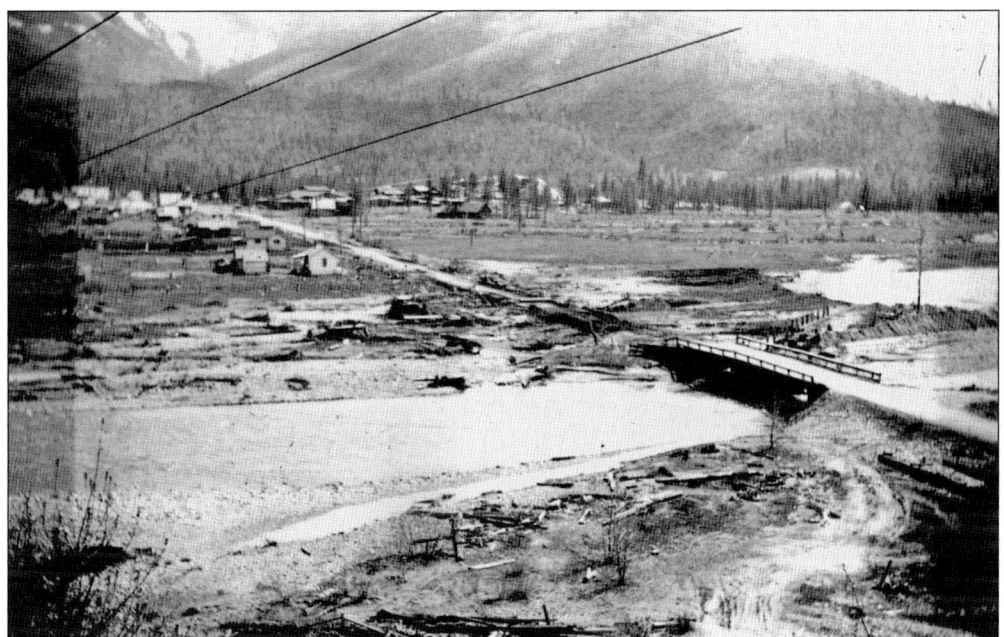

This flood in Pinehurst in 1938 was one of many. Between cutting timber for the tunnels underground and the Great Fire of 1910, the mountains lacked trees and brush to help hold the snow and moisture back. Some winters would be marked with Chinook winds. A Chinook is a very warm wind that comes suddenly and can melt an entire snow pack in just a couple of hours. If the ground is frozen when this happens, there is nowhere for the water to go. This picture of Division Street shows that Pine Creek took it over when it flooded.

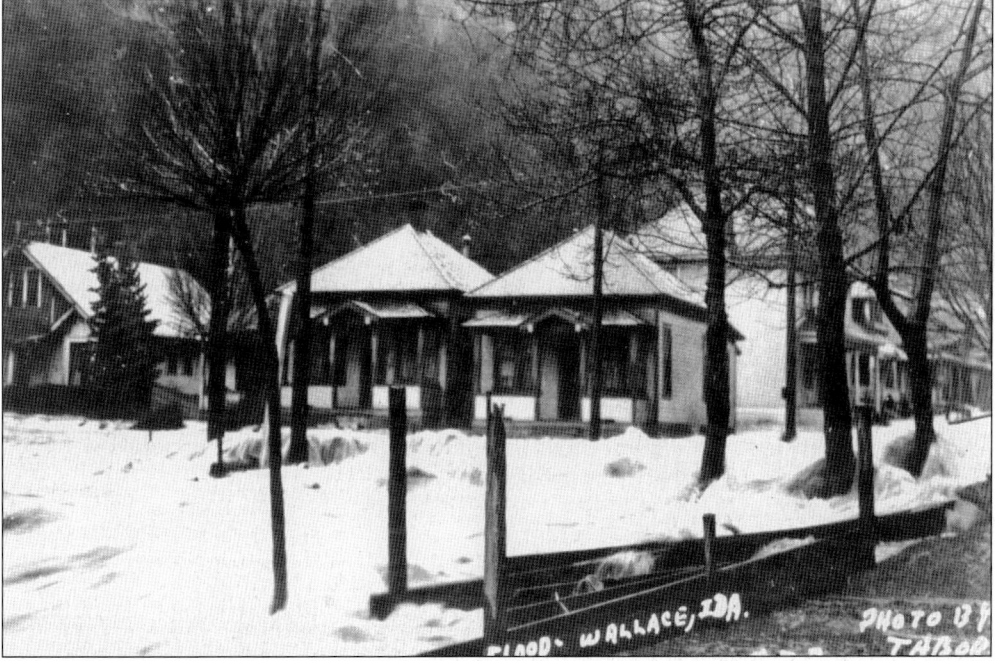

This photograph taken by Tabor is of King Street, during the Placer Creek flooding in 1933. Note the waves.

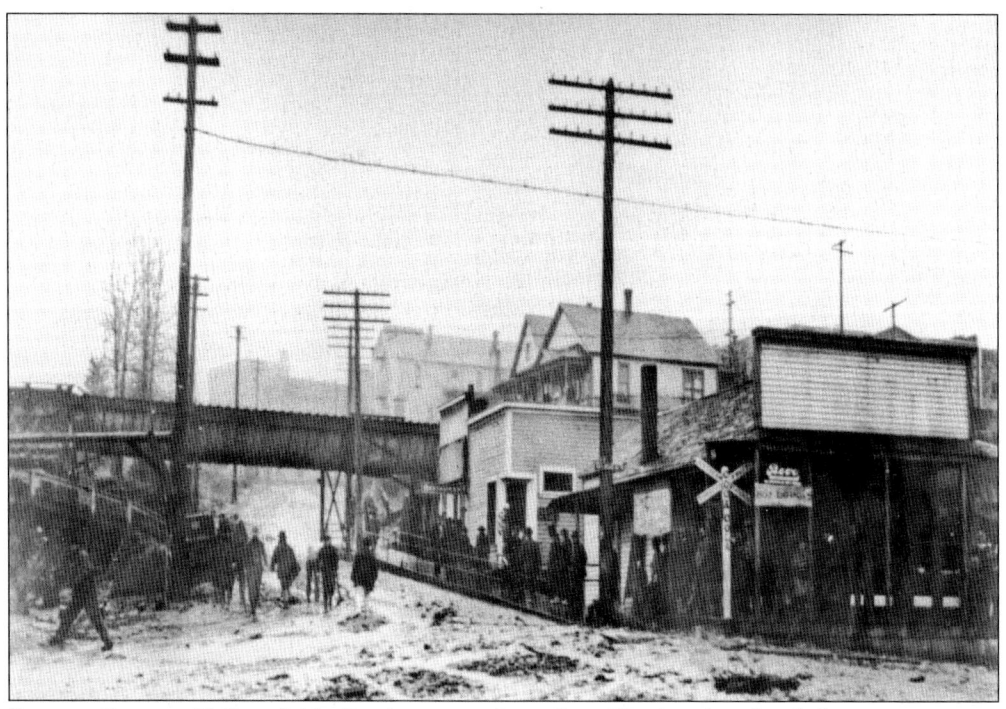

Division Street in Kellogg, Milo Creek coming down from Wardner has flooded many times over the years. It now runs under ground through large piping system.

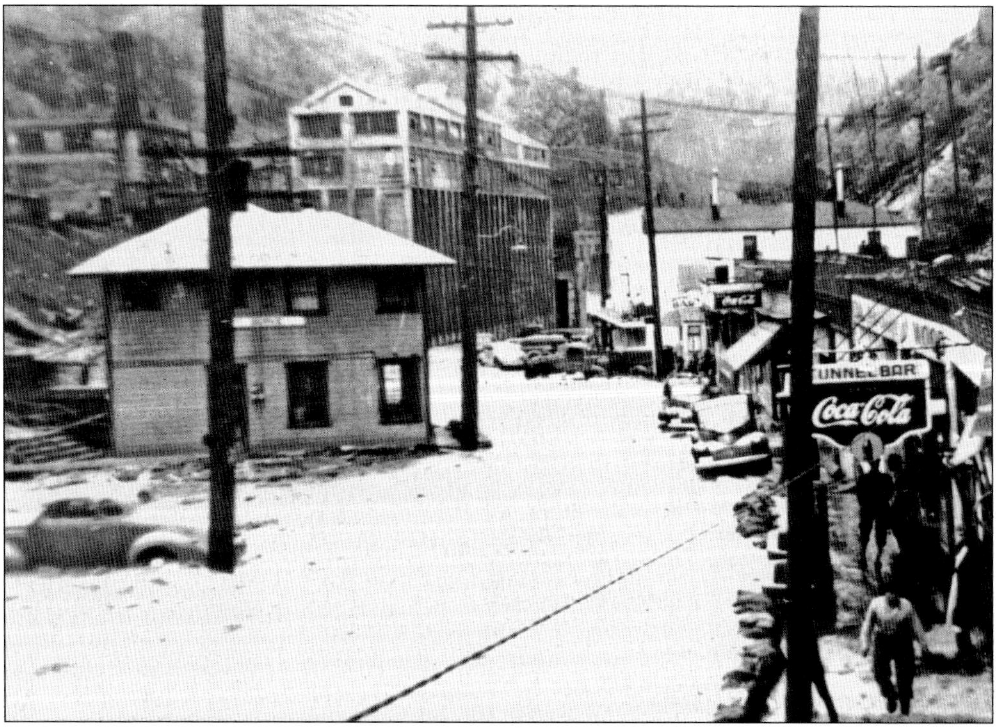

This photograph shows the aftermath of another flood in Burke Canyon. Hecla's Star Mine is in the background.

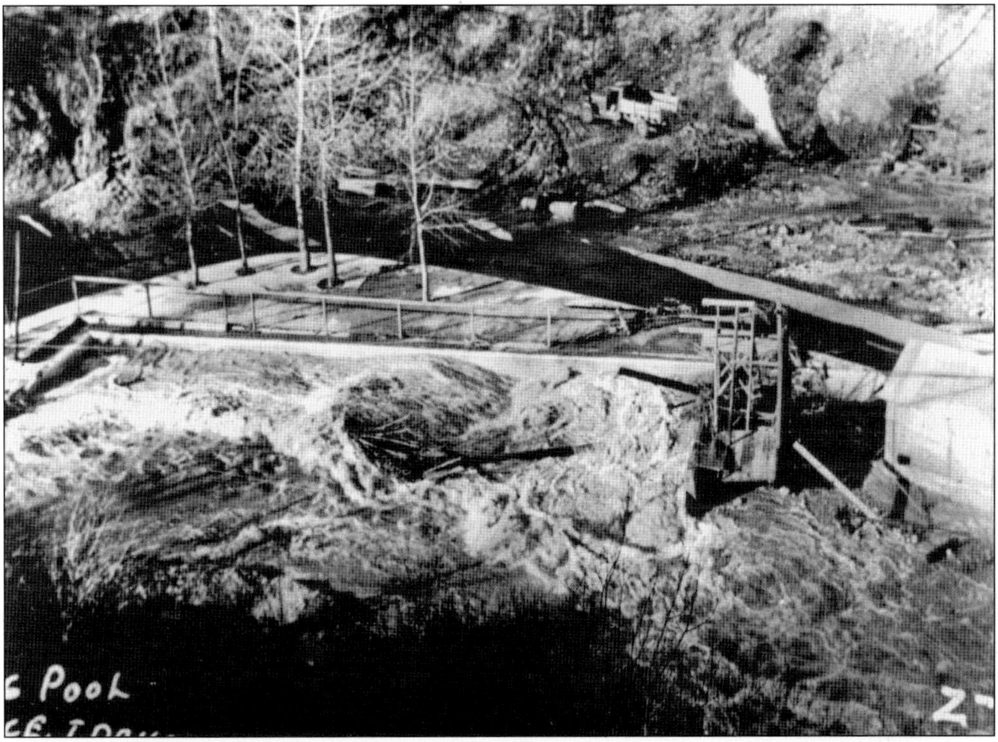

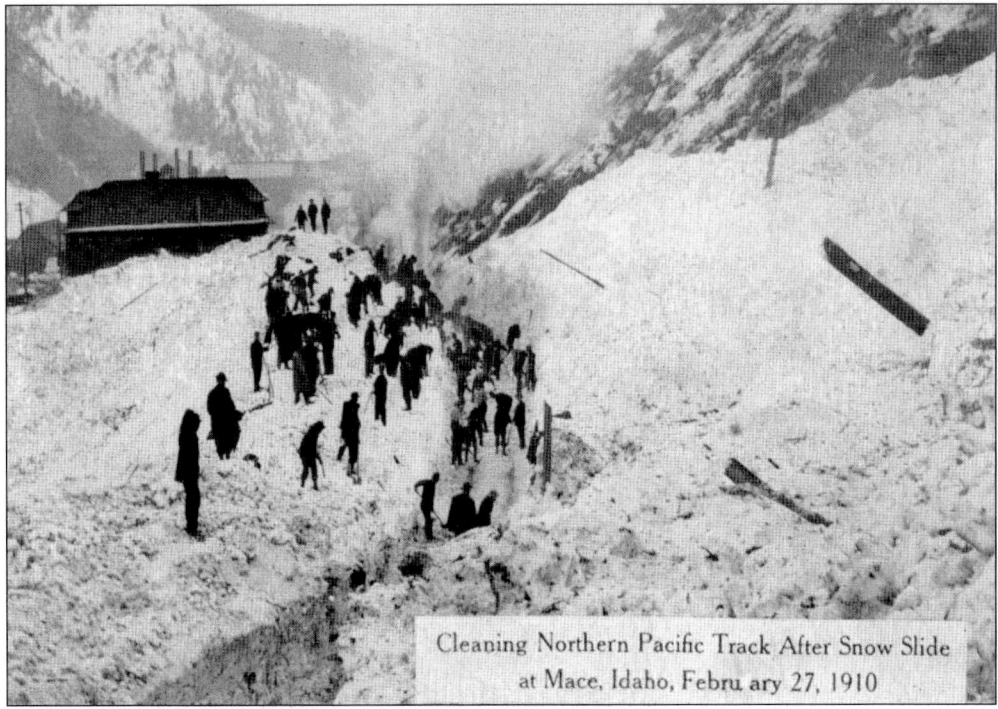

This is the Wallace city pool in 1933, flooded by Placer Creek.

Cleaning Northern Pacific Track After Snow Slide at Mace, Idaho, February 27, 1910

This snow slide easily earns the right to be called an avalanche. Here they are shoveling through over 80 feet of snow to reach the train tracks.

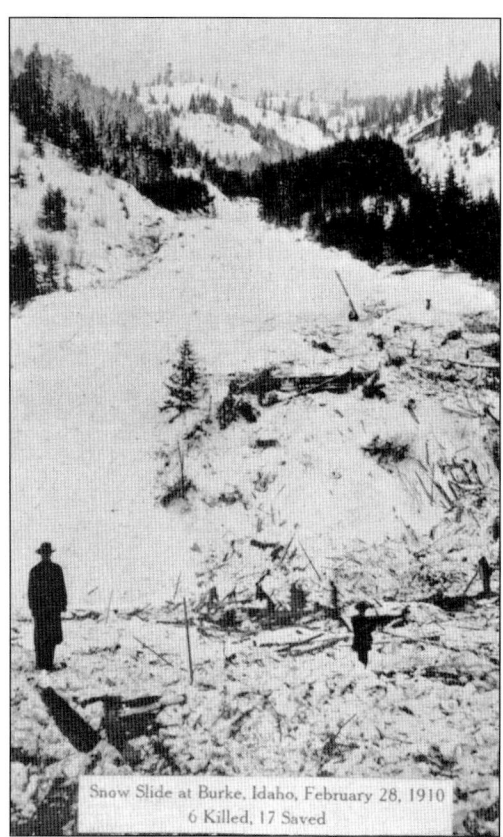

Snow Slide at Burke, Idaho, February 28, 1910
6 Killed, 17 Saved

The snow slides at Burke on February 28, 1910 reduced homes to kindling.

On the back of this photograph is a note written by a woman in Burke to a friend in Wallace: "We're awfully frighted but none were hurt the back side of the house were crushed but we only got the edge of the slide and the force was spent on the house above us where three were killed. I wrote you all a card the wires were down. This card is where Mr. & Mrs. Gibsons & 15 other homes were destroyed and 12 killed outright & one died afterwards. Gibsons are out of the hospital now but Red is not entirely well yet. Mrs. Kittrell two babies were killed in their house. There were 11 homes destroyed in the Burke slide & 5 people killed & two are in the hospital. The Burke people were warned after the Mace slide & left their homes or they would have all been killed. But we were at the Mace slide helping Red's & did not know of the warning & went back home only about an hour before the slide."

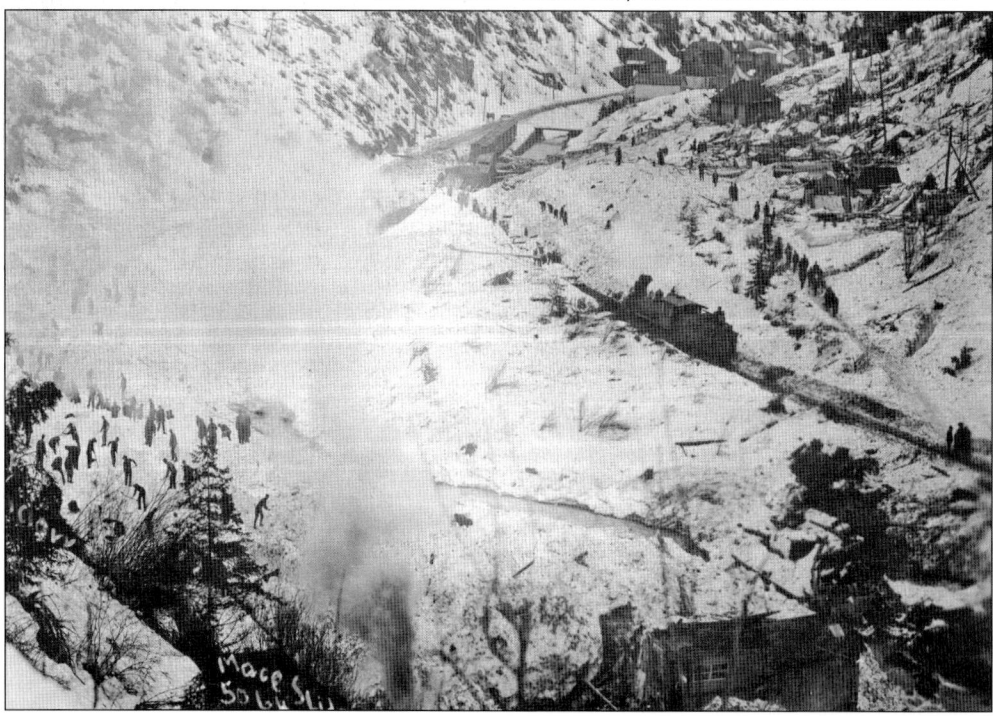

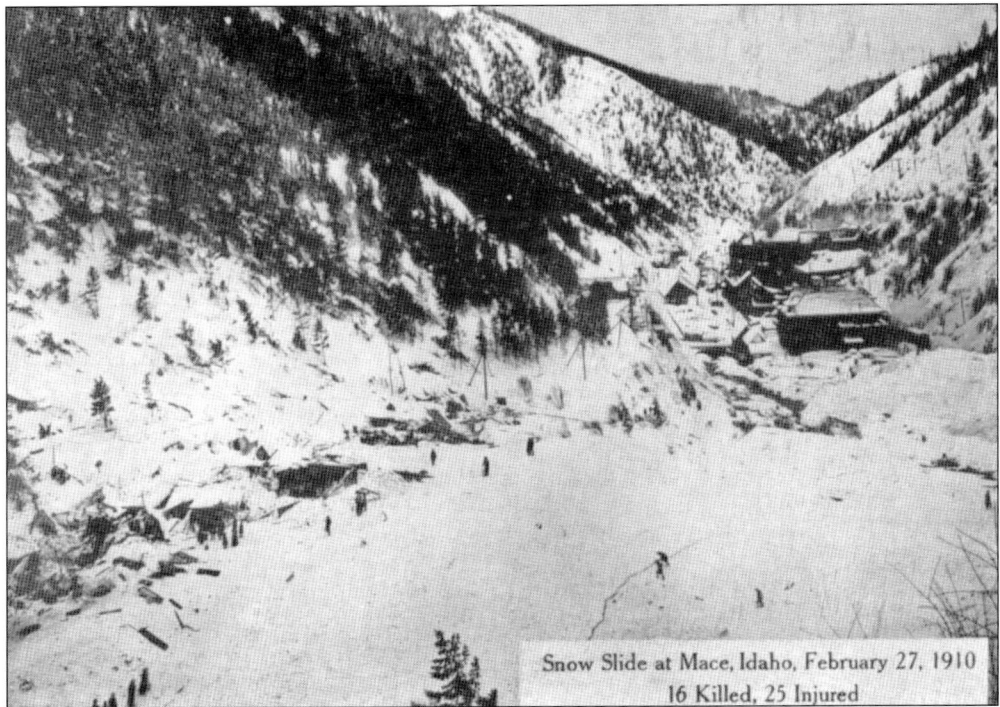

The people of Burke Canyon were made up of great strength. After a night filled with terror, the survivors were up and working to salvage whatever could be saved.

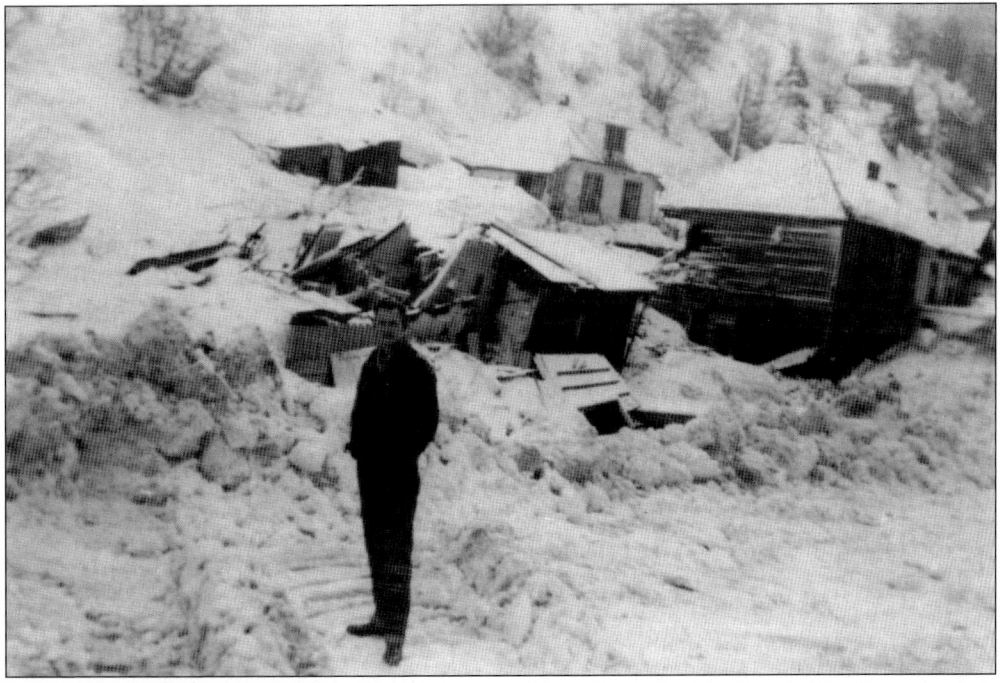

Snow slides in Burke Canyon, destroyed homes, such as the one pictured in this 1950 photograph with Rance Rummelhart. During one such slide, a house that came down the mountainside intact was simply pulled down the road to a vacant spot and pushed in.

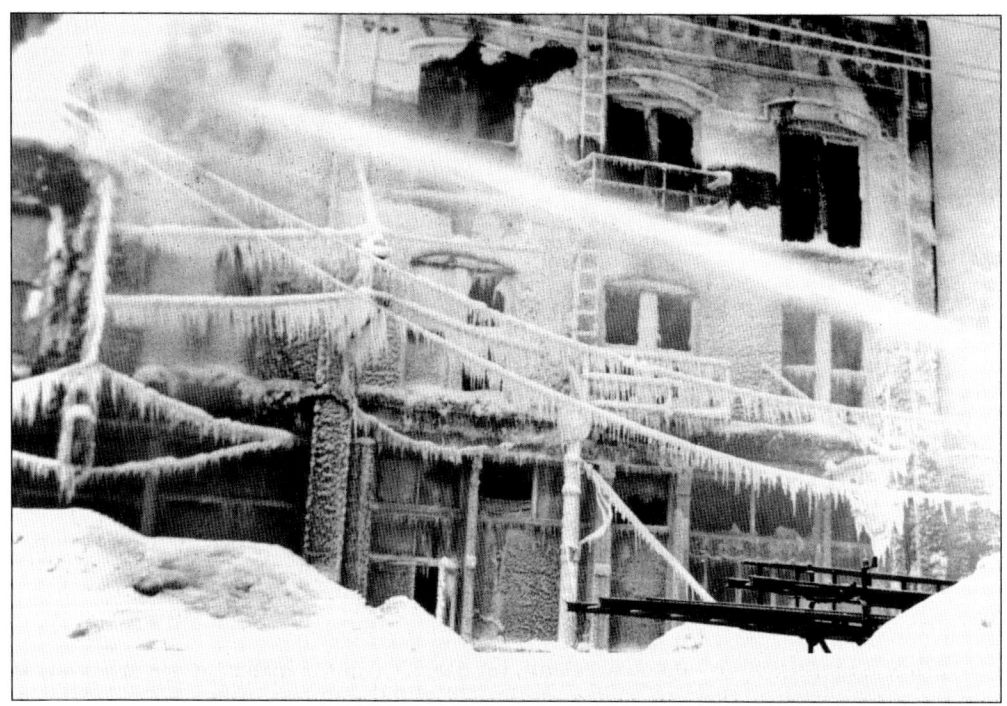

This photograph shows the 1933 Tabor/Ryan Hotel fire. Note the ice hanging from the power lines and the buildings. The water from the fire hose is freezing as fast as it hits the building.

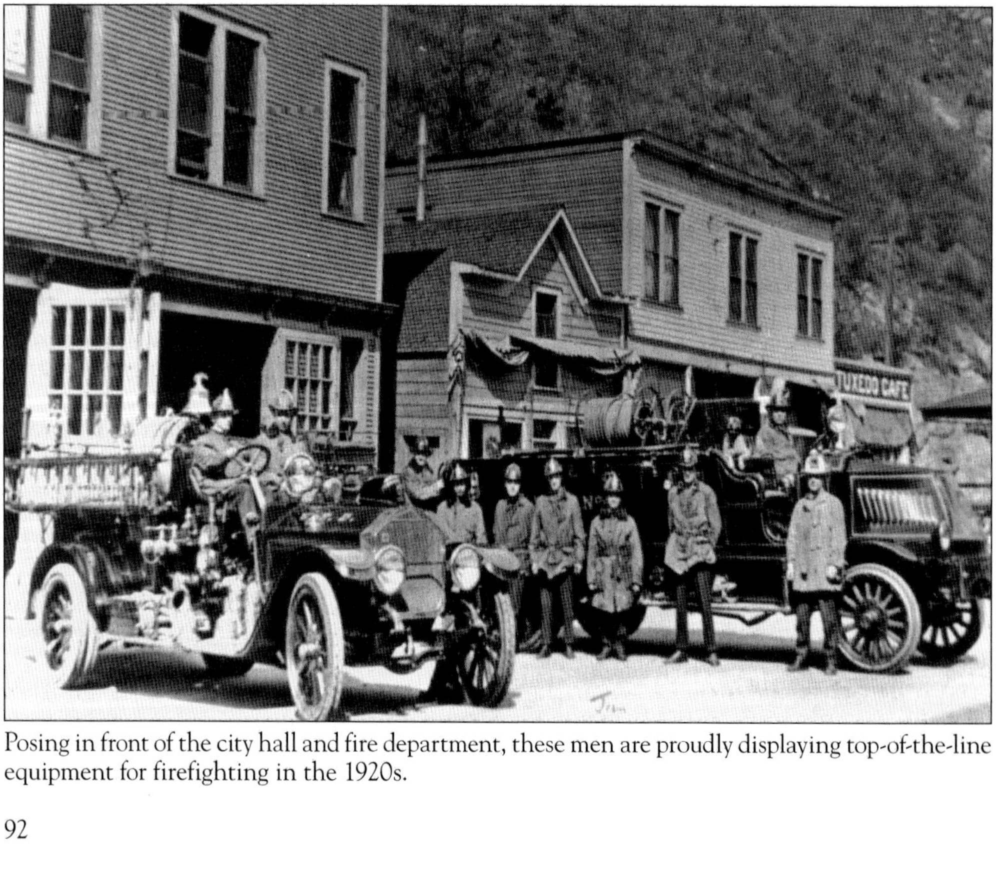

Posing in front of the city hall and fire department, these men are proudly displaying top-of-the-line equipment for firefighting in the 1920s.

# Eight
# FAMOUS AND INFAMOUS

The Silver Valley has been blessed with both the famous and the infamous over the years; its women as colorful as its men.

Wallace Forest Service Ranger Pulaski led a group of firefighters to safety in a mine tunnel just south of Wallace during the Great Fire of 1910 and later invented the Pulaski tool used by firefighters worldwide.

May Arkwright Hutton worked alongside her husband, Levi. They would find their mother lode with the Hercules in Burke. She would work to get women the vote and welcomed men like Clarence Darrow into her home. She would run for the Idaho State Legislature in 1904, when few women were even thinking about being able to vote. In her memory her husband started the Hutton Village, a place for orphans, in Spokane.

Lana Turner, the "sweater girl" of the 1940s, was born Julia Jean Mildred Frances Turner in Wallace at Providence Hospital on February 8, 1921. She would return with a war bond tour in June 1942. Norma Zimmer of the *Lawrence Welk Show* was born Norma Larsen in Larson near the current town of Mullan.

In 1925, the silent film *Frivolous Sal* was filmed in Wallace, considered an epic film in its day. In the summer of 1979 Kris Kristofferson filmed *Heaven's Gate* here—a western that required dirt streets, something Wallace had not had since 1917. *Dante's Peak*, with Pierce Brosnan and Linda Hamilton, was filmed here in the summer of 1996.

In the late 1960s, *Sky King* came to Osburn with the Carson and Barnes Circus. The lead in the television show was played by Kirby Grant from Butte, Montana. From 1967 to 1970, he traveled with the circus. He would fly his plane, the *Song Bird*; he landed here and took off from Interstate 90.

During the 1800s, Calamity Jane, Wyatt Earp, and Molly B. Damned came to the goldfields of Murray.

Because of photographers such as Harry English, Arthur Faye, and the photographers from the Barnard/Stockbridge and Tabor studios, we are one of the most photographically documented areas in the country.

Each of the famous, infamous, and forgotten have brought with them and left behind them something of themselves, so they still touch our lives with their spirits.

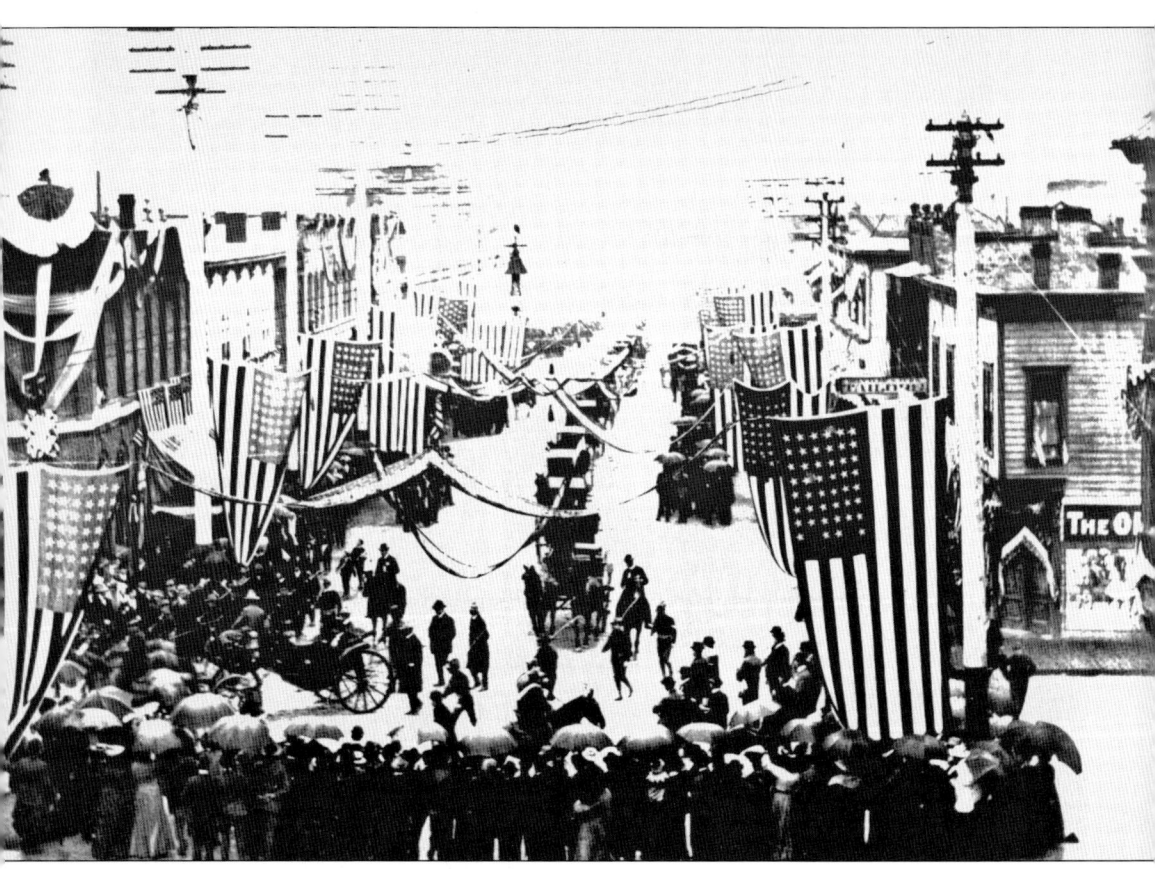

On May 26, 1903, Pres. Theodore Roosevelt came to Wallace. He arrived at the Northern Pacific Depot on Sixth Street. As seen in this photograph, the parade came down Sixth Street, turned on Bank Street, and ran through the residential area of town, ending at the school grounds where "Teddy" addressed the crowd.

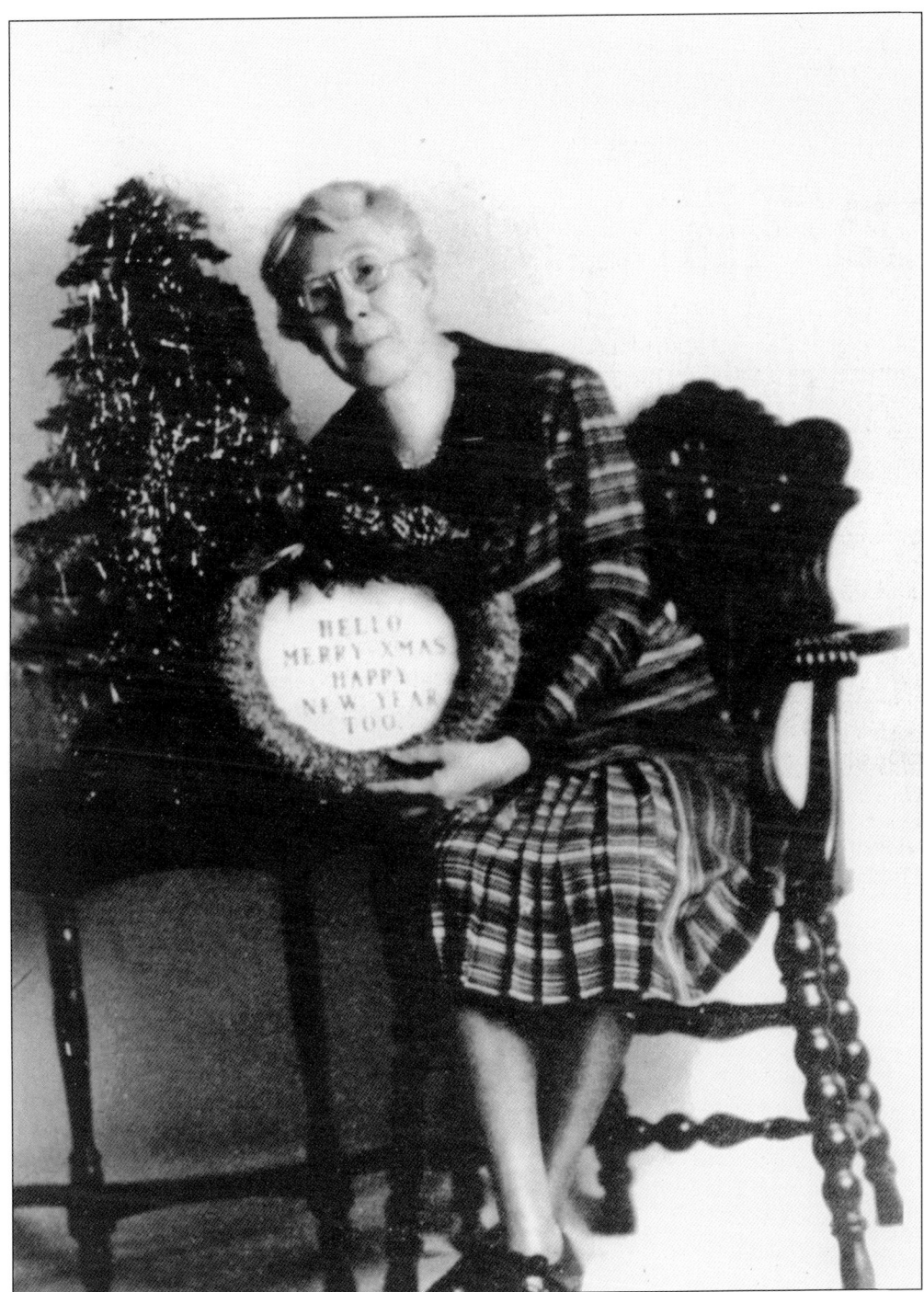

Nellie Stockbridge spent over 60 years documenting the valley with her camera. Miss Stockbridge photographed everything for everybody. She was taken into the mines to photograph a new piece of equipment or ore veins for a mining company annual report. She photographed weddings, babies, graduates, growing families, and a growing mining camp.

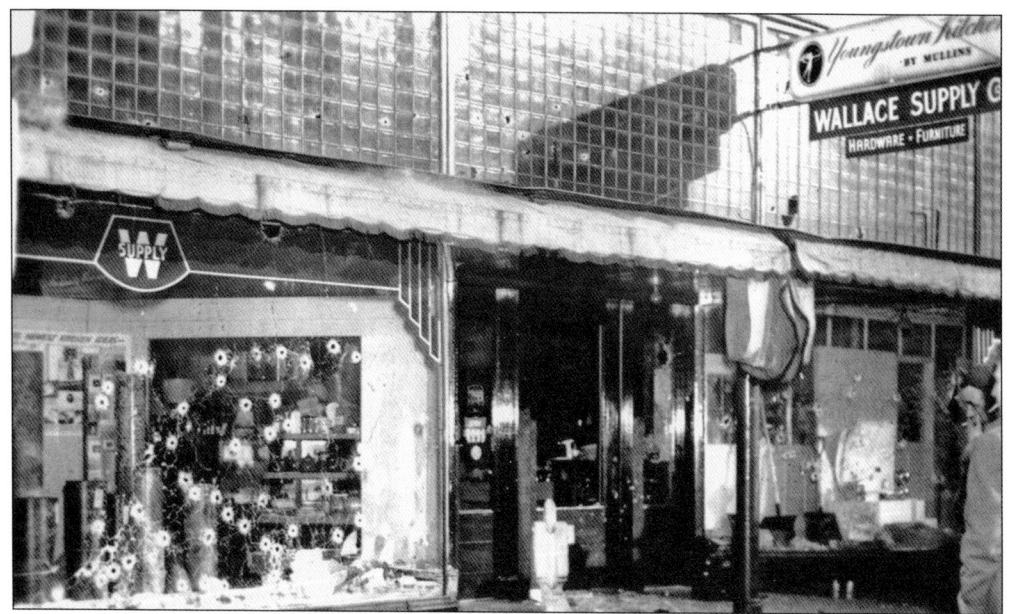

From the number of holes, it is easy to see that plenty of firepower was used during the valley's St. Valentine's shoot-out. Today the bullet traces are embedded in the floor.

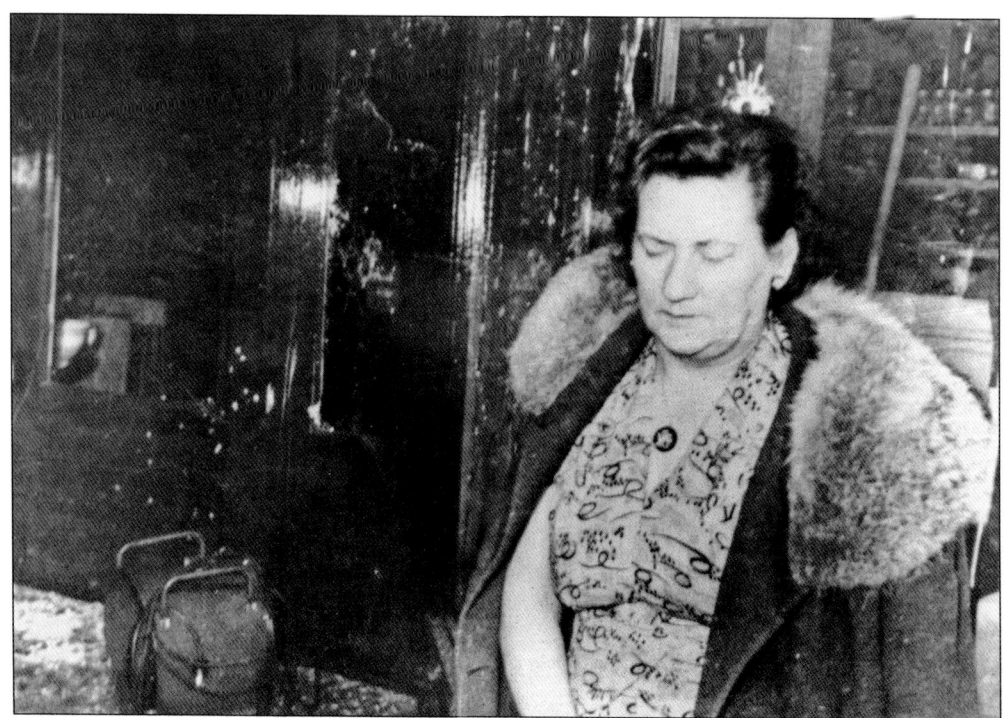

Mary Hinton, the woman that started it all, had a date with two men in one night but ended up alone after one beau was killed by the other—and then he was killed by the police.

Chief Mace McCoy and two other officers are pictured with the body of John Stoddard. John didn't like sharing Mary.

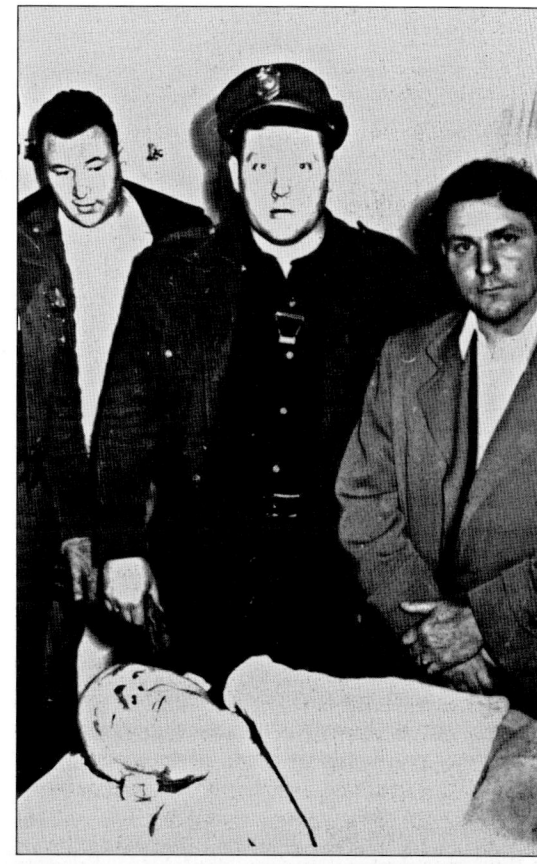

Gov. Cecil Andrus addresses the crowd at the formal dedication of the relocated Northern Pacific Railroad Depot Museum. Looking on are local dignitaries Coleen and Harry Magnuson, Archie Hulsizer, and Michael Alldredge.

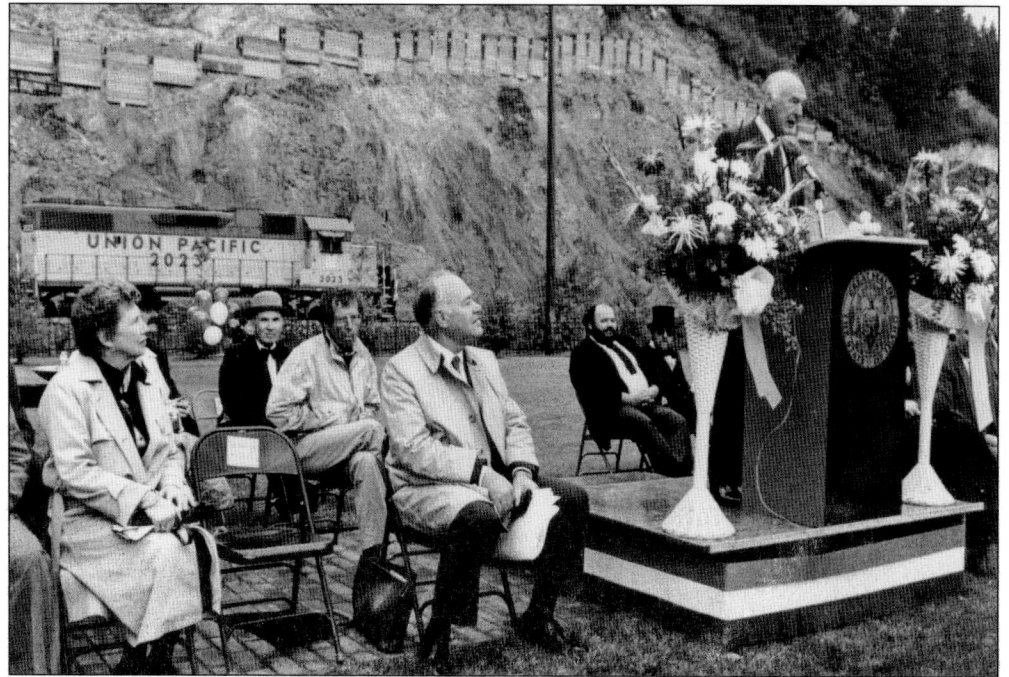

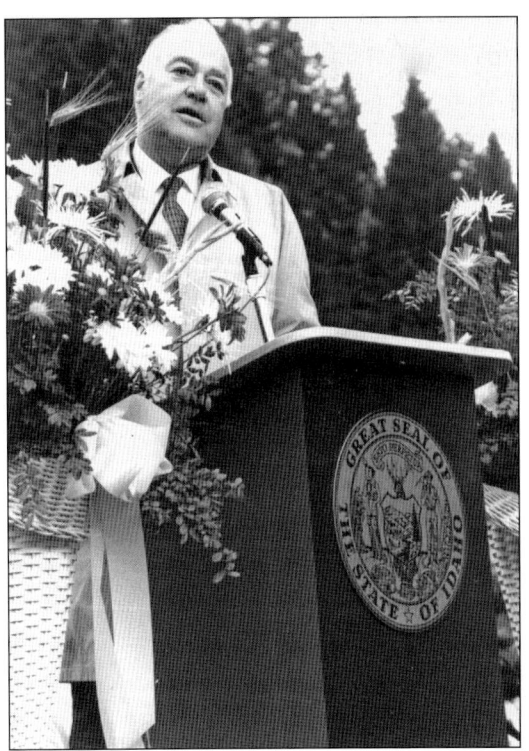

Pictured here is Harry F. Magnuson, a Wallace native and president of the Northern Pacific Railroad Depot Foundation.

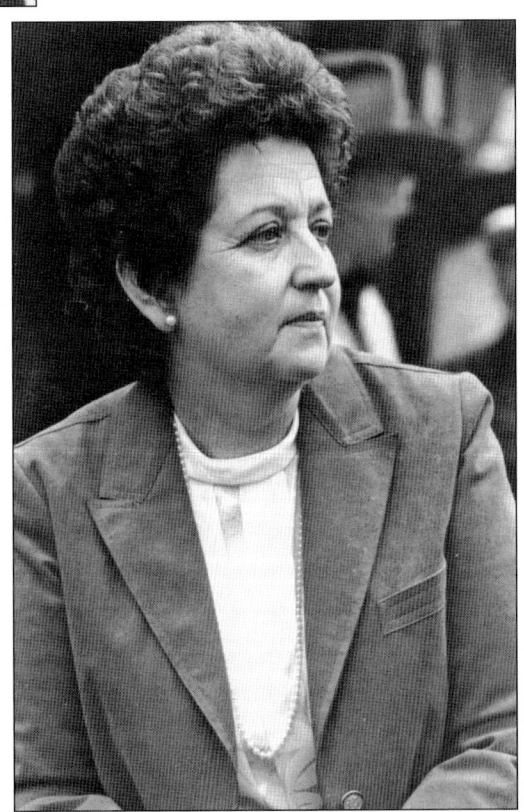

Pictured here is Joan M. Sellars, great-granddaughter of Col. William R. Wallace.

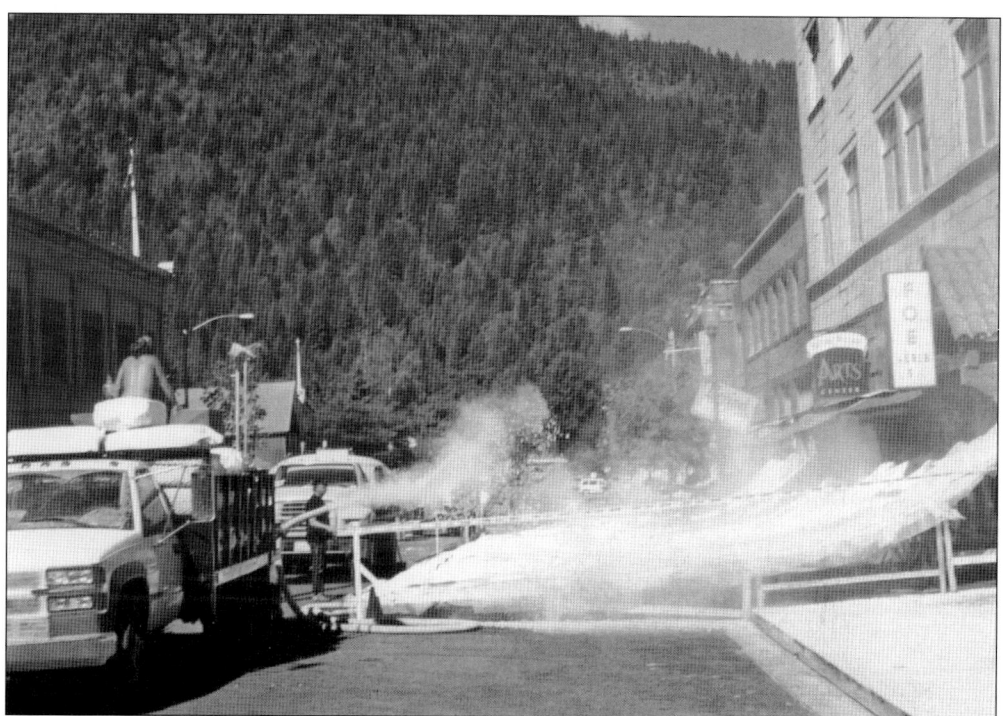

The crew of *Dante's Peak*, 1996 is pictured spraying the scaffolding to hold the "piles of volcanic ash" in downtown Wallace.

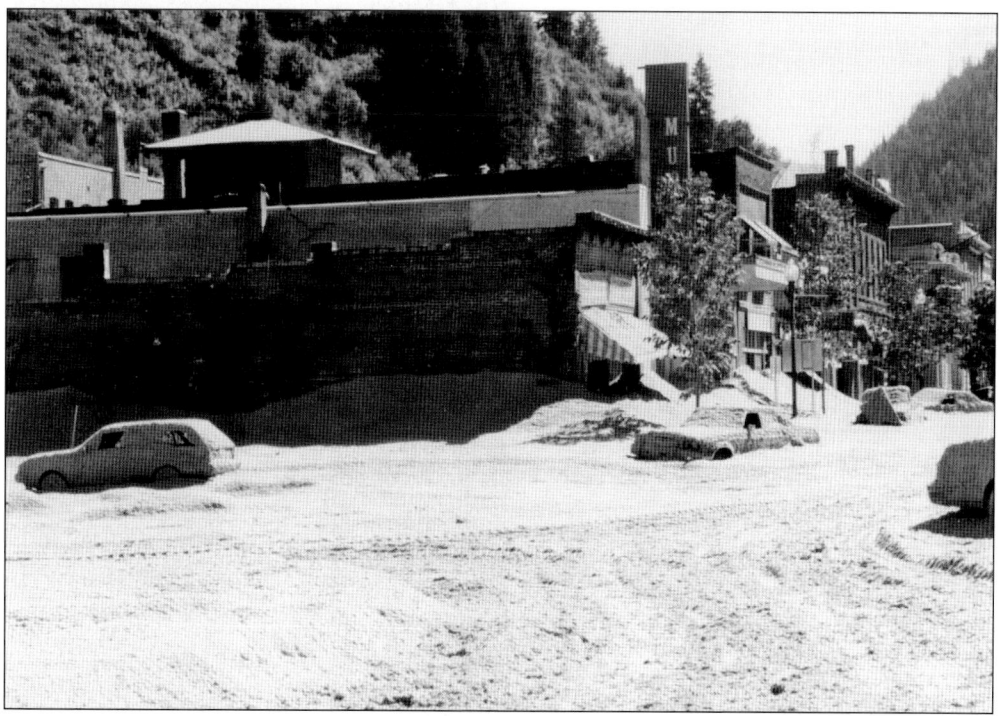

Bank and Fifth Streets are buried in volcanic ash, ready for an evening of filming for *Dante's Peak* in June 1996.

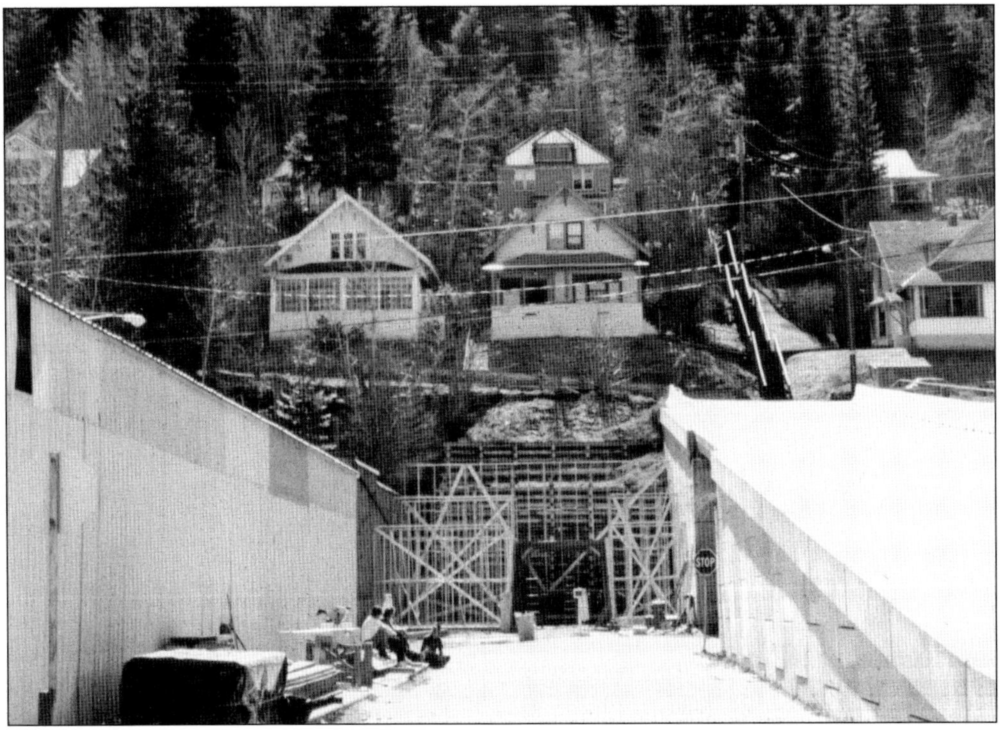

Pictured is the construction of the mine adit that "saves" the family in *Dante's Peak*. The movie stars Pierce Brosnan and Linda Hamilton.

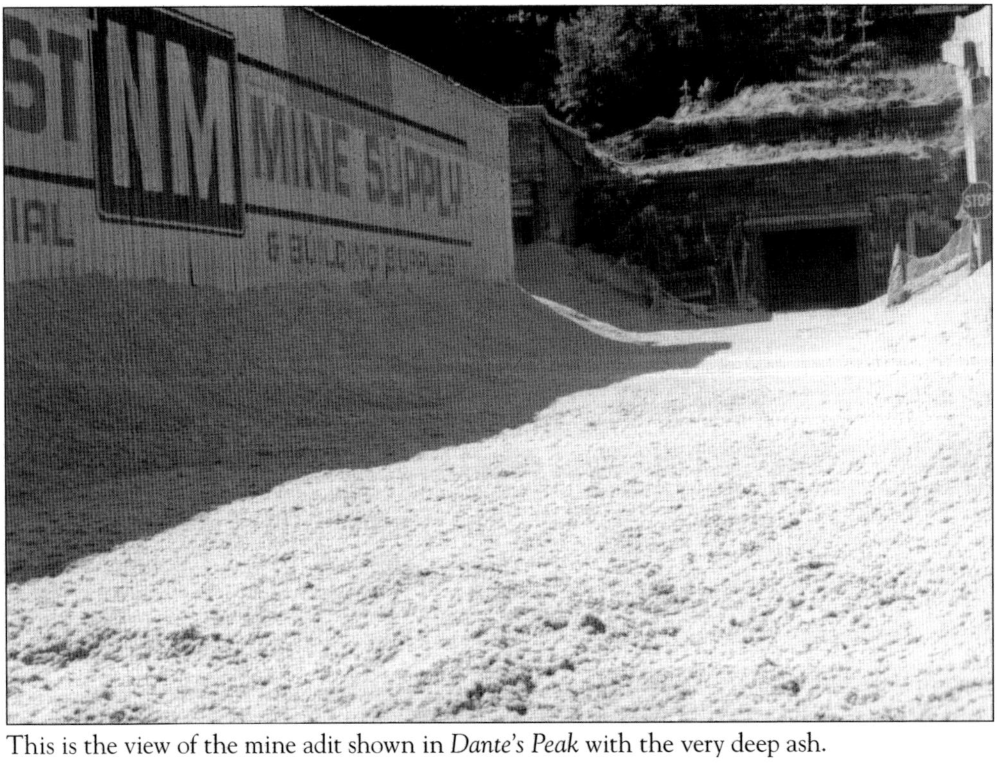

This is the view of the mine adit shown in *Dante's Peak* with the very deep ash.

# *Nine*
# SILVER VALLEY MINES

The Silver Valley's Coeur d'Alene Mining District has been the source of more than 1 billion ounces of silver over the past century and is poised to produce another billion ounces in the next. A billion ounces of silver would produce enough silver dollars to encircle Earth. The district also has produced more the 8 million tons of lead, more than 3 million tons of zinc, 2 million tons of copper and a half-million ounces of gold, and continues to produce those metals today.

After the Civil War, gold was discovered in streams near what would become Murray. It was the lower 48's last gold rush. As those claims panned out, miners moved 20 miles south and discovered silver, lead and zinc outcroppings in the forested hillsides, pursuing those veins down to today's depth of 7,000 feet below the surface.

Active mines in the Coeur d'Alene District include Lucky Friday, Galena-Coeur, Golden Chest, New Jersey, and Bunker Hill. Now idled, the Sunshine Mine is expected to return to production.

"Muck" (mineral-bearing ore) is blasted from veins underground and hauled by rail or truck to vertical haulage-ways, called shafts—the single-deepest being the Lucky Friday's Silver Shaft, which extends from the surface deeper than 6,000 feet.

Once on the surface, mineral-bearing muck is fed into a mill, or concentrator, where it is crushed and ground into a powder, and then to a battery of flotation tanks where the waste rock and the mineral-bearing material are separated. The waste sand is slurried back down into the mine to fill mined-out areas, while the mineral-rich concentrate—assaying as high as 2,000 ounces of silver per ton—is dried and shipped to the smelter for refining into pure metal.

Mining as practiced today is safe and coexists easily with other human activity such as tourism. Mine water must be as clean or cleaner than drinking water when it leaves the property, ensuring a vibrant fishery here. Because of their small footprint, silver mines make a negligible impact on the aesthetic virtues of the Silver Valley.

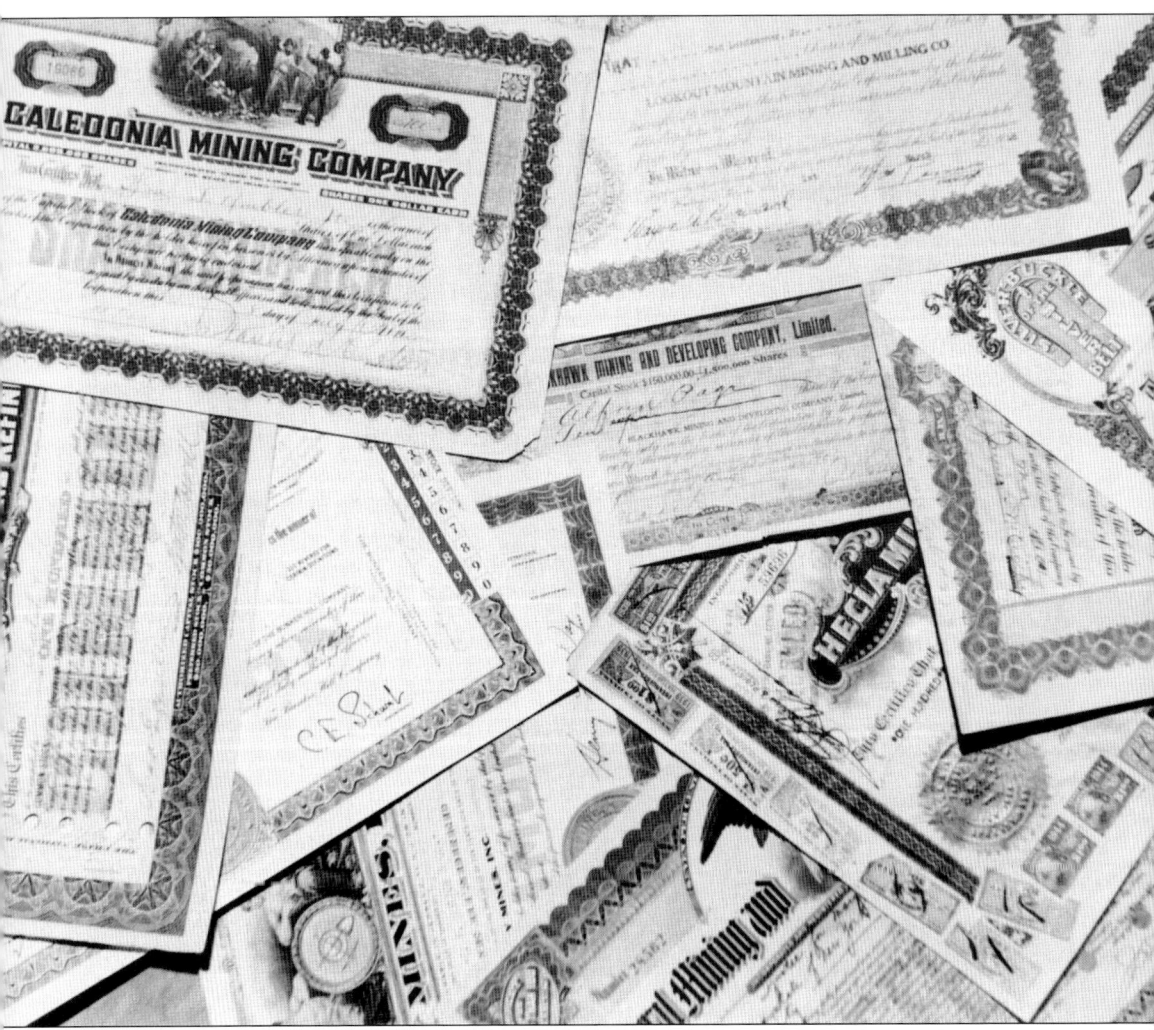

The lifeblood of any new mining district is its stock certificates. Investors put up the money for exploration and development, and miners extract the rich and precious ore out of the ground. Investors would be given stock certificates as proof of their investment. Ornately decorated, they these numbered certificates stated the quantity of shares the owner possessed. The total shares owned and the value of the share price determined the amount of return on the investment.

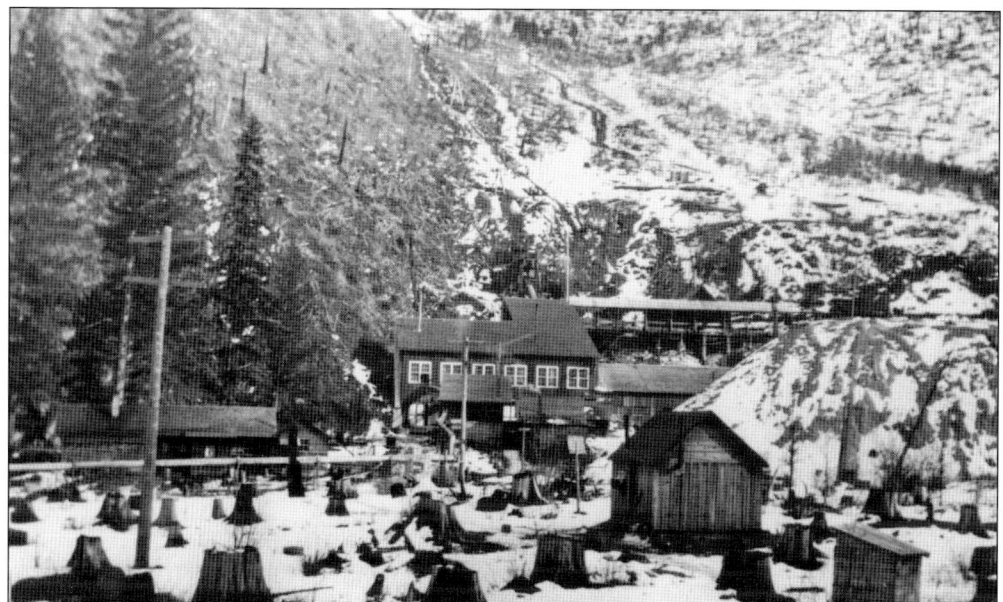

In the early days, mining companies would use the trees close to where the mine was located. These trees would be used to build their buildings as well as for timber in the tunnels, drifts, and stopes. The trees have all come back. The Sunshine (pictured here in 1926) would become the world's premier silver mine, with over 300 million ounces produced to date.

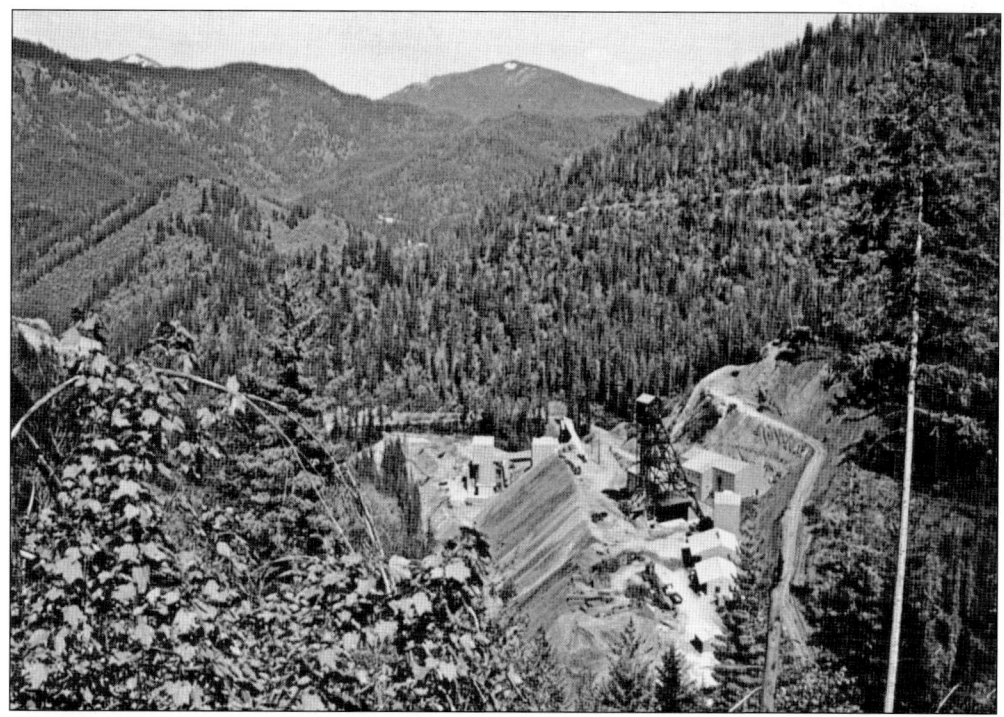

The Coeur was the heart of Coeur d'Alene Mines for many years. With each year, the mines grow larger underground while their above-ground footprint rarely changes.

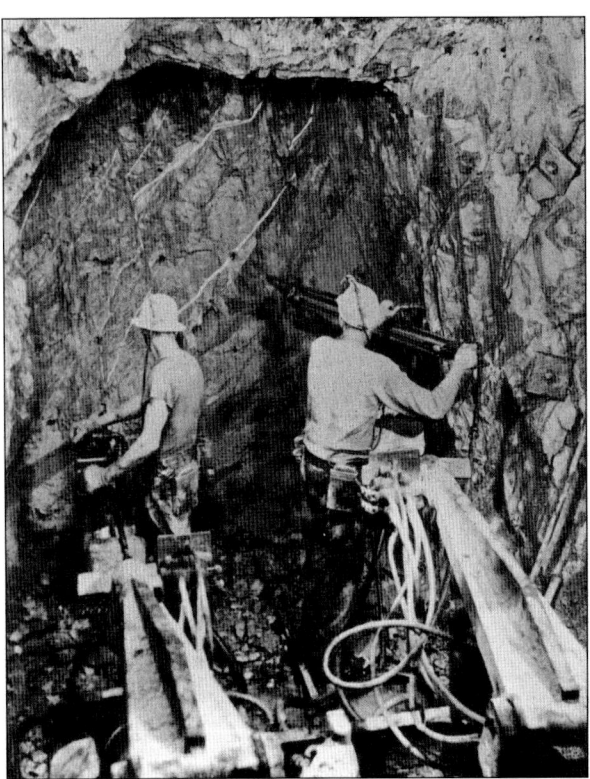

Drifts follow ore veins, they will continue opening up the drift as long as there is a vein to follow. ASARCO drift miners Ed Arthur, on the left, and Bill Erickson are pictured at the Galena Mine in 1961.

To get the leverage right for the drill position, sometimes a step or platform need to be built. Notice the water and air hoses attached to the drill, and the extra drill steels leaning against the rock walls.

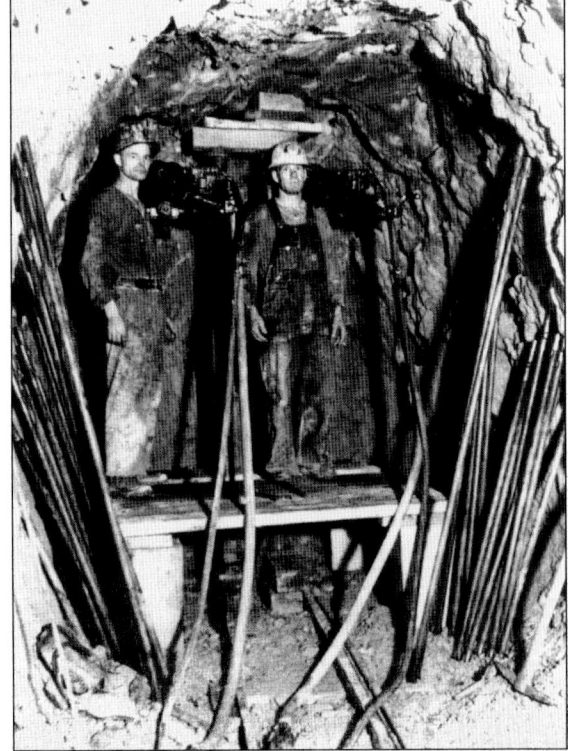

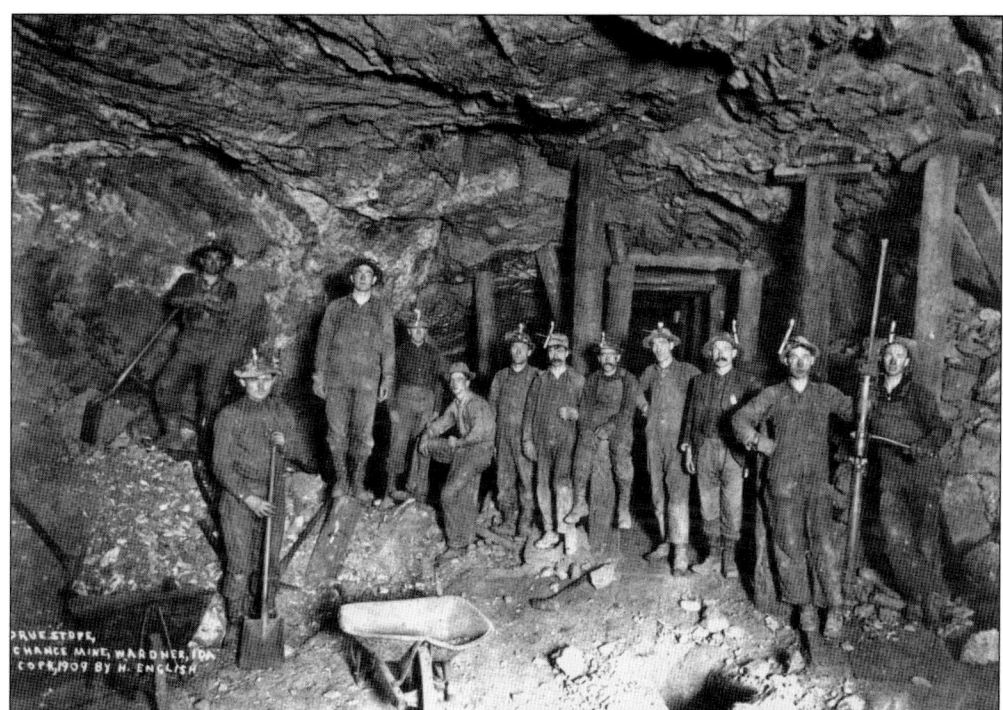

Mining is not the kind of job that you wear your best clothes to do. These miners are using candles for light on soft hats in the Drue Strope in the Chance Mine in this 1909 photograph by Harry English. Early American miners used grease lamps burning whale oil to see in the dark mines and eventually candles in metal holders that could be pushed into the walls of the mine tunnels.

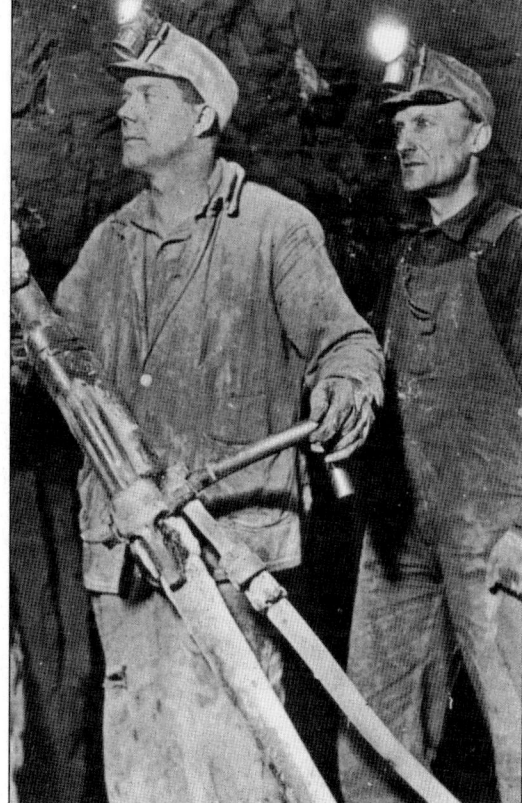

By 1914, electric cap lamps would make lighting the work area easier. The drillers in this c. 1920s image, posing with a "widow-maker," are still wearing cloth caps, before the time of hard hats.

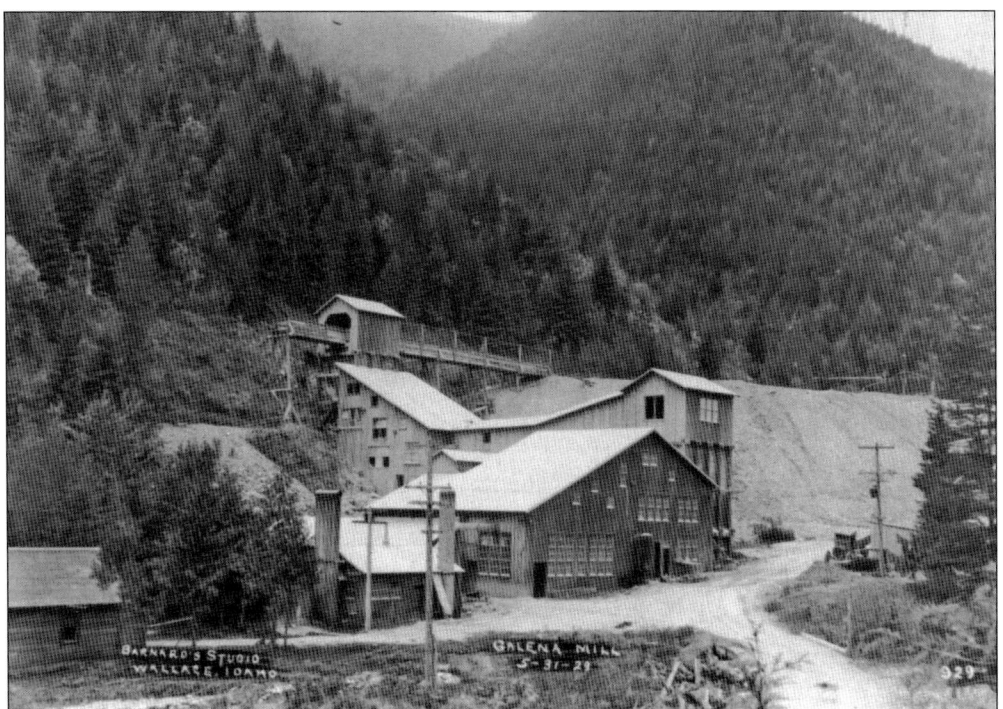

Pictured here is the Galena Mill in 1927, located in Lake Gulch of the Coeur d'Alene Mining District. It is now owned by U.S. Silver Corporation.

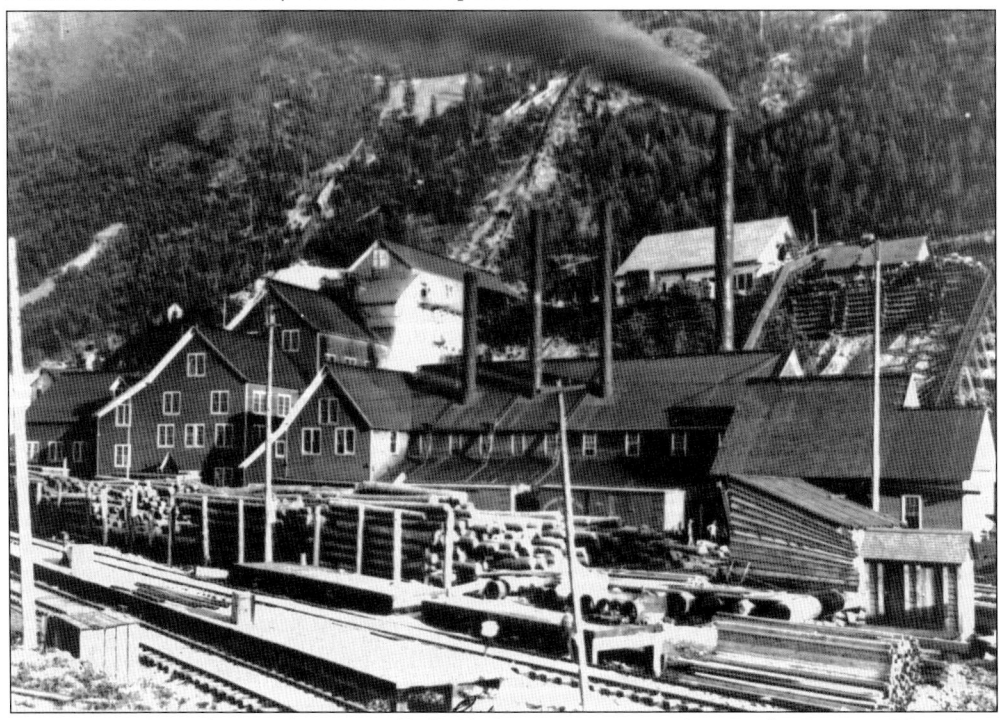

Pictured are the Helena and Frisco Mills (left) along Canyon Creek in Burke Canyon. The white building on the right is the Frisco Mine in 1904.

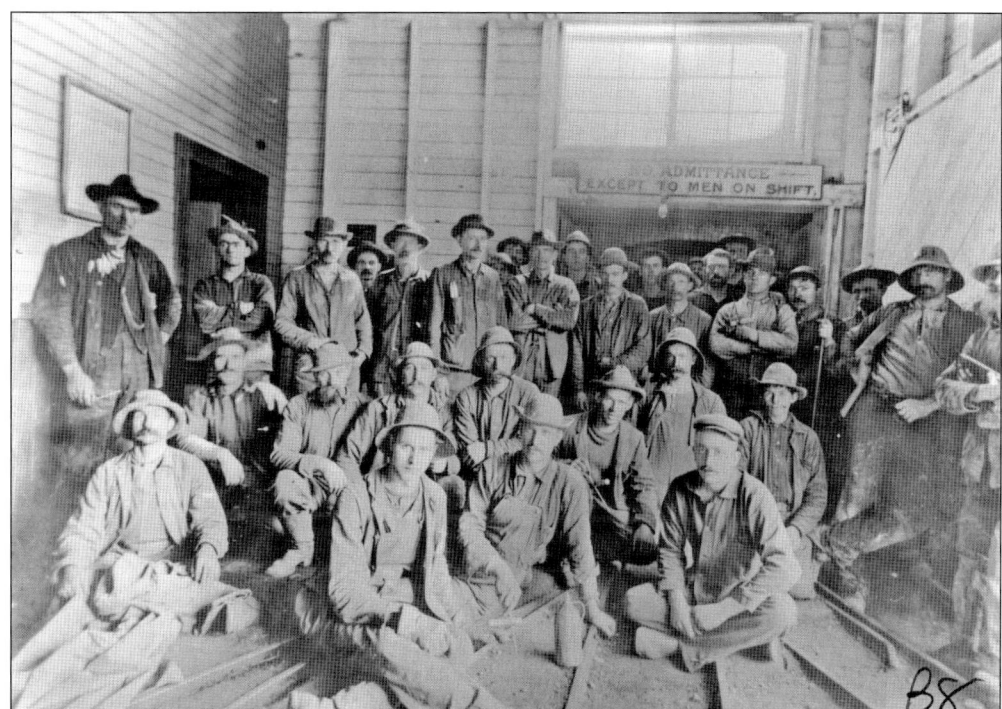

A group of working miners at the entrance of the Frisco Mine in this 1905 photograph, likely taken by Frank Hess, who worked for The Barnard Studio in Wallace.

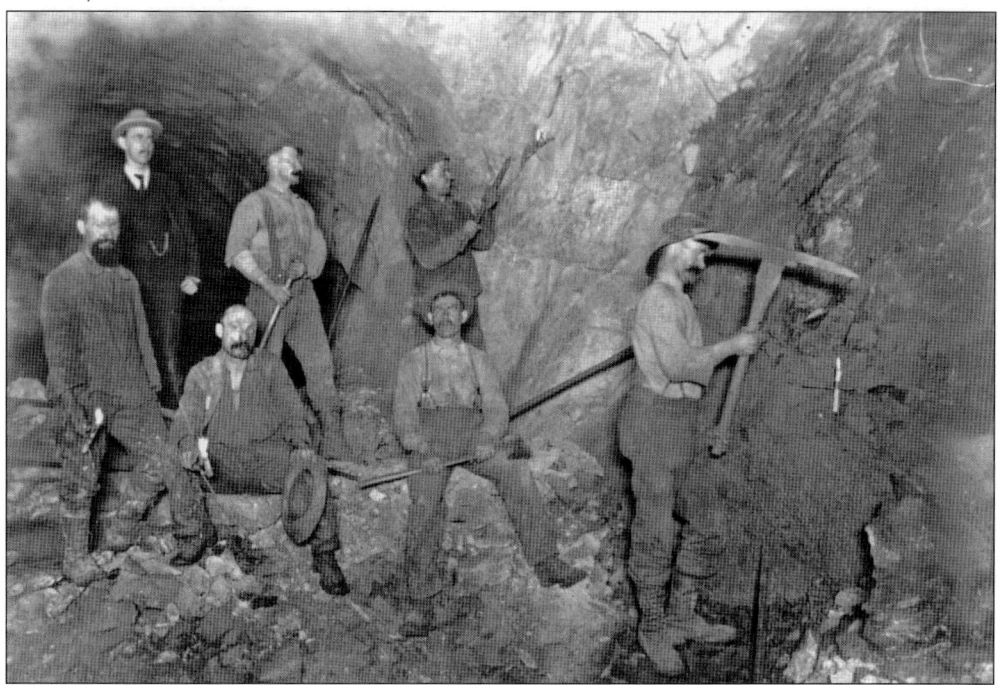

A staged photograph shows miners in a stope with management at the Frisco Mine in 1905. This photograph was likely taken for the company's annual report. It was easier to make a photograph of the underground work than to describe it. Candles are stuck in the rock to light the work area.

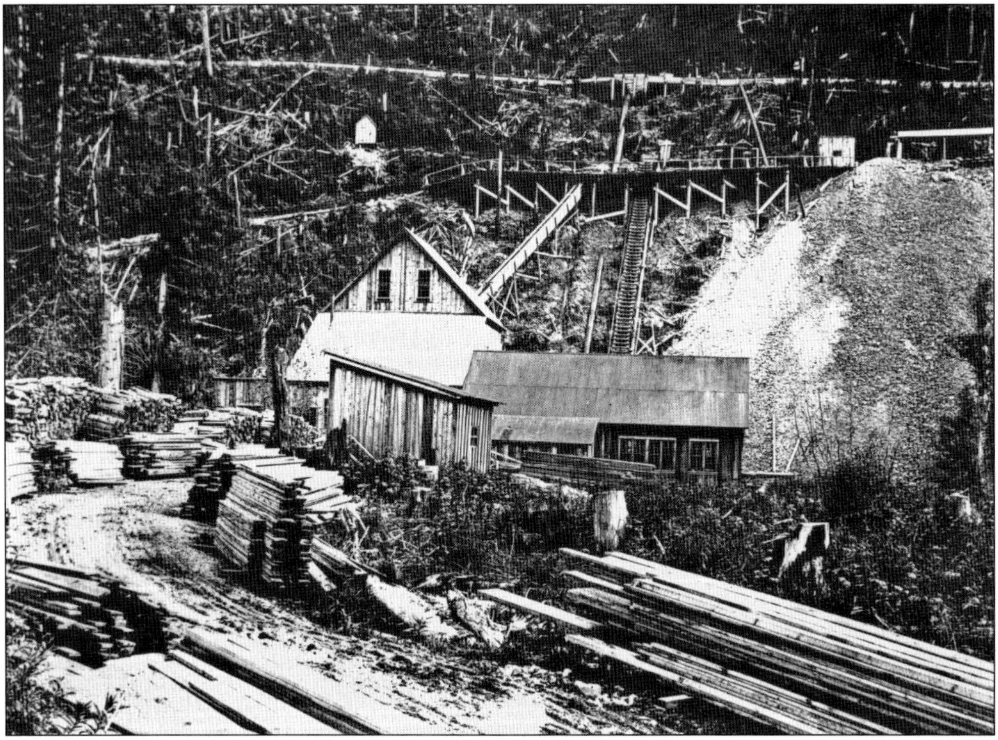

Pictured in 1910 is the Monarch Mine and Mill, east of Murray.

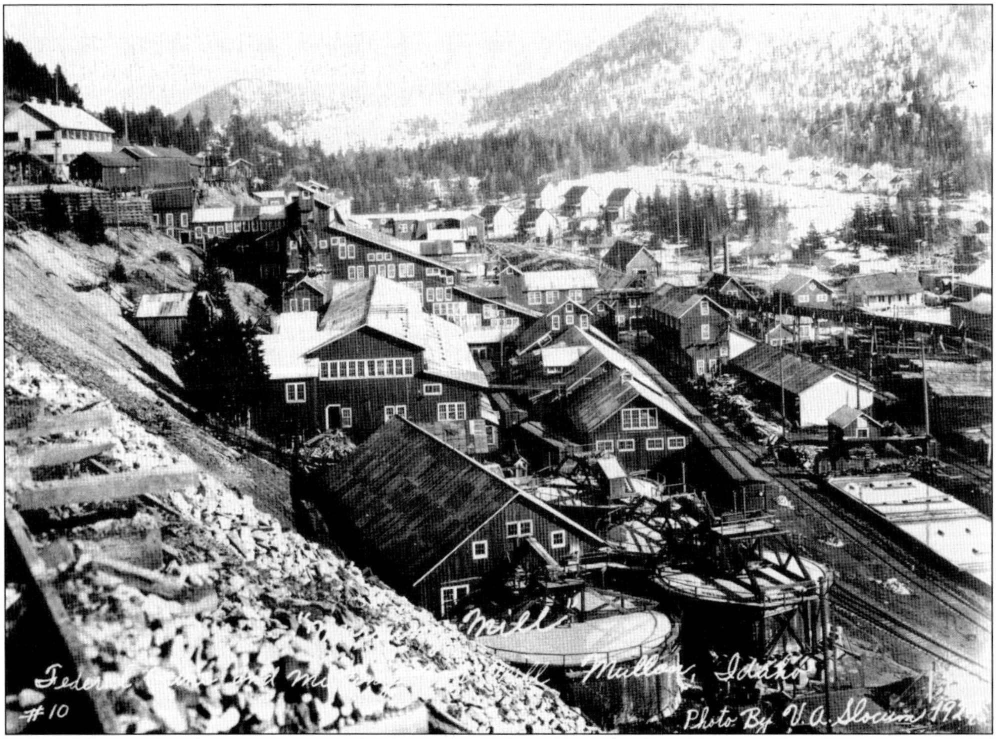

This c. 1924 photograph shows Morning Mill, just west of Mullan in the Morning District.

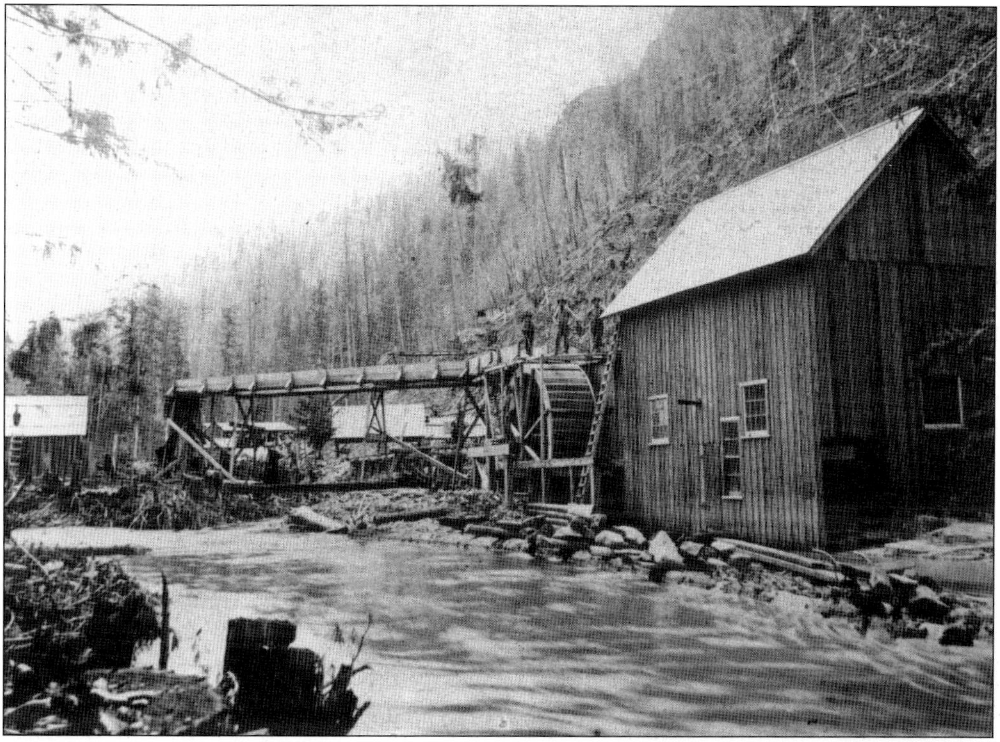

The pelton wheel at the Mother Lode Mill east of Murray in 1888 was the source of power for the mill.

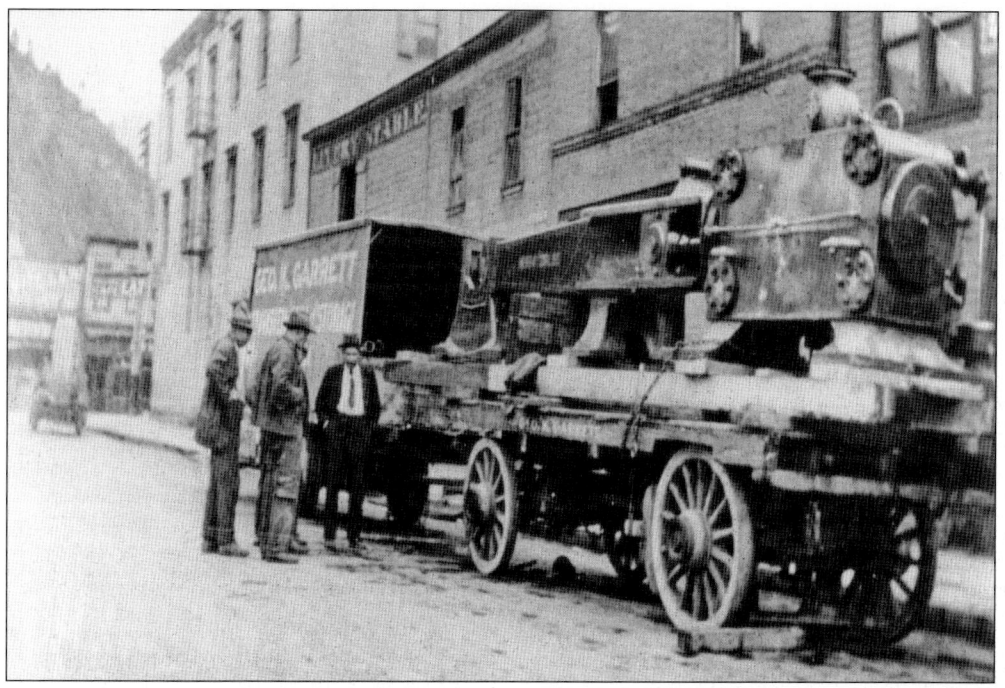

The compressor is headed for the Galena Mine, being delivered by Garrett Trucking in 1927. It is parked on Pine Street in front of the Livery Stable and The Jameson.

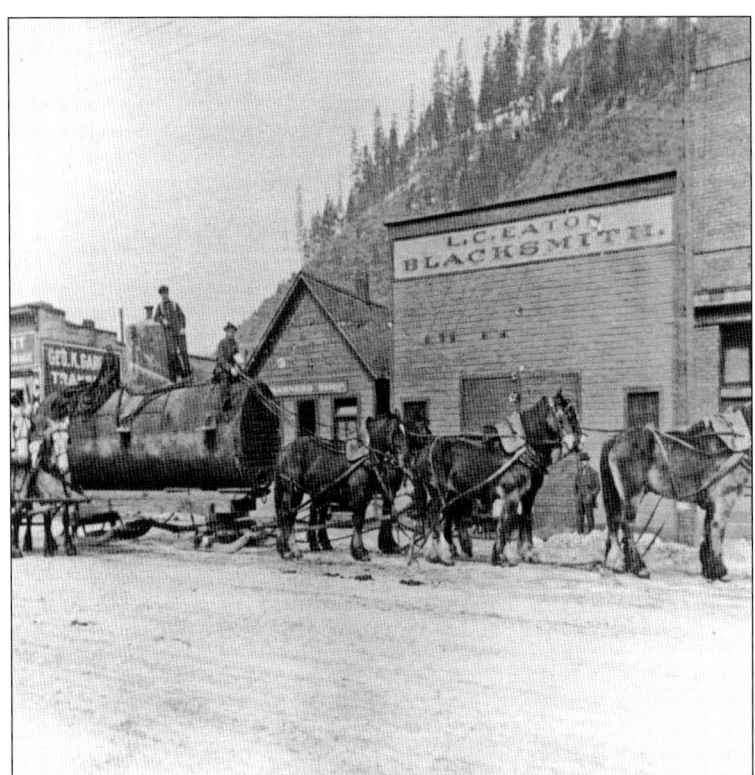

Another part of the compressor is being delivered to the Galena Mine in 1927. This piece is parked on the south side of Pine Street.

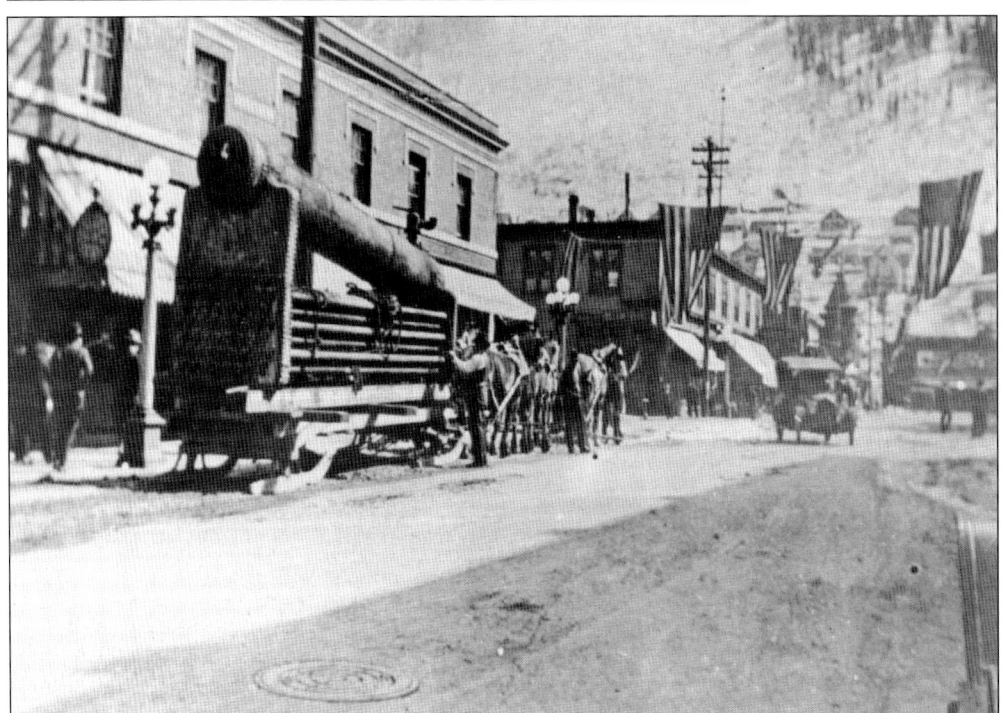

This is the third part of the compressor for delivery to the Galena Mill in 1927. This piece is parked on Sixth Street on the northeast corner near to the Arment Building.

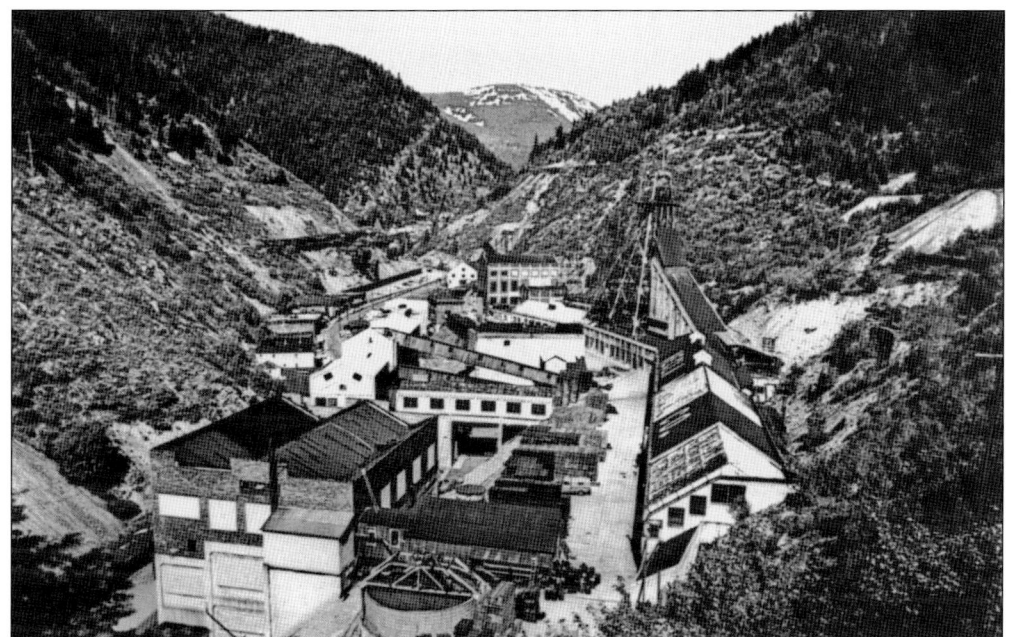

Founded in Wallace in 1891, Hecla Mining Company is the Silver Valley's largest mining employer. Pictured in 1947 is Hecla's mine at Burke, looking north.

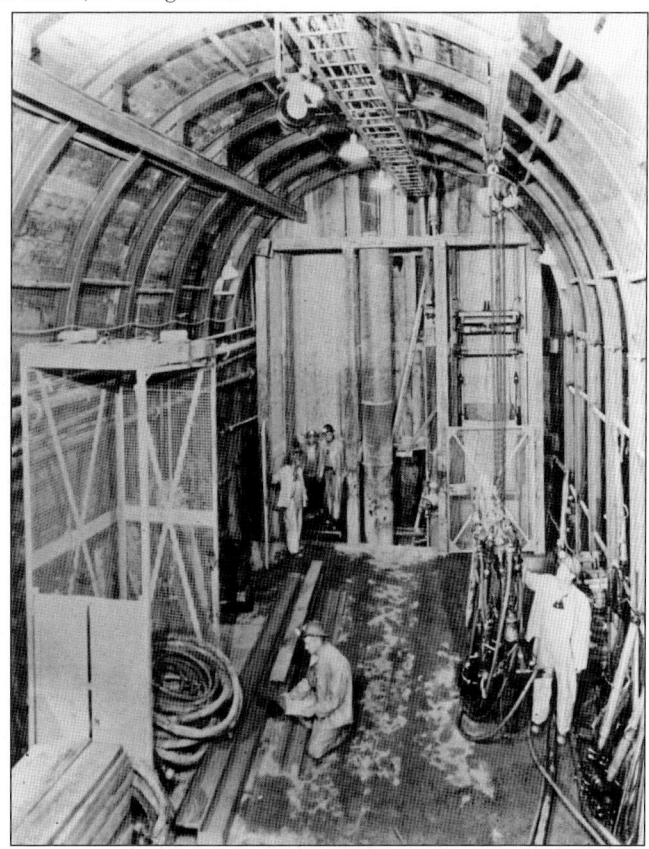

At a level of 2,400 feet, this station serves as a staging ground for all underground equipment and supplies. With its high arch, this large room gives the feeling of being in a cathedral.

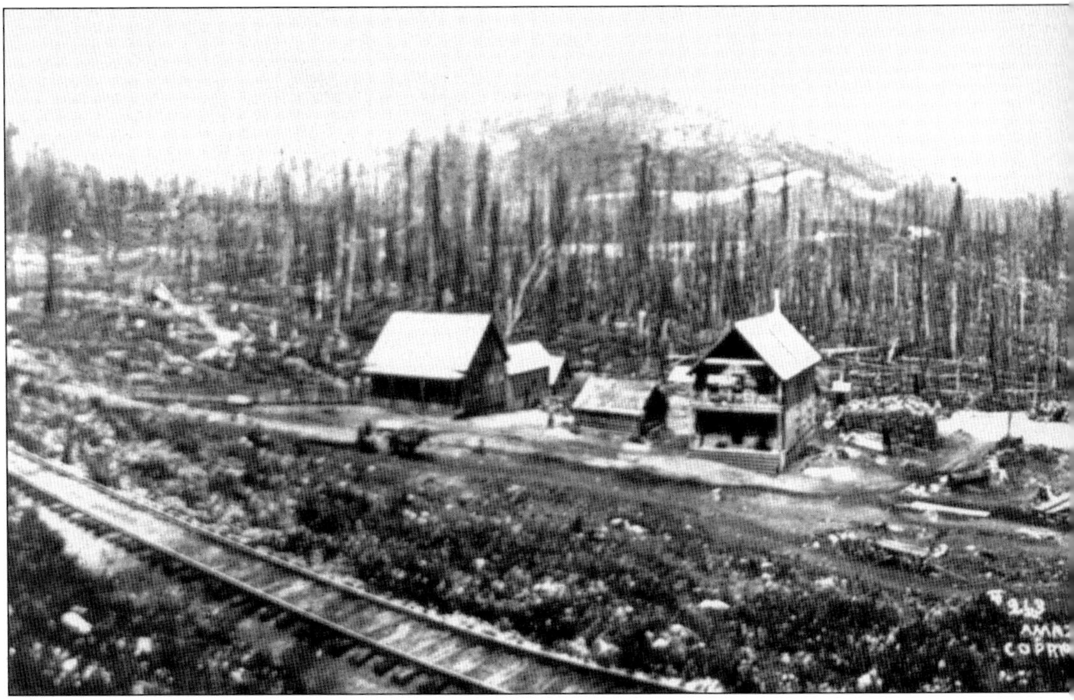

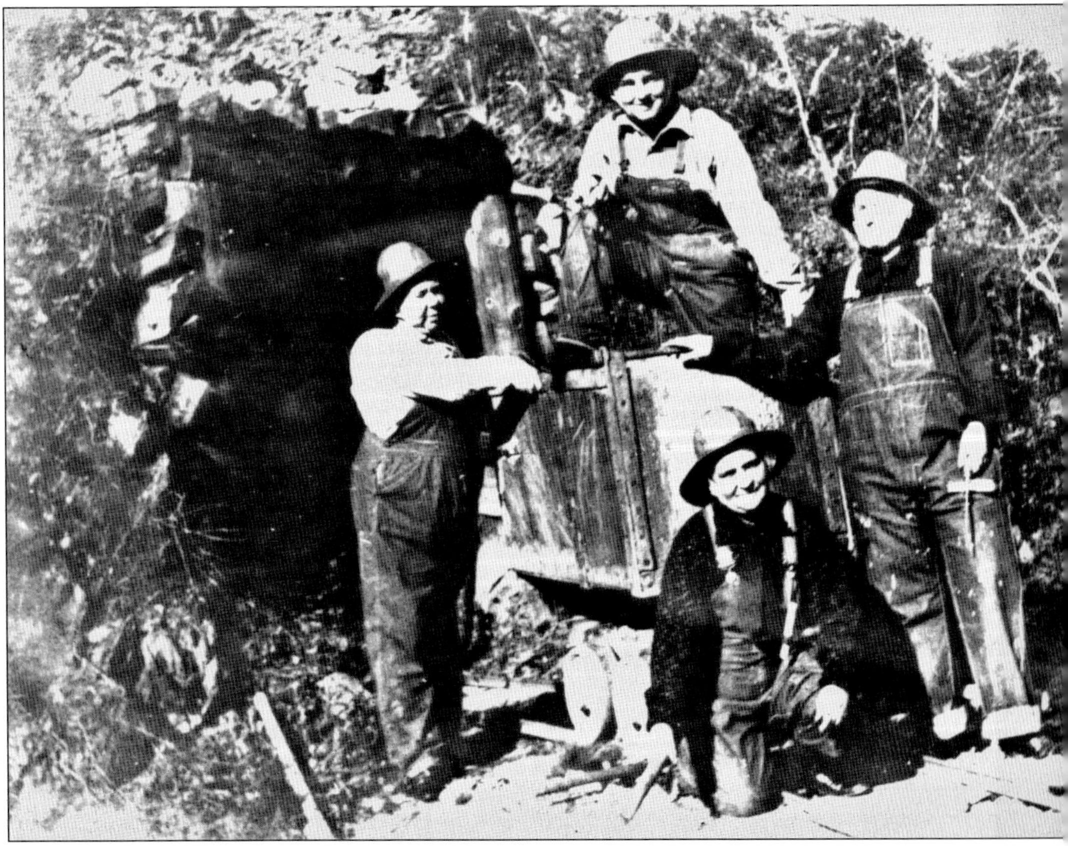

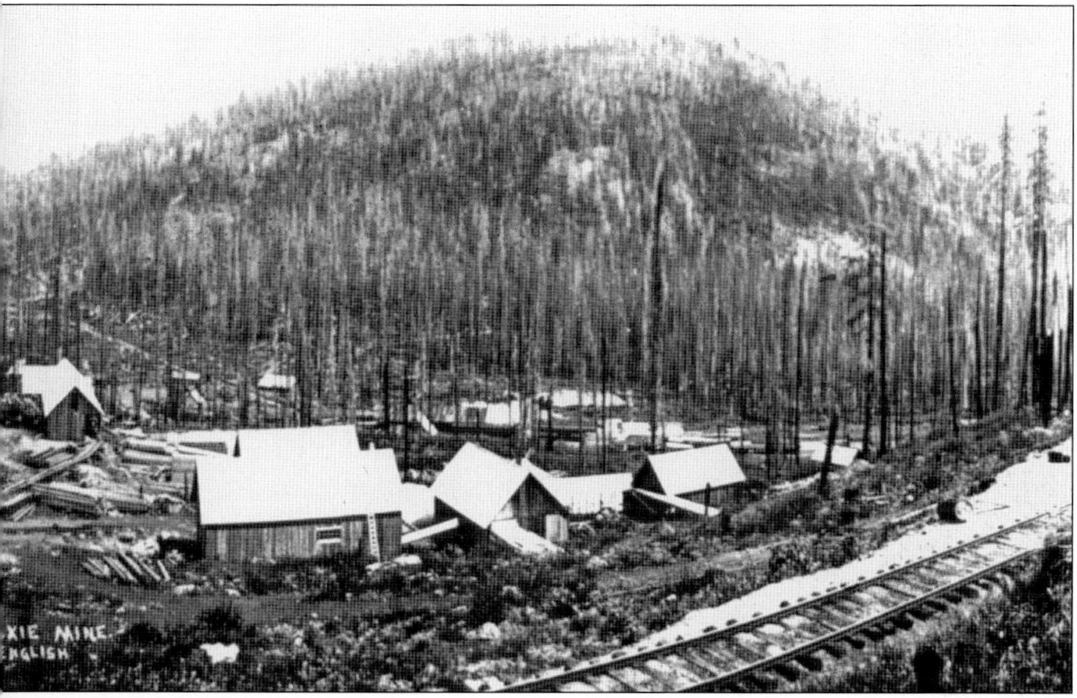

This is Amazon Dixie, located in Montana a mile east of Lookout Pass, in 1909. Although located in the state of Montana, it was considered part of the Coeur d'Alene Mining District: ore beds do not recognize state boundaries.

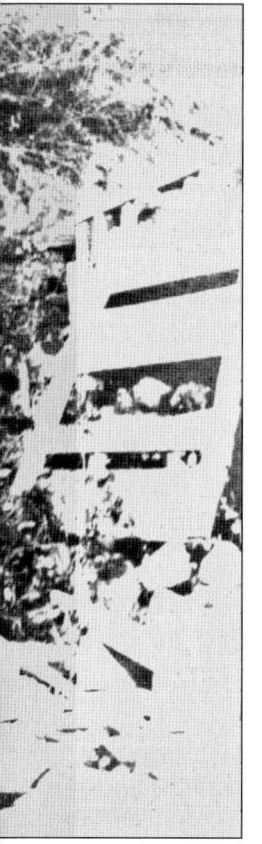

These "Women of the Hercules" worked alongside their husbands, finding and building the great Hercules Mine.

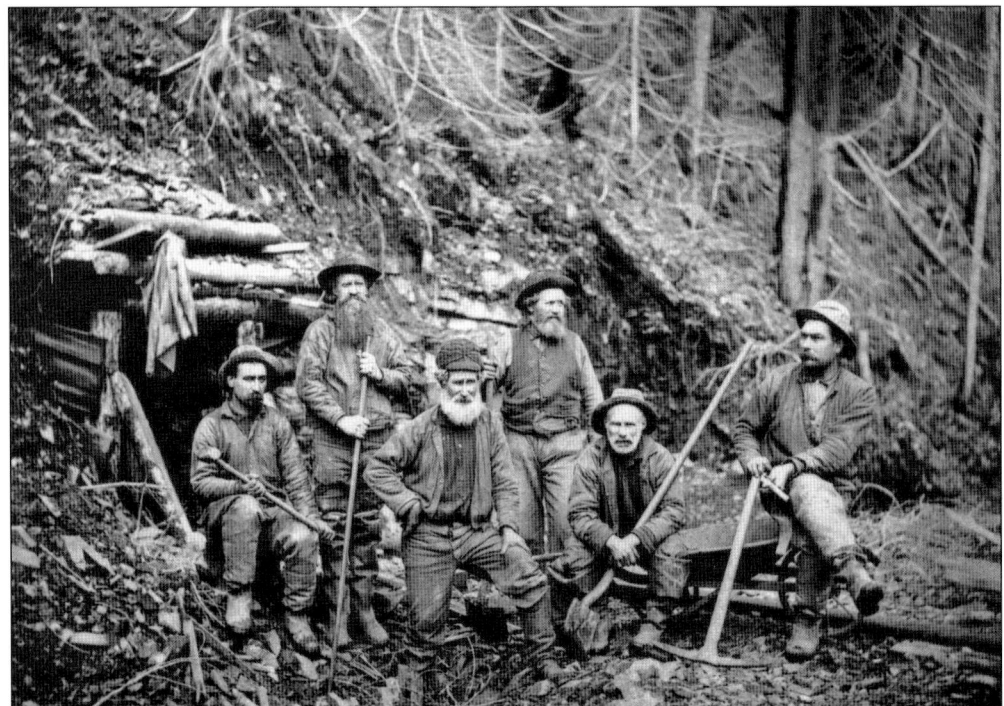

Mother Lode Boys were photographed by T. N. Barnard in the spring of 1889. Identified from left to right are Dan Segar, Paddy Moran, Dixie Wentz, Uncle Billy King, Albert, Otto, Frank Seigar [sic].

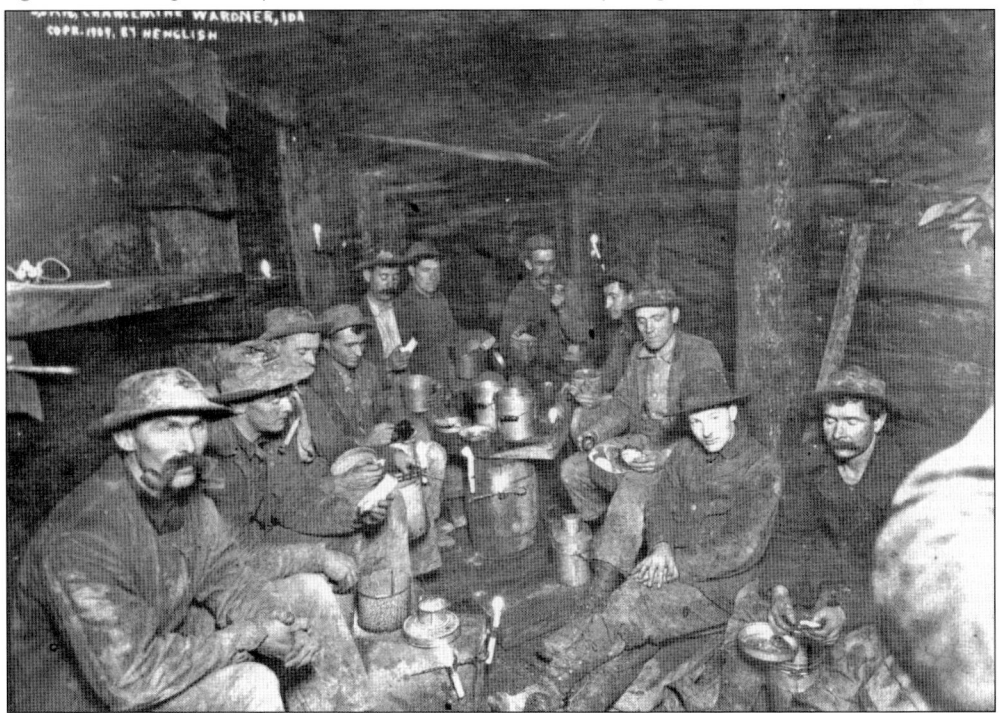

Harry English photographed a lunch break at the Chance Mine, located on Milo Creek, in Wardner in 1907.

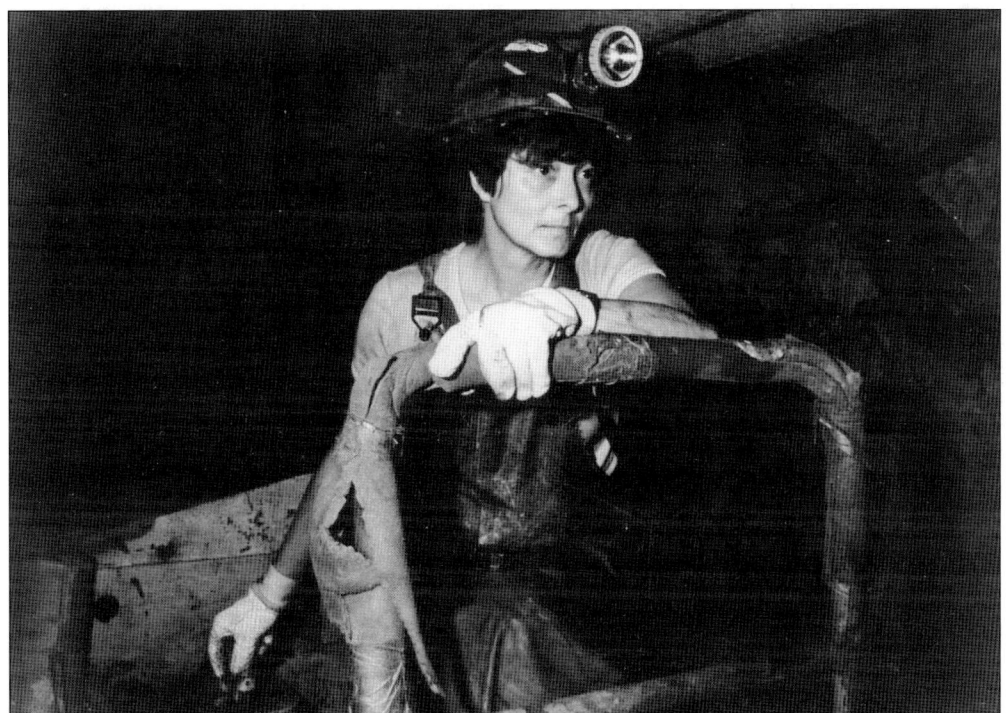

"White Glove" Cheryl is captured running the motor in the Lucky Friday Mine in 1986. (Courtesy of Shauna Hillman.)

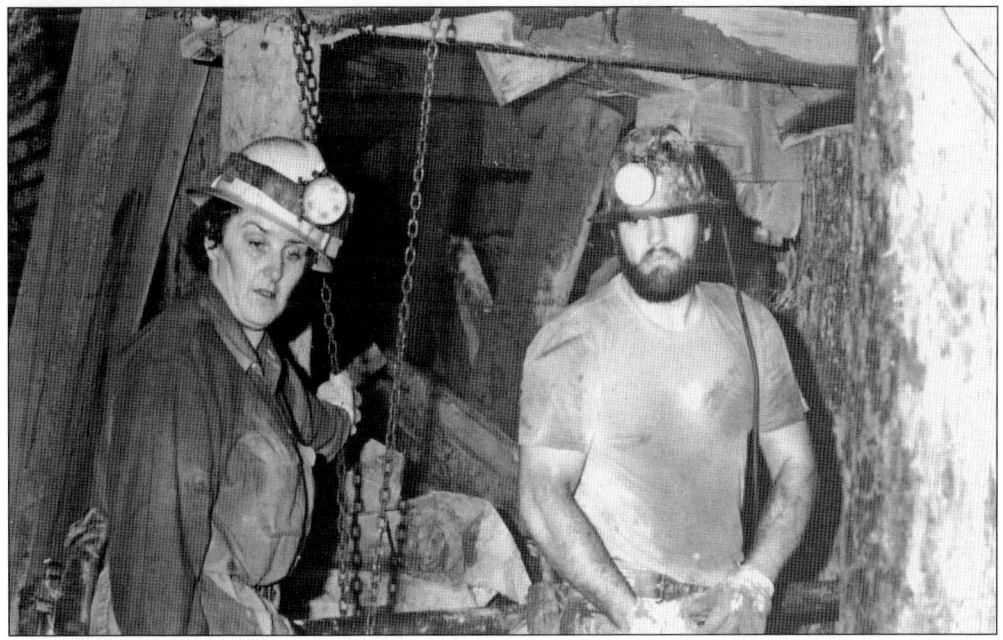

Women have worked alongside their husbands since the beginning of mining. At first, many old-timers were not supportive, but they soon learned these women could do the job, such as in this 1986 picture of Betty Scott with a miner in the Lucky Friday Mine in Mullan, Idaho. (Courtesy of Shauna Hillman.)

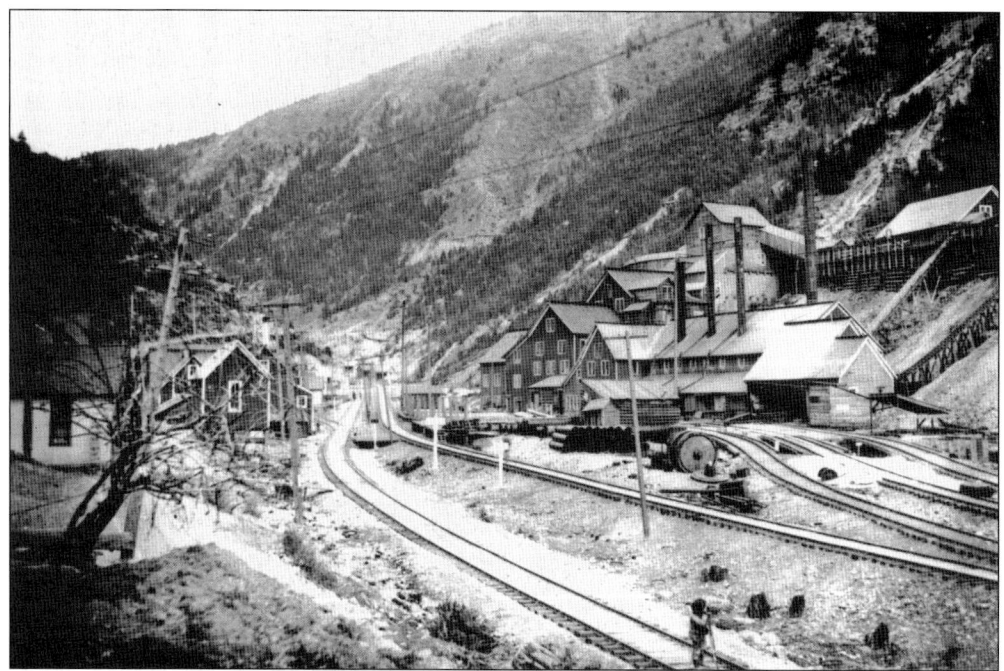

Pictured in 1898 are the Helena and Frisco Mills, on Canyon Creek. Frisco Village is situated straight across the creek and railroad tracks.

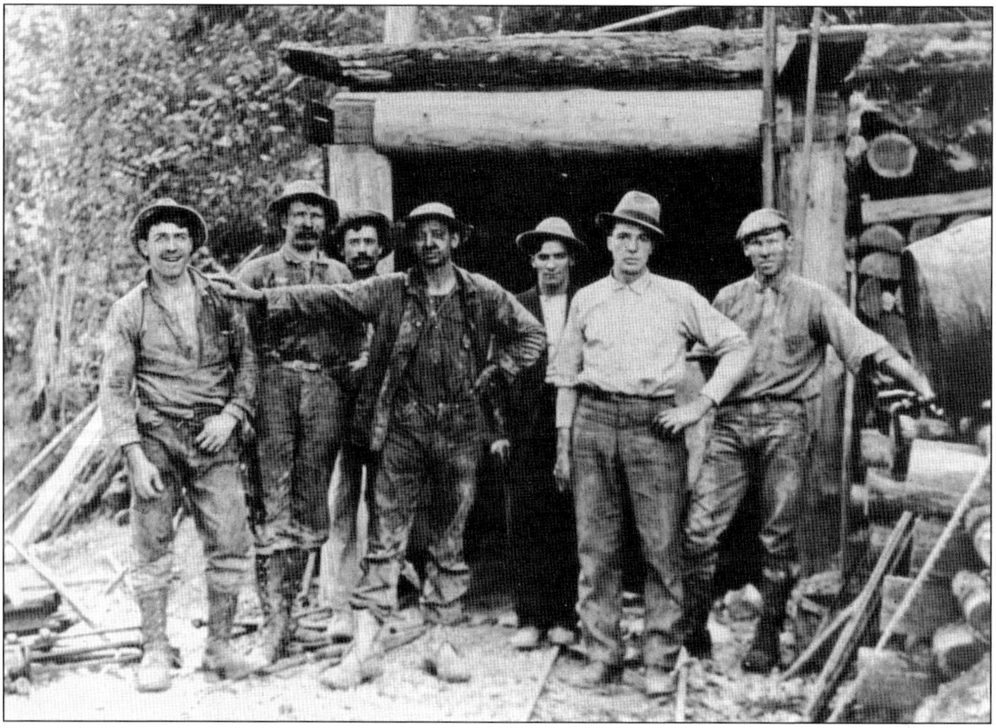

Identified from left to right at the Haywire Mine at Gem in 1920 are Dan Albertini, Bart O'Rouke, George Albertini, Larence Parisotto, Albert Albertini, Jim O'Neal, and Paddi McNeal [sic]. The barrel under Paddi's hand was kept full of whiskey.

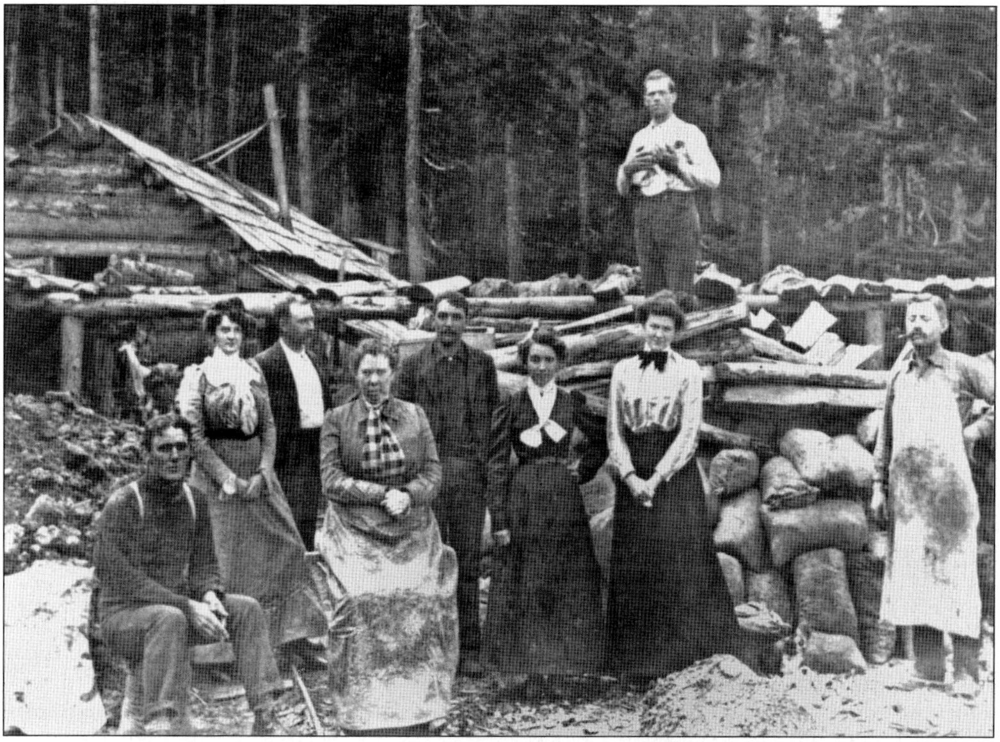

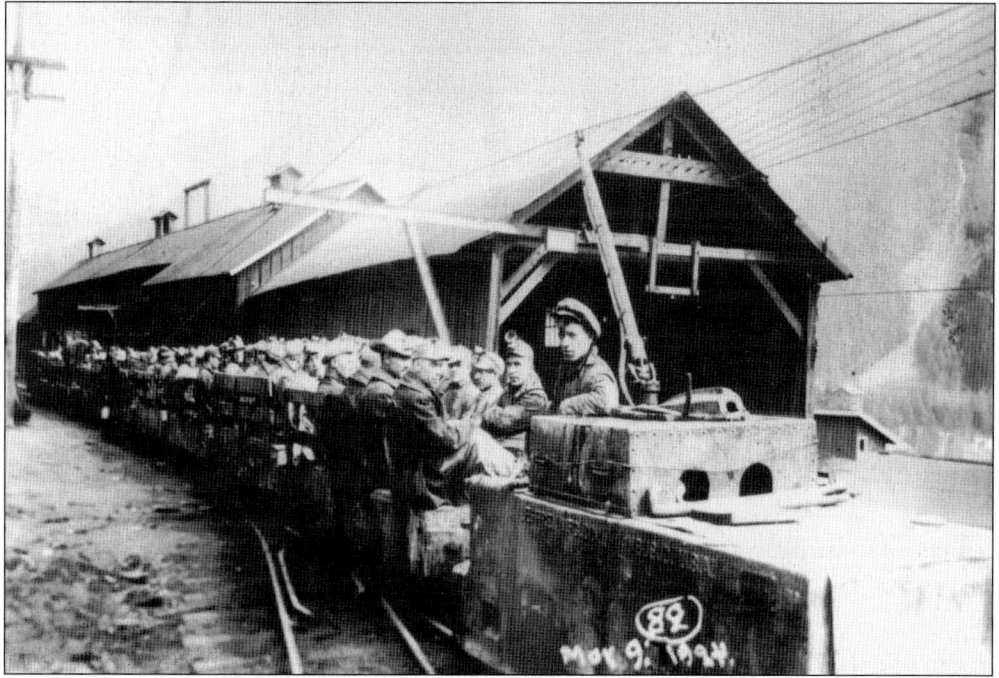

The partners in the Hercules Mine pose for a *c.* 1890 photograph. May Hutton is seated with the checkered scarf. The pile of ore in the foreground is an example of the high quality silver "ash" discovered by Harry Day.

Pictured is the man train at Mullan's Morning Mine in 1924.

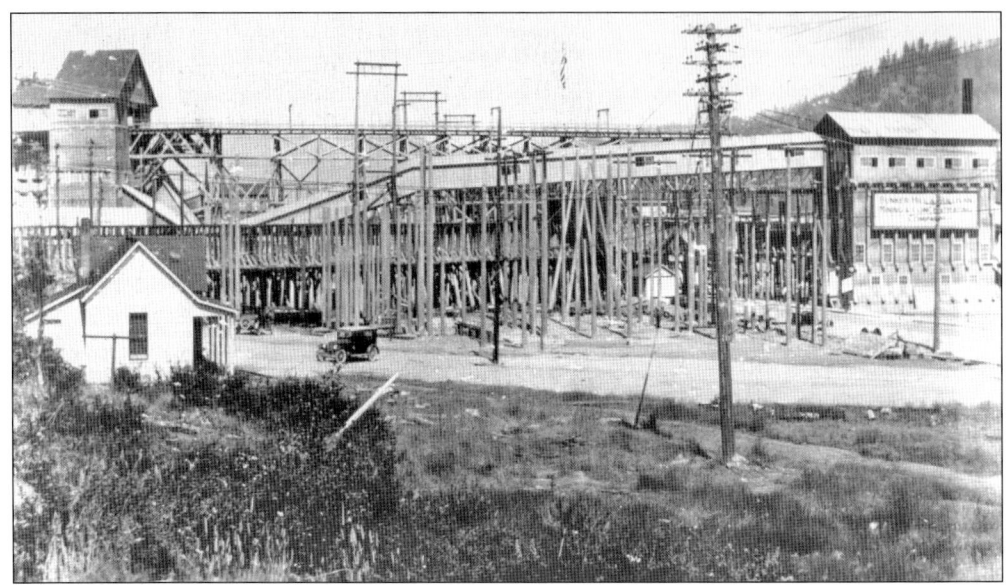

This c. 1920 photograph shows the Bunker Hill and Sullivan Mining, Milling, and Concentrating Company.

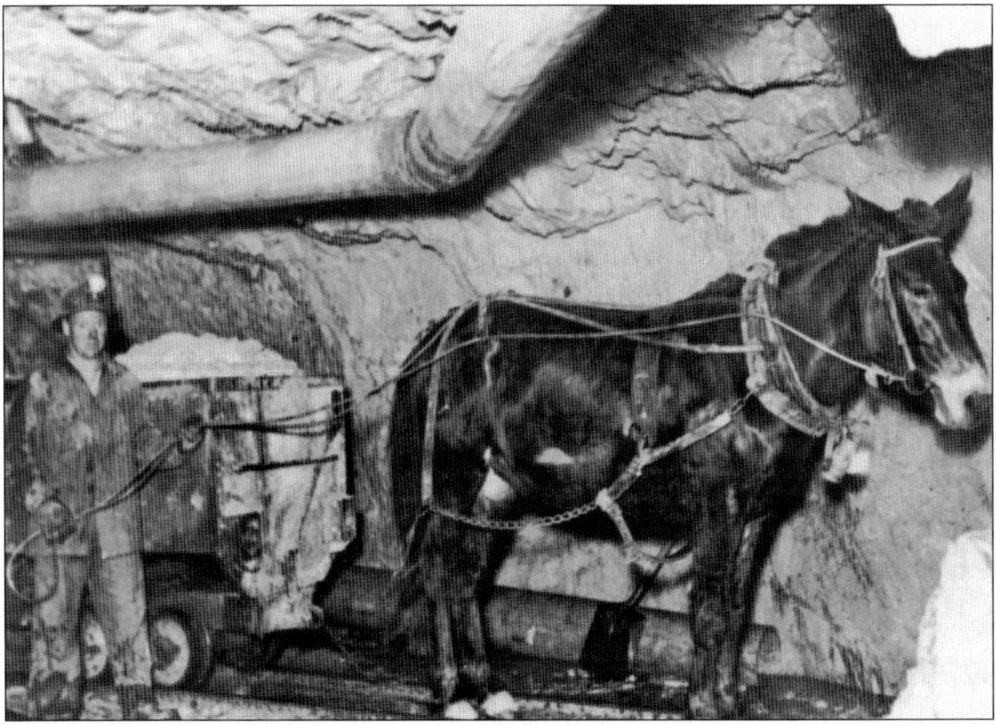

The interior of the Silver Dollar Mine is the backdrop of this c. 1880 image.

This photograph shows "muck" being pulled from the No. 2 chute at the Galena Mine in 1961.

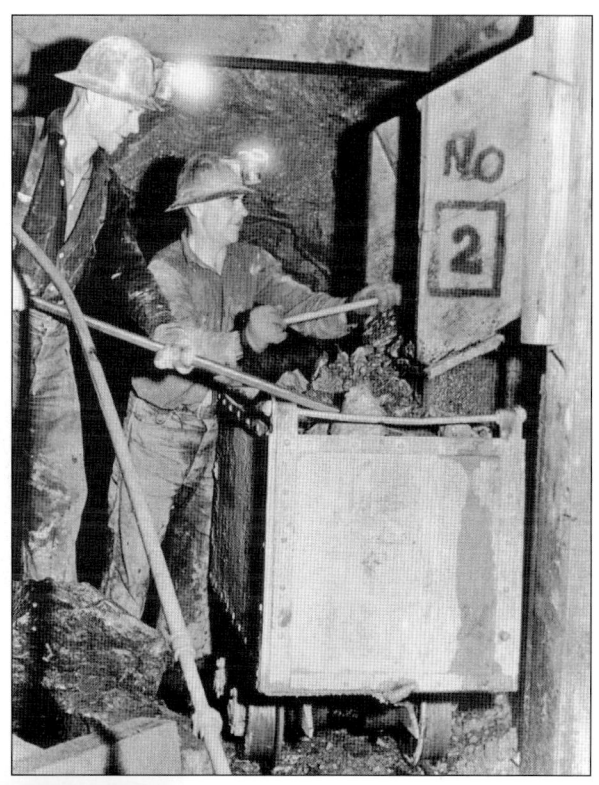

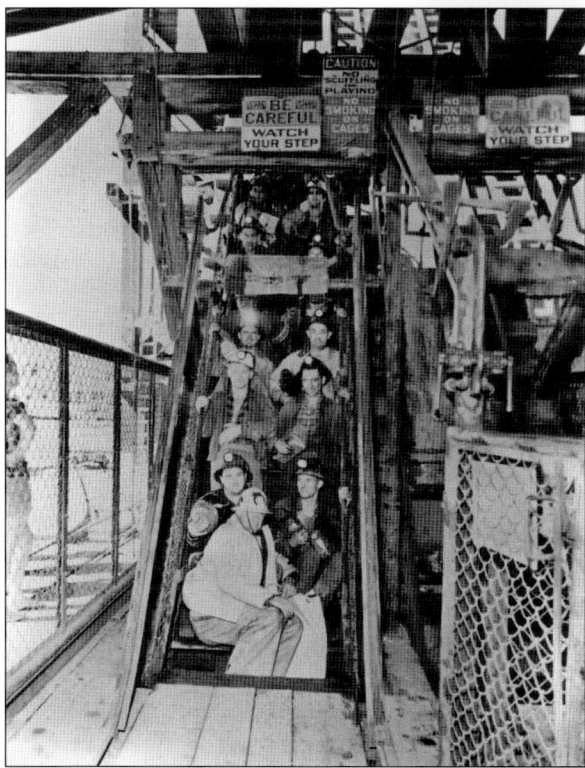

This 1961 image shows the Page Mine incline shaft, another method for transporting men, muck, and equipment into the mine. This mine was owned by American Smelting and Refining Company. (ASARCO.)

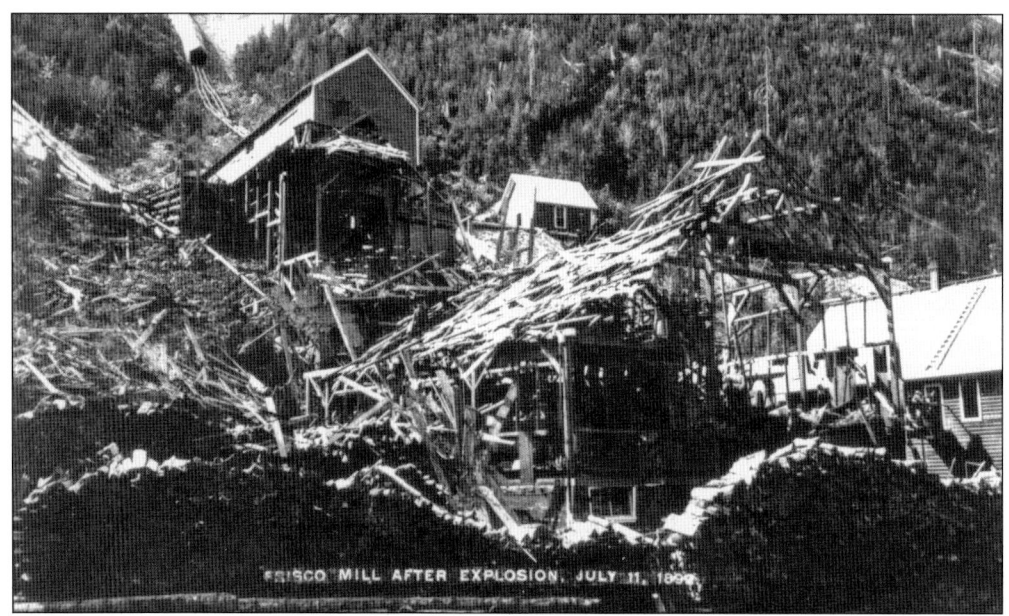

This is the Frisco Mill after the explosion of July 11, 1892. Dynamite was loaded into ore cars and sent down the tramway to the Frisco Mill after Gem miners were denied a raise for carmen and shovelers from $3 to $3.50 per day, and following the discovery of Pinkerton spies.

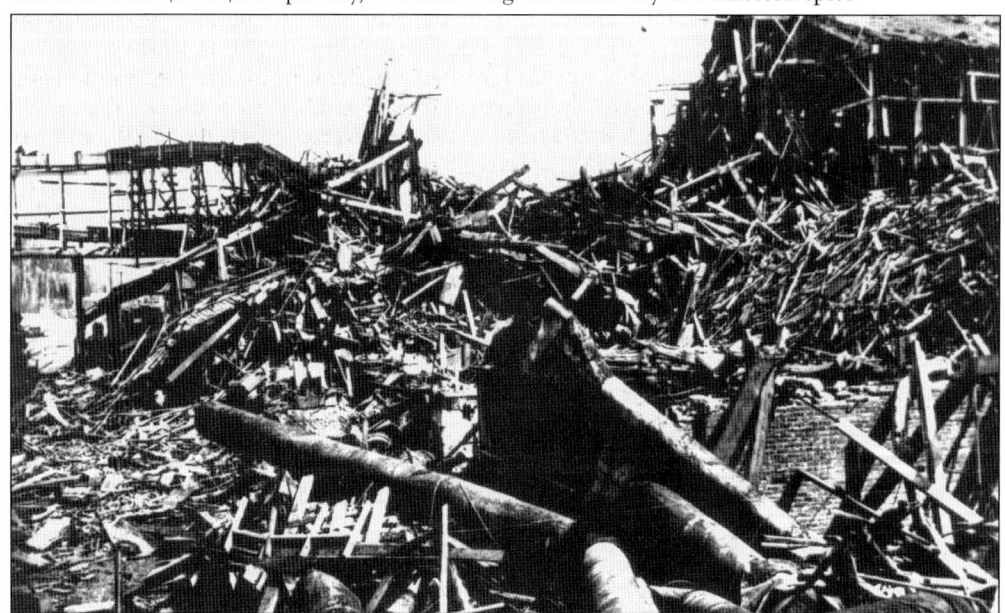

This is the Bunker Hill and Sullivan concentrator, after the explosion of April 29, 1899. Miners hijacked the Northern Pacific Train at Burke, proceeded down Canyon Creek, picking up more men and boxes of dynamite. The "dynamite express" traveled down along the South Fork to Kellogg. The concentrator was destroyed. A thousand men were herded in to an old barn, and three died from the conditions. Union sympathizer Emma Langdon charged in a 1908 book that Gov. Frank Steunenberg received $35,000 from mine owners at the time. Over the ensuing years, even though Bunker Hill would become known as "Uncle Bunker" by valley residents, its labor relations never recovered.

# *Ten*

# MINING WARS AND DISASTERS

The 1890s were a troubled time for the country as a whole because of the depression that hit in 1893. Idaho, having just become a state in 1890, was still in its infancy, trying to establish its political and economic base. As prices for produce fell, everything from banks to mining companies closed their doors. In 1887 trouble hit when the Bunker Hill and Sullivan Mining and Concentrating Company reduced the wage from $3.50 to $2.50 for a 10-hour day at the Bunker Hill mine. The miners struck, and while the company backed down, the men formed the Wardner Miners Union in November 1887 to protect their jobs. In January 1892 the Mine Owners' Association announced that it had to close most of the mines because of an increase in freight rates. By March the rates were restored and though mines would be reopened, owners stated that there would be pay cuts. Miners balked. By July 11,1892 fighting had escalated and the Frisco mill was dynamited to pieces. In 1894 the Bunker Hill and Sullivan was battling with its miners over 50¢ a day, even employing undercover agents to identify union men, and by April 1899 martial law had to be established. It is worthy of note that the notorious International Workers of the World (the "Wobblies") regarded the miners of northern Idaho far too radical.

In the 150 years of the Silver Valley's history, hundreds of casualties have been recorded; the first in 1887, when 25-year-old Lyman Wilson did not wait long enough to check an unblasted round, when it exploded. In 1919 five men were killed in a hoist (the elevator used to haul men, ore and material in and out of the mine) accident when the operator sent the hoist in the wrong direction. In the early days of electricity men were electrocuted when their metal tools came in contact with the wires. With each new innovation in mining came knowledge that helped to make it safer both for the miners and the environment. But like most advances, knowledge comes at the precious cost of human life. On May 2, 1972, a total of 91 miners perished in a fire at the Sunshine silver mine. The Sunshine Mine Disaster of 1972 led to significant improvements in safety policies at hard-rock metal mines around the world, and to formation of the Mine Safety and Health Administration.

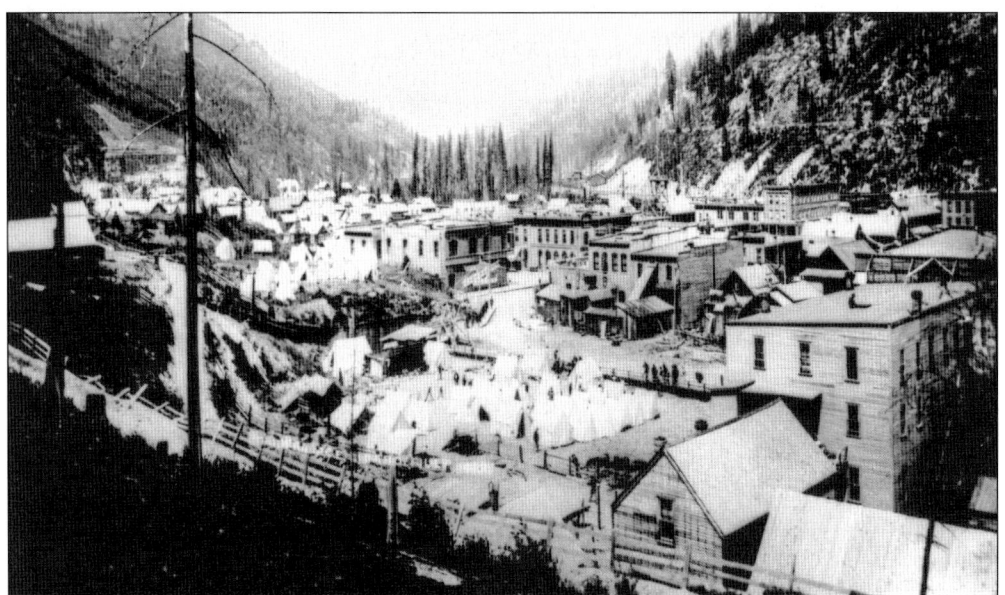

A military encampment on Hotel Street just off Bank Street in downtown Wallace. Shoshone County was declared under martial law after the explosion of the Frisco Mill on July 11. Mine owners appealed to Gov. Norman Willey. He answered their call by sending in National Guard troops and requesting federal troops from President Harrison, who responded with Black conscripts. Some 600 union officers, members, and sympathizers were arrested and locked up in warehouses and storehouses dubbed "bull pens." By March 1893, they were all freed and returned to their homes.

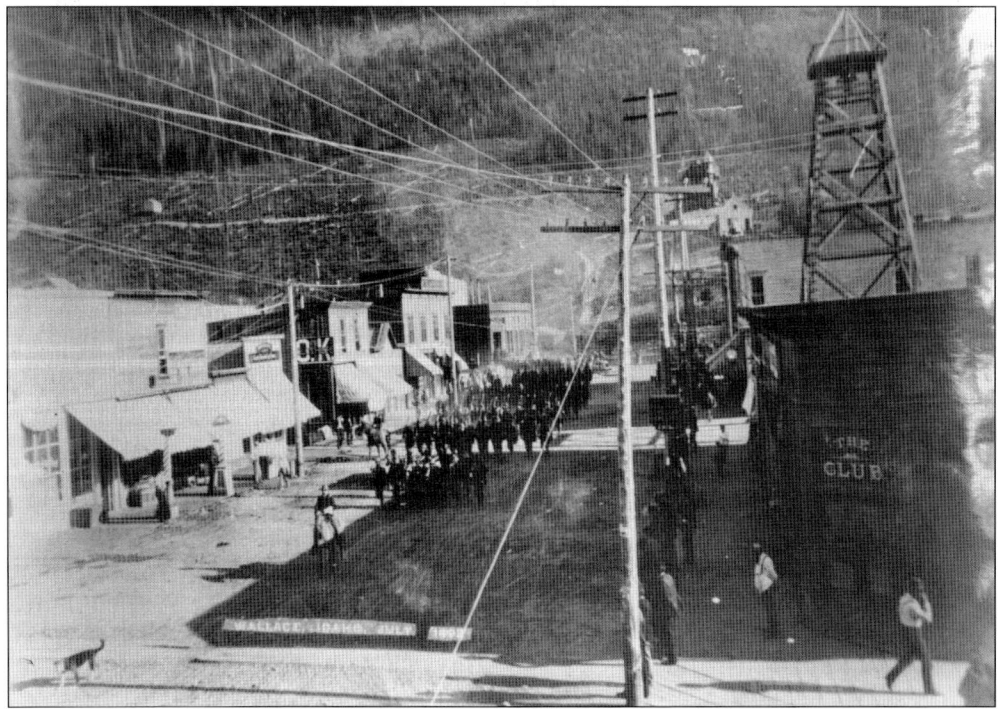

Troops march through Wallace on Sixth Street in July 1892.

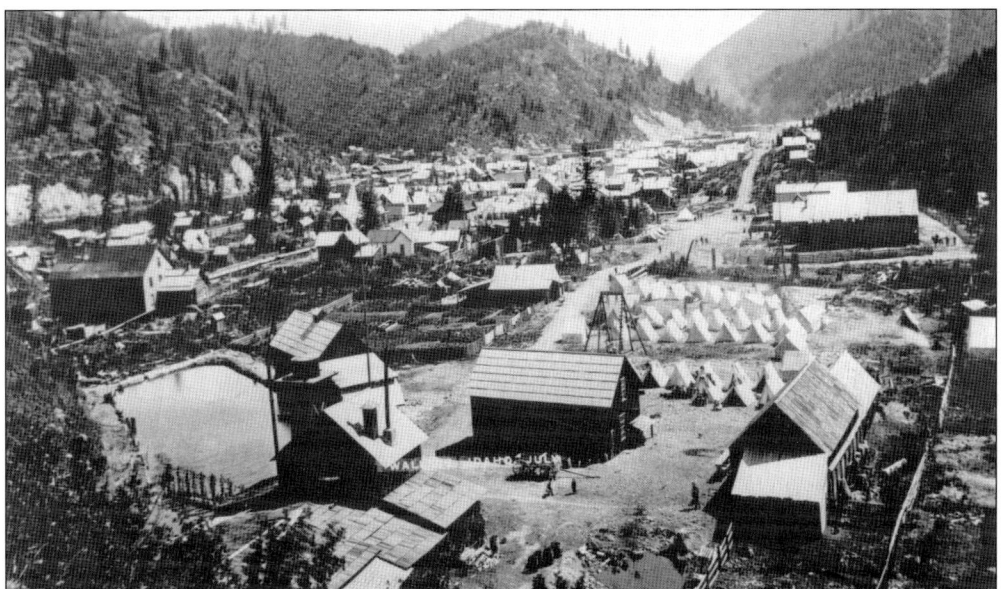

Another military encampment in 1892 at the corner of Bank and King Streets on the west edge of Wallace. The pond and large buildings on the left are part of the Mallon Family Brewery.

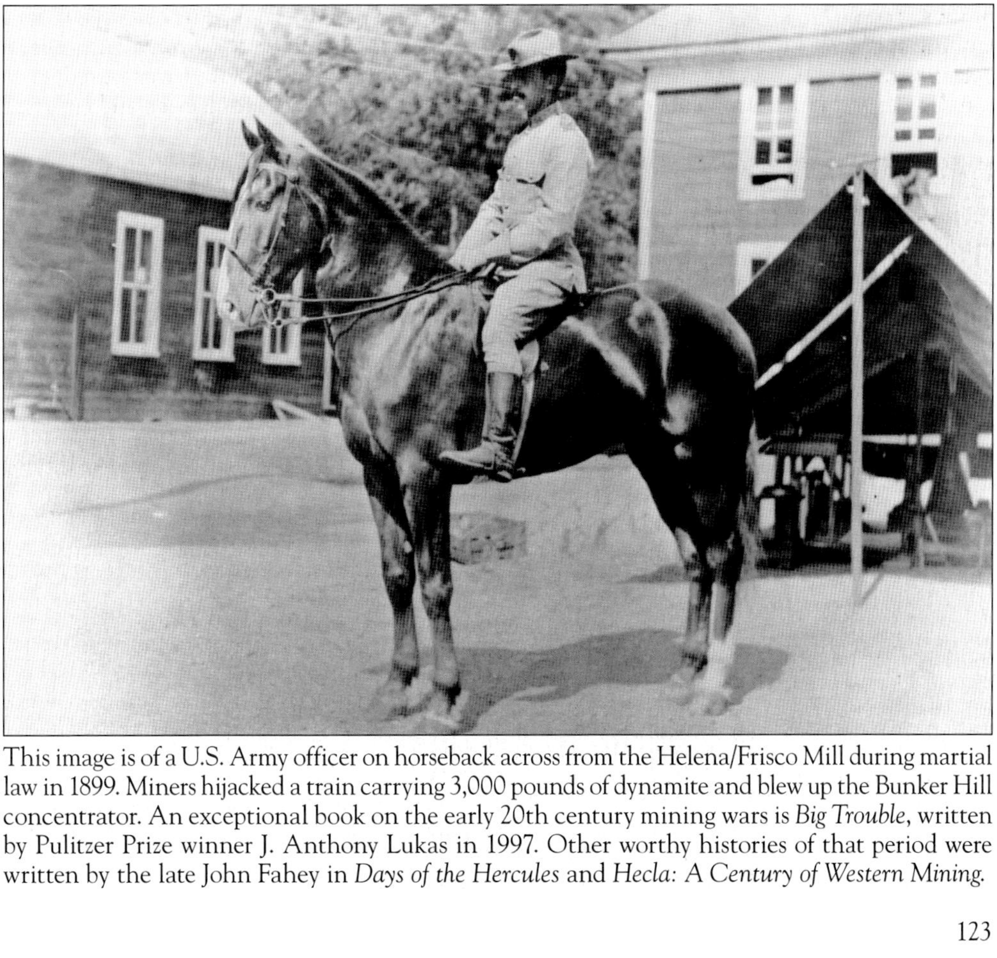

This image is of a U.S. Army officer on horseback across from the Helena/Frisco Mill during martial law in 1899. Miners hijacked a train carrying 3,000 pounds of dynamite and blew up the Bunker Hill concentrator. An exceptional book on the early 20th century mining wars is *Big Trouble*, written by Pulitzer Prize winner J. Anthony Lukas in 1997. Other worthy histories of that period were written by the late John Fahey in *Days of the Hercules* and *Hecla: A Century of Western Mining*.

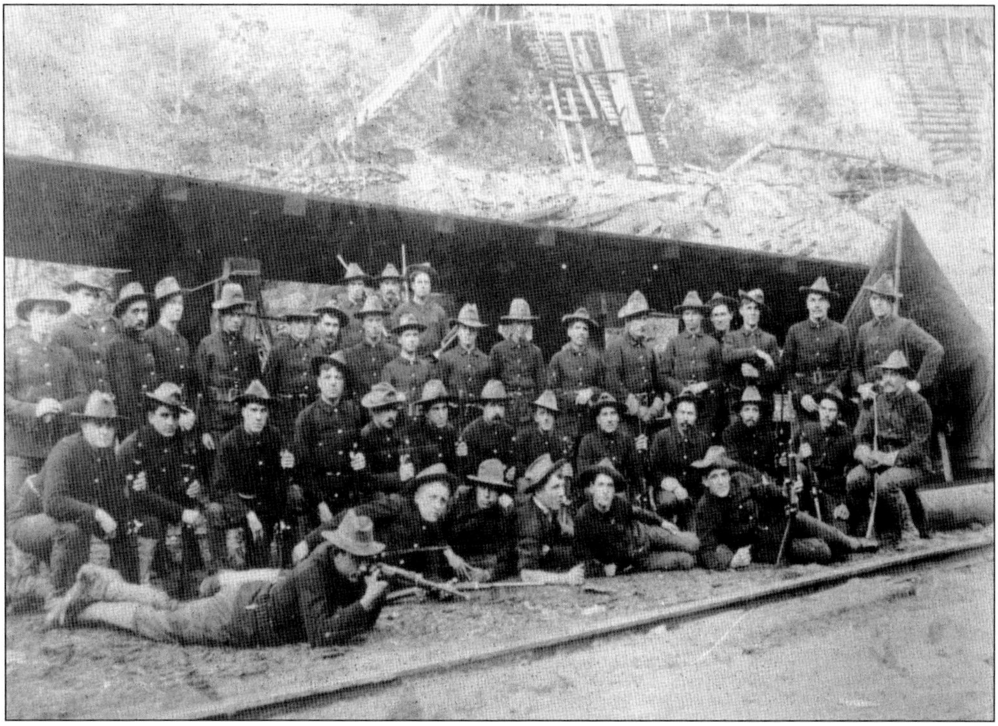

This 1892 photograph shows soldiers at the site of the Frisco Mill explosion.

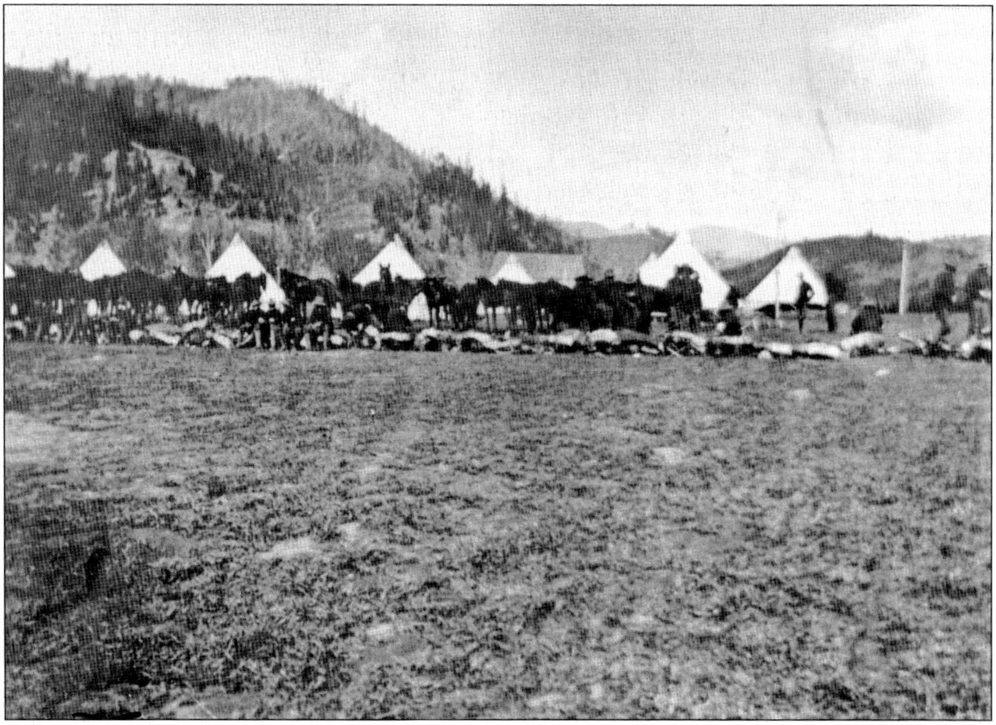

Pictured is a military encampment at the mouth of Canyon Creek in 1892.

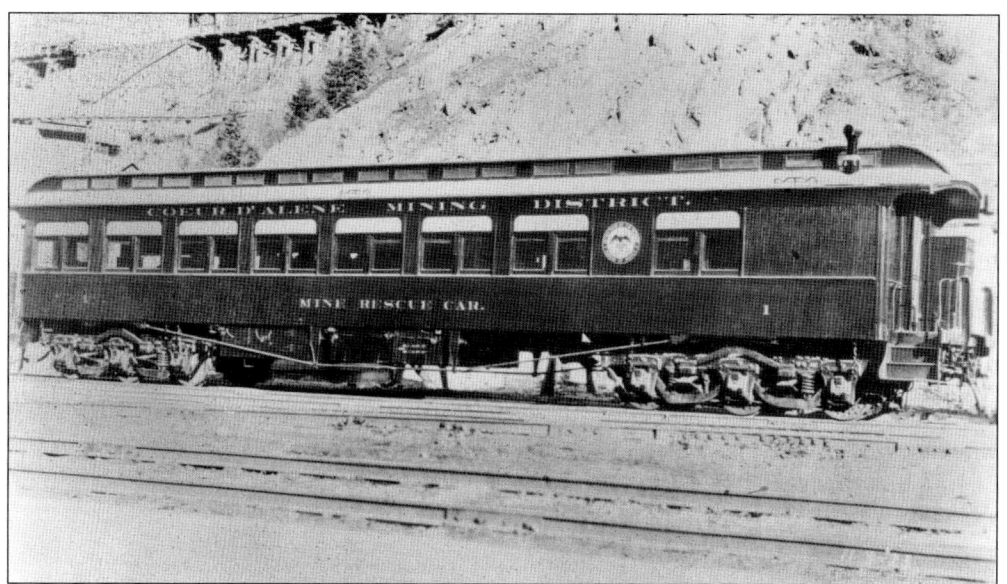

Mining companies in the Coeur d'Alene Mining District put together this train car, labeled "Mine Rescue Car," that could be quickly taken to the site of mining accidents.

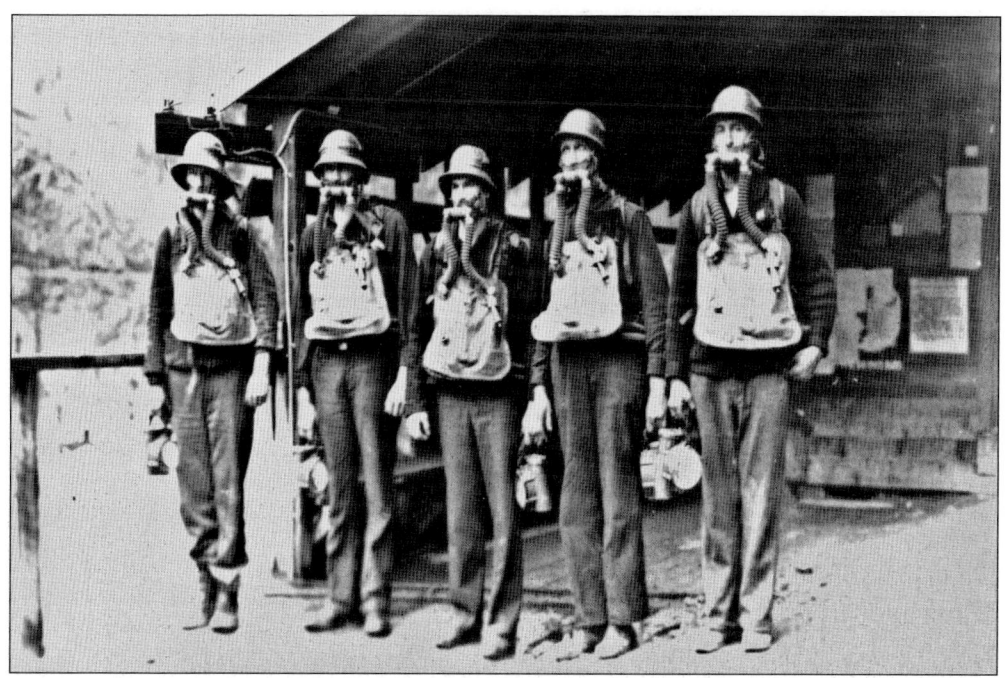

Rescue breathers from the 1930s were very bulky and were worn by rescue workers going in looking for injured or trapped. We do not take these accidents lightly, nor do we forget those who paid the price.

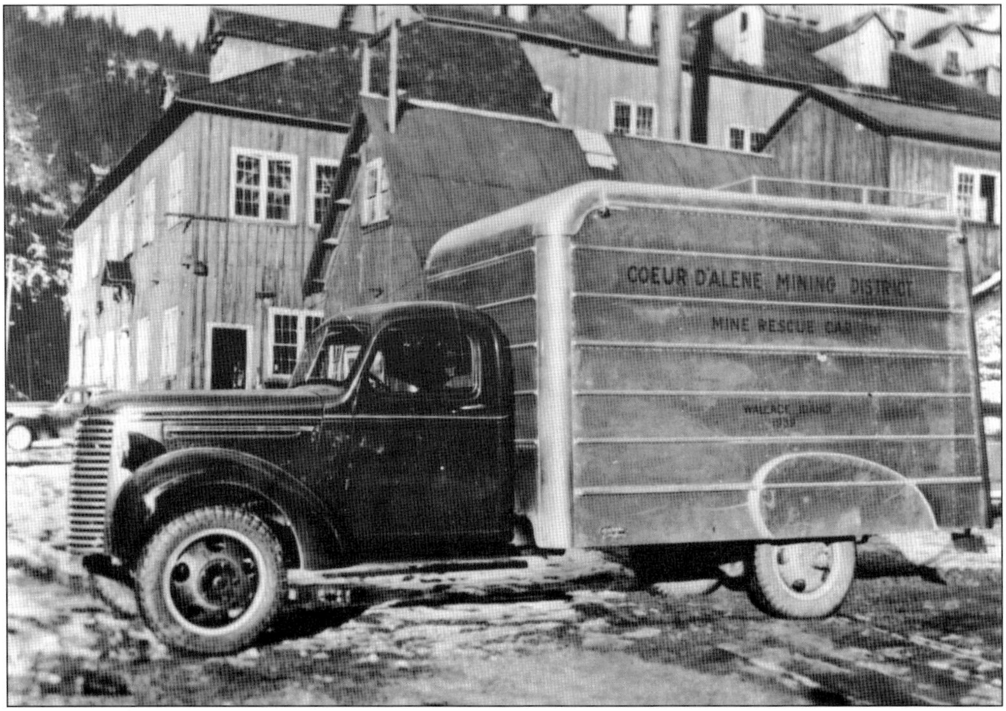

This safety truck was equipped to be ready to respond to mine accidents at a moment's notice.

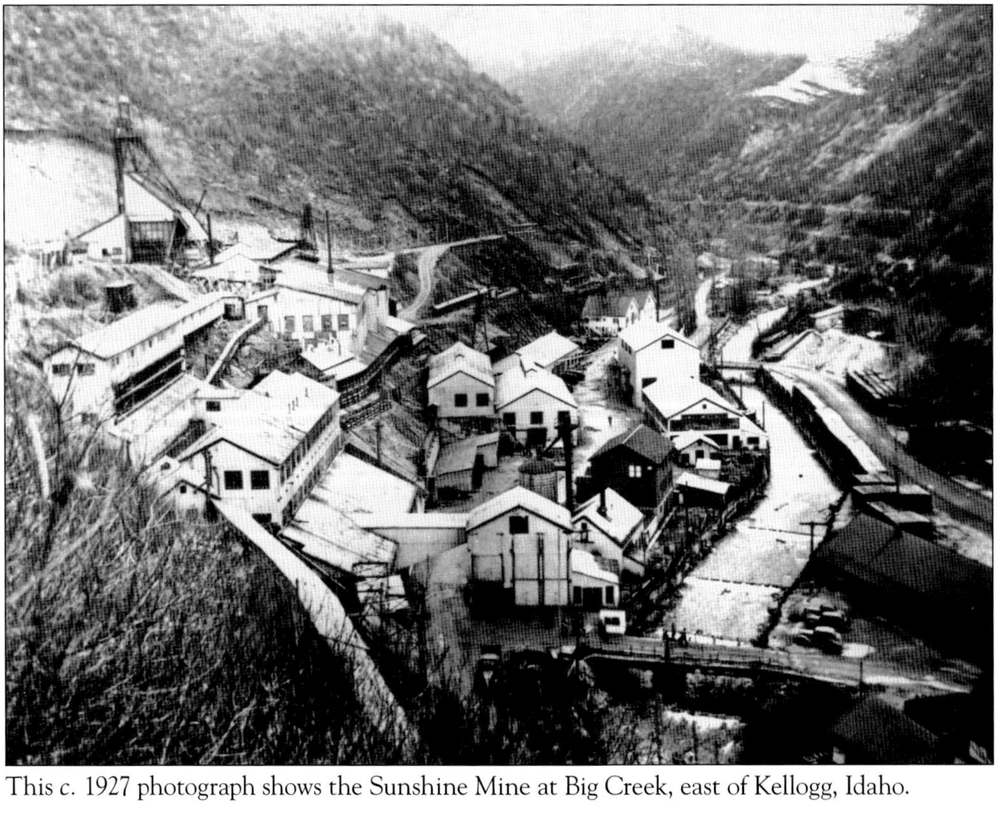

This *c.* 1927 photograph shows the Sunshine Mine at Big Creek, east of Kellogg, Idaho.

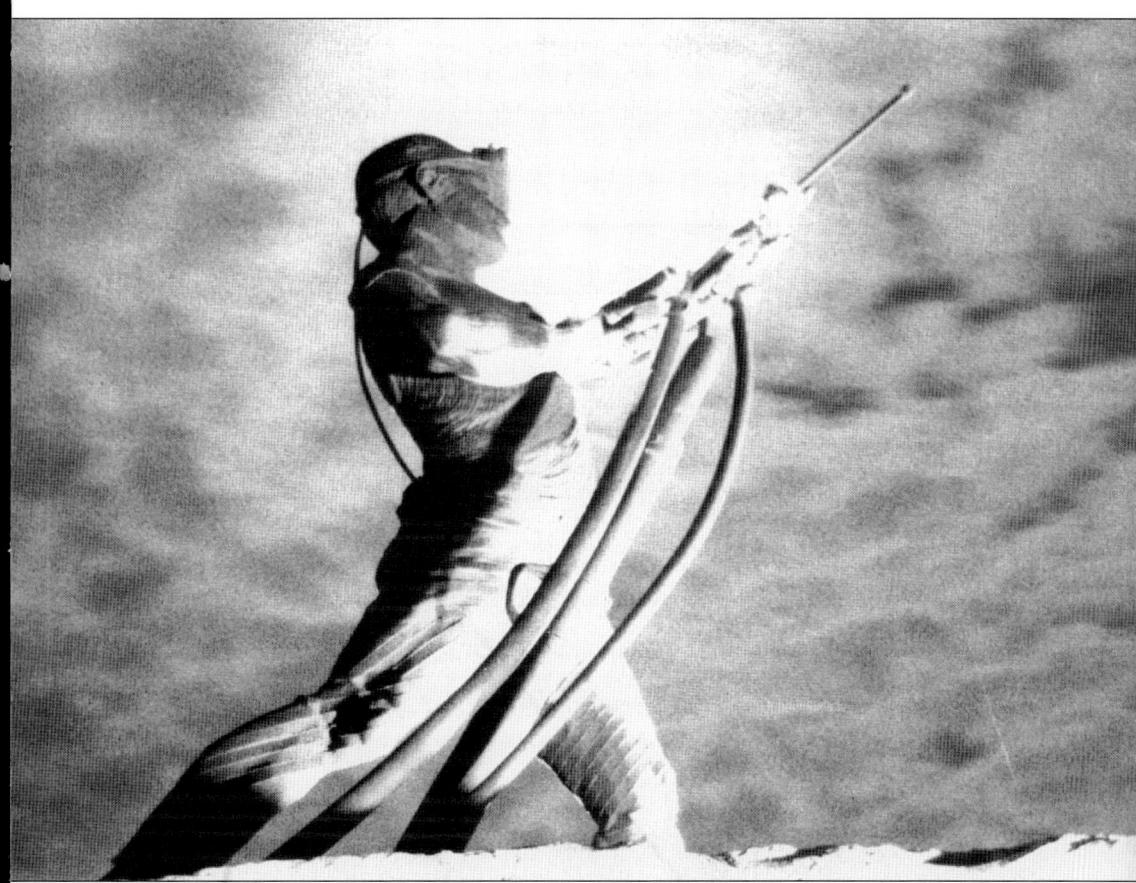

The Miners' Memorial, pictured in 2000, stands at the mouth of Big Creek looking south toward the Sunshine Mine, dedicated to those lost on May 2, 1972. Deadly carbon monoxide and gas from a burning polyurethane foam bulkhead swept throughout the underground workings by the mine's state-of-the-art ventilation system. The Sunshine Mine, at the center of the valley, is over 6,000 feet deep. With 179 men on the day shift, only 88 would escape, including two who were trapped for nearly a week. The Miners' Memorial has become not just a place to meet to mourn their loss but also to remember the heroism of those who died trying to rescue the miners. The miners' story of that dreadful day, and the effects it had on the communities of the Silver Valley, is told in Gregg Olsen's 2006 book, *The Deep Dark: Disaster and Redemption in America's Richest Silver Mine*. The full moon increases the intensity of the miner's headlamp, which is forever burning, reminding us that at our darkest moments we will find light together. The Sunshine disaster knitted Idaho's disparate farming, lumbering, ranching, and mining sentiments together. These sentiments were best expressed in a poem cast in bronze at the base of the Miners' Memorial and written by southern Idaho onion farmer (and future Idaho governor) Phil Batt, entitled, "We Were Miners Then": (in part) "Our tongues have not tasted the bitter dust / The roar of the drills has never reached our ears / Unfelt to us is the darkness of the shafts / Yet we are Idahoans / And we were miners then . . . / Yes we were miners / We waited in Spirit at the mouth of the pit / Ached in unison at the news of the dead / Joined in the jubilation at the rescue of the living / Marveled at the poise of the tiny community / And we became strong / The flux of the widow's tears / Welded your strength into our bodies / And we were all Idahoans / And we were all miners / And we were all proud." (Courtesy of Shauna Hillman.)

# www.arcadiapublishing.com

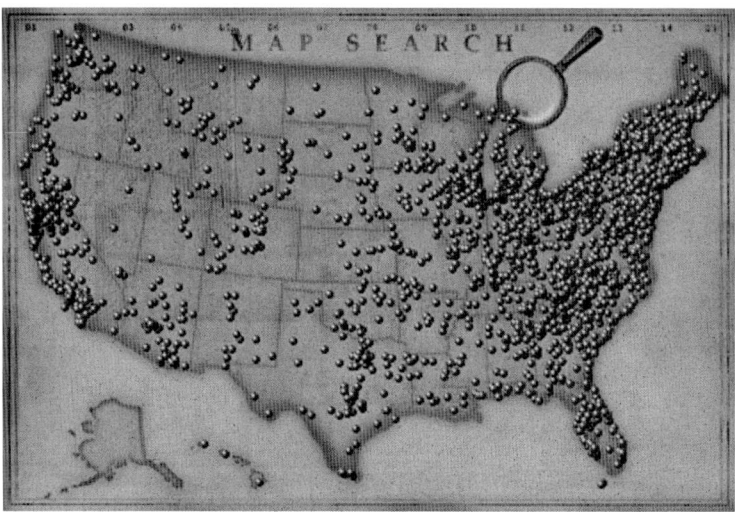

Discover books about the town where you grew up, the cities where your friends and families live, the town where your parents met, or even that retirement spot you've been dreaming about. Our Web site provides history lovers with exclusive deals, advanced notification about new titles, e-mail alerts of author events, and much more.

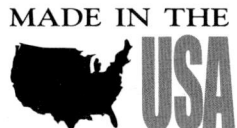

Arcadia Publishing, the leading local history publisher in the United States, is committed to making history accessible and meaningful through publishing books that celebrate and preserve the heritage of America's people and places. Consistent with our mission to preserve history on a local level, this book was printed in South Carolina on American-made paper and manufactured entirely in the United States.

This book carries the accredited Forest Stewardship Council (FSC) label and is printed on 100 percent FSC-certified paper. Products carrying the FSC label are independently certified to assure consumers that they come from forests that are managed to meet the social, economic, and ecological needs of present and future generations.

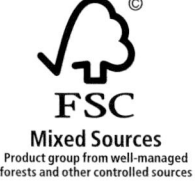

**Mixed Sources**
Product group from well-managed
forests and other controlled sources

Cert no. SW-COC-001530
www.fsc.org
© 1996 Forest Stewardship Council

*Find Your Place in History.*